MIGRANT IN THE CITY

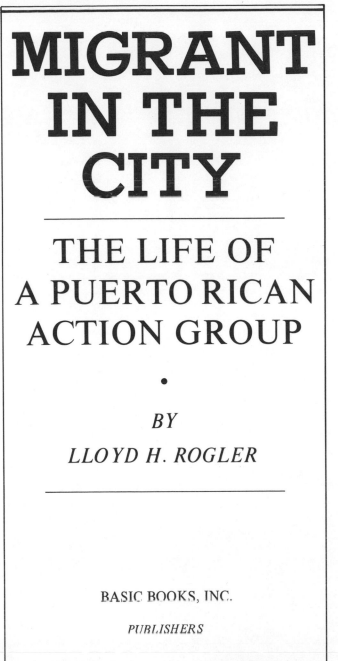

MIGRANT IN THE CITY

THE LIFE OF A PUERTO RICAN ACTION GROUP

•

BY

LLOYD H. ROGLER

BASIC BOOKS, INC.

PUBLISHERS

NEW YORK   *LONDON*

DEDICATION

To the Hispanic Confederation of Maplewood,
its members, and all groups that give a voice
to persons scarcely heard, and to my father,
Charles C. Rogler, for having taught me that
the study of society is itself a major cultural
value.

FOREWORD

I felt a little awkward when I was first asked to write this introduction because I have never been able to understand why good and literate books should begin with words written by someone other than the author. Once I had read the manuscript, though, I began to feel that I might have a role to play here after all.

Lloyd Rogler is a modest man, and the book he has written persistently understates the size and significance of his accomplishment. In the first place, he does not employ any of the conventional sociological strategems for drawing a reader's attention to what an author has done: he does not talk about models, theories, or hypotheses and he does not give us a lengthy set of instructions as to where his work fits into the rest of the sociological literature. In the second place, he does not provide any more than the sparest description of himself and the relationship he had with the people he was studying. On both of these counts, it seems to me, a brief introduction by someone else is in order.

One of the traditional tasks of the sociologist is to infer something general about social life by looking carefully at a particular sample of it. When sociologists go to the trouble of interviewing people or looking at the passing human scene, then, they are usually trying to look *through* those people and scenes in an effort to glimpse larger patterns in the background.

Migrant in the City is something else. It is a patient, sensitive account of what goes on in one small corner of the social universe where people live out their lives and try to make sense of their surroundings. This kind of sociology is difficult to do well because it requires meticulous craftsmanship, an ability to regard the social scene one is observing as important in and of itself, and a willingness to let the subjects of the study set the tone, pace, and rhythm of the research. Professor Rogler did not use the group he was studying to fill in the gaps of some larger sociological vision; he used the insights and methods of sociology to help him understand the character of the group. And in the process he has given us a double gift. *Migrant in the City* is one of the best "natural" accounts of life in an ethnic ghetto available in the literature, yet it is so sensitive to the best thinking in sociology that it also offers a real contribution to several of the dominant concerns in the field.

If I were a librarian, I would have a difficult time trying to decide how to catalogue this book. It offers a number of rich insights into group dynamics and deserves a place among the best works in that area. It also contains a good deal of valuable material about Puerto Rican life styles and would fit logically alongside the works, say, of Oscar Lewis. And it tells us enough about the new urban politics to belong on the same shelves as the growing literature on community power. *Migrant in the City* is difficult to catalogue because it stands by itself. It is not "about" group dynamics, Puerto Rican life styles, or the new urban politics; it is "about" the Hispanic Confederation of Maplewood. And it comes alive as a narrative exactly because Rogler focused on the group itself, and not on a vague set of generalizations lying somewhere in the distance.

Lloyd Rogler, the sociologist, is also too modest to tell us any more than he absolutely has to about Rogler Canino the participant-observer. He offers a few laconic remarks about himself because his sense of method required him to do so, and he describes one moment of "outburst" when he began to fear that he may have "departed from the norms governing the participant-observer role." Beyond that, though, he says almost nothing about the qualities of warmth and quiet strength that are necessary to live as he did through the long months of research. I am only guessing, of course, but I doubt that Rogler could have been half so good an observer if he had not been so sympathetic a participant. The most skillful actor in the world could not have survived ten minutes in that quick, sensitive milieu — only a good and generous friend.

I am not saying this to praise or embarrass an esteemed colleague but to make a note on method, for one of the strengths of this book is that no matter what his original intentions, Rogler became absorbed by the particularities of the group he was studying and the humanity of the people in it. He cared about them, felt for them, respected them — and the result is a compelling portrait informed not only by the discipline of a sound sociological mind but by the insight of a concerned and empathetic observer.

Sitting where I do, in a university town not far from Maplewood (and having once been profoundly unsuccessful in a research project not unlike this one), I cannot help reflecting that it takes a special person to do what Rogler managed to do. As his account reminds us again, a lingering self-doubt is one of the most perverse results of America's long history of inhospitality to minorities. A sympathetic observer is bound to notice that groups like the one studied here suffer greatly from what the participants themselves call "lack of confidence" or "inferiority complexes," but what others might simply call "low self-esteem." Yet this is far and away the most difficult matter for a well-meaning friend to deal with. How can one be sensitive to the fact that others have been exposed to years of humiliation without adding to the humiliation oneself? How can one take into account that others have been patronized all their lives without being patronizing in the process? And worse, how can one remain aware of these things and relate to them honestly without seeming or feeling superior?

There is not a trace of this difficulty in Rogler's book, and I think I know why. Real dignity of person depends upon recognizing the dignity of others, and it is clear from Rogler's account that he had this kind of relationship with the people he was studying. It is a rare and fine thing.

Kai T. Erikson

PREFACE

Two events, both unexpected, led to the study upon which this book is based. The Puerto Rican action group, whose story is told here, was the unplanned result of one man's attempt to bring Puerto Ricans in the neighborhood where he worked into American civic groups and voluntary associations. In turn, my study of the organizational life of the migrant in the city was the accidental result of being in the right place at the right time. Having studied families in the slums of San Juan, Puerto Rico, I wanted to see what happened to such families when they migrated to the United States; my main interest was the impact of the assimilative process upon Puerto Rican families. To plan the study I became actively involved in Maplewood's Puerto Rican community. As I participated in the migrants' activities I learned of the many unsuccessful efforts made by Puerto Ricans to develop organizations to represent their interests in the city. When I was told that another organization, the Hispanic Confederation, had recently been formed, I joined as a participant-observer.

Sometime later, I had to abandon plans for the study of the assimilation of Puerto Rican families because I could not secure adequate financial support. By then, however, the confederation itself had captivated my interest and I was determined to continue studying it. Unplanned as these events were, they did lead to more than three years of field work on the confederation and the members' struggle to band together to pressure Maplewood's governmental and service organizations into helping their ethnic group.

The confederation's story covers a 44-month period, from the inception of the group when the members were docile and unsure of themselves to that point in time when they became avowedly militant in their negotiations with city officials and hostile toward the establishment. The story is told in two ways: From Chapters 2 to 11 and in the Epilogue, the narrative of events is presented, from the members' viewpoint and my own, as a chronological account of the development, internal and external problems, social change, and eventual success of the action group. Chapters 5 and 8 are first-person accounts of the same material from the viewpoint of the Puerto Rican political boss of the city and from the point of view of the second president of the group, two strong community leaders whose personalities were shaped by their ethnic experiences. The remainder of the book, Chapters 12 to 15, is devoted to methodological explanation and sociological interpretation, complete with statistical analyses of patterns of group support and social change among the membership.

No individual can conduct a field study and write a full-length report of it on his own. Many people cooperated with me, assisted me, and advised me. Some who cooperated with and supported the study must remain nameless because of my obligation to preserve the confidentiality of the material. This in no way reduces my debt to them. To the others I wish to express publicly my most sincere gratitude and appreciation.

The investigation was aided by a grant from the Foundations' Fund for Research in Psychiatry; without the grant it is doubtful that the study could have been made. I wish to thank Clark J. Bailey for his support and steady encouragement. I also wish to acknowledge the support provided me by Case Western Reserve University for the time to devote to the writing of the manuscript.

Victor Thiessen and Roy Treadway gave me advice and help in the computer analysis of the data presented in Chapter 14. Hubert M. Blalock also gave me advice on the statistical analysis of the data. I thank them for their contribution to this work.

At one time or another, the following persons gave me valuable assistance in research or performed important secretarial duties: Eileen Abricki, Christine Bennett, Pamela Degler, Carolyn Durway, Barbara Hartford, Patricia Howard, Djelal Kadir II, Patricia A. Martin, Patrick Plesqunas, Joanna Ruickholdt, William Schallert, Lillian Smith, Janet Vining, and Gwen Williams.

I wish to thank Lee Ann Cooper for typing the final manuscript, and William R. Cooper and M. Audrey Kachelski for their help in proofreading.

While field work was in progress, Carmen Sylvia García came from San Juan to Maplewood to assist me in the study and to serve an apprenticeship in field research. During her year's stay in Maplewood she helped in the development of the interview schedule used in the study, conducted systematic and intensive interviews, assisted in the translation of data from Spanish into English, and collaborated with me fully as a participant-observer in the confederation. Since then, she has completed her doctorate in social work and has returned to Puerto Rico where she has become a leader in social research. I am much indebted to her for her generous and unstinting help in the study and for her criticisms of the chapter on research methods.

It is a pleasure to express my special thanks to Sona Mahakian Caro for her many contributions to the study. She became my assistant-in-research when Miss García left, and she collaborated with me in almost two years of field work. She helped in the painstaking work of translating tape-recorded interviews from Spanish into English; also she did the difficult work of checking the reliability of my analysis and interpretations of the tape recordings of the confederation's meetings. After I left Maplewood, she helped me keep in touch with my friends in the city's Puerto Rican community. I thank her too for her useful suggestions on the chapter on research methods.

I wish to express my gratitude to my good and wise friend and former collaborator in research, August B. Hollingshead, for his many years of help, and to Jerome K. Myers for his steady support and intelligent advice. I am grateful to Gilbert W. Merkx for his sensitive and valuable criticism of the manuscript and for the many other ways in which he graciously helped me. I am thankful to my mother, Carmen Canino, for discussing with me her insights into Puerto Rican culture. In addition, Reuben Hill gave me advice for which I am thankful.

Janet Turk is the person to whom I am most indebted for indispensable help. Mrs. Turk has worked with me on two major books during the past decade. She reworked copy, edited, and reorganized much of the material. She gave me competent and wise advice. Her enthusiasm was always a source of encouragement; her standards of excellence, an inspiration. I am deeply grateful to her.

A study such as this, with its requirements that night and day, weekends and holidays, be devoted to field work, to the consuming tasks of translating data from Spanish into English, to data analysis, and to the drafting of the manuscript, unavoidably takes much from one as a husband and father. My wife Elaine, my daughter Lynn, and my son Lloyd have understood this problem with exceptional sensitivity and always gave me their wholehearted support. I owe them an unmeasured debt of gratitude.

LLOYD H. ROGLER

Cleveland, Ohio
1972

CONTENTS

PART V
RESEARCH METHODS, INTERPRETATION, AND CONCLUSIONS

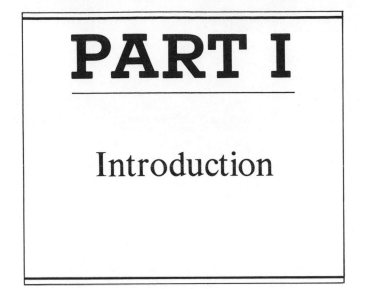

PART I

Introduction

1

The Research Problem

•

That group? Ha! They have no life, no discipline,
no organization!
          — One of Maplewood's
            Puerto Ricans

This book tells the story of a small group of Puerto Ricans who banded together to form the Hispanic Confederation of Maplewood in an attempt to secure for their ethnic community a voice in the affairs of the city. Many times before this, the Puerto Ricans of Maplewood had tried to develop civic, religious, political, and social groups, but with little success. Some efforts came to an end before the groups were even given a name. In a 13-year period, 15 groups developed to the point of being named, but only two survived. In brief, the desire to become organized was offset by the inability of the groups to endure.

This was a surprising and interesting finding because in three years of intense research field work in the slums and public housing developments of San Juan, Puerto Rico, I had never seen such determined efforts to form organizations.[1] The Puerto Rican residents of both San Juan and Maplewood had a Catholic-Hispanic cultural background, were at the bottom of the socioeconomic heap, and had been swept into urban life by forces common to developing societies. They also shared a tradition which neither provided nor valued secondary, grass-root organizations.[2] The San Juan Puerto Ricans had families, friends, and acquaintances, joined Spiritualist and Pentecostal churches, and were part of street-corner, neighborhood, and *cafetin* ("a small combination grocery store and bar") groups, but they had little, if any, of the organizational zest of their compatriots in Maplewood. This observation led to the study of the Hispanic Confederation of Maplewood.

Maplewood is a middle-sized, eastern city, an economically affluent industrial, urban-surburban complex with an economic base in institutions of higher learning, factories, trade, and commercial enterprises, almost all of which place a premium upon the highly developed skills or advanced education of their employees. Historically, the city has been the recipient of repeated waves of migration from the Old World; in addition, many blacks came from the southern United States. Over the last century or so the Irish came, as did the Germans, the Danes, and the Swedes, followed by Italians, Russians, Polish Jews, Slavs, and others. With the exception of the few who brought skills in the developing crafts and wealth, each most recent migrant group took on the jobs at the bottom of the occupational ladder.

Puerto Ricans, comprising the newest immigrant group of major size in the United States have characteristics which set them apart from preceding migrants: they are American-born citizens, albeit with a different language and culture; they cover the spectrum of racial differences and, historically, have practiced racial intermarriage; although Catholic, they did not bring their own clergy with them; and they are the first airborne migration of people into the United States.[3] At the present time, Puerto Ricans are the least assimilated minority of significant size in the United States.[4]

Maplewood's estimated 4,500 Puerto Ricans live in the inner-city neighborhoods and comprise an important part of the city's silent laboring force. They are the dishwashers, busboys, janitors, garbage collectors, and form the bottom rung of unskilled workers in the local factories. Few have ascended to performing skilled manual work and fewer still have joined the ranks of the white-collar workers.

Although to Maplewood the Puerto Rican arrival is a repetition of the recurring pattern of the most recent migrant entering the occupational structure at the bottom of the ladder, to the Puerto Rican, the city presents a welter of new experiences, not at all like those he had in his island home. He sees great diversity of occupations, differences in religion, new variety of ethnic groups. The racial dichotomy between black and white that splits the city's social life intrudes into his own and makes new demands upon his capacity to adapt. Although he is culturally and linguistically marginal to a highly differentiated social setting, he must, tacitly or overtly, actively or passively, confront the bewildering experience inherent in it.

The confining influence of de facto residential segregation conspires with the sting and indignity of prejudice and discrimination to prod the Puerto Rican into a new awareness. His social life extends into his own group, not horizontally into the world of the neighboring blacks, and not vertically into the world of the more economically advantaged second- and third-generation ethnic groups. The awareness of ethnicity is the main axis upon which his orientation pivots as he scans the American and Puerto Rican worlds in the host society. Thus, facing the intricate mosaic of the city's social organization and sharing experiences with persons of his own kind, the Puerto Rican develops a root identification as a member of a distinct cultural group, as a part of *la raza* ("cultural community"), as an *Hispano* ("Hispanic").

When the Puerto Rican looks outward at the American world, he sees Maplewood's numerous social, ethnic, and racial subgroups as cohesive units pushing their own interests through organized action and competing successfully for the city's resources. Because Maplewood is nationally renowned for its urban rede-velopment and antipoverty programs, he sees rich resources given to those groups who, with a strong organized voice, bring pressure upon the city's decision-making circles. In the migrant's words, *"Si no lloras, no mamas la teta."* (If you don't cry, you don't suck the tit.) His frequent though incorrect references to the Mafia as an organization which thrusts the Italians into the solid comforts of an affluent society expresses a view of the solitary individual's impotence and of the need for organizations in the host society. The incentive to form groups evolves out of the migrant's awareness of his ethnicity into an ever expanding conception of how selected groups come to be favored in the host society.[5] The main adherents of this view are those who have taken steps toward assimilation into the new culture but are still confined socially, economically, and residentially to the new ethnic group.

As he looks inward to the city's Hispano world, the migrant sees his compa-triots conducting themselves badly; he often describes their conduct in strongly derogatory terms. When he compares them to the more successful groups in Maplewood and measures them against the norms, lifestyle, and requirements of the host society, he finds little pride within his new ethnic awareness. With the exception of when he compares Hispanos and blacks, the identity of the Puerto Rican is devoid of ethnocentric sentiments although there are nostalgic, romantic memories of life on the island. The prevalent feeling is that of being uprooted from the island-based community of warm, convivial, primary social relation-ships.

In Maplewood there are few institutions that bind the migrants together into a unified emotional whole: a few small Pentecostal churches with their own lay clergy perform this function for a handful of members, and the Catholic church takes an occasional interest. Organizations of whatever kind as long as they are Hispano represent collective efforts to compensate for the loss of communal life. They express the yearning that somehow a piece of the island home can be im-planted in Maplewood. They are attempts to restore what was once experienced and is still valued but is now sorely missed.

Thus, the sentiments and views associated with the Hispano and American worlds converge upon the migrant's ethnic awareness to create a wish for the de-velopment of organizations. This is a departure from tradition and it distin-guishes the city's Puerto Ricans from their peers on the island. Nevertheless, most migrants are not joiners, for they have had, at best, only casual or transi-tory contacts with organizations. Many life experiences, attitudes, and values keep the prevailing wish from conversion into a solid, widespread commitment to support organizations. Not the least important reason is that in looking back upon their organizational efforts, the migrants are disillusioned by a history of group failure.

As a sociologist, I looked upon groups in general as having much greater stability than the migrant organizations displayed. Much of the literature on voluntary organizations coincided with this impression: it dealt with associations as imbedded in the social structure, as "already there."[6] The research questions and theoretical propositions in this literature took as a point of departure for the sociological task at hand the existence, stability, and endurance of such groups although there was recognition that associations do change and some even die out. Nothing in the literature prepared me for the surprisingly volatile and anomic character of Maplewood's Puerto Rican organizations. The observation, therefore, invited questions about the conditions under which emergent groups form, evolve, and vanish as human constructs, not over a long historical period as do general social movements, but over a comparatively short period of time. Such questions were central to the Puerto Ricans' organizational problems.

To uncover the problems, I had many talks with Puerto Ricans who had participated in groups in Maplewood. They alluded to many things: funds that were pilfered, political take-overs, conflict and factionalism among the members, lack of group discipline, loss of interest, and intrusions by the Catholic church. The explanations tended to remain discrete and fragmented, despite my determined efforts to probe more deeply. Often, it appeared that the person's memory had dimmed the experience of participation or that he consciously wanted to forget what had turned out to be an unrewarding experience. The accounts suffered many of the limitations of information recalled in retrospect. The result was that I could not develop from them a holistic view of what had happened to a group, over time, as it proceeded to do its business. Adequate as a base for the original observation, the accounts did not provide satisfying answers to the questions that they themselves raised. Fortunately, at that time I was told about another group getting under way, the Hispanic Confederation of Maplewood. I joined the group as a participant-observer.

The first purpose of this book, therefore, is to present the history of the Hispanic Confederation as it confronted internal and external organizational problems while seeking to represent the interests of Maplewood's most recent migrants. The book narrates what happens when an ethnic minority with a different language and culture and little or no power attempts to achieve a voice in the affairs of an affluent city. It is guided by the need for detailed knowledge of the way in which such a minority copes with the host society. The more prominent field studies on Puerto Ricans have focused upon the culture of the migrants, the problems they confront, and the motivations associated with the Puerto Rican migration.[7] These research studies have added to our knowledge of factors relevant to assimilation, but they have had little to say about the social structural incorporation of the migrant into the urban setting, as channeled and mediated by ethnic organizations.

On the other hand, the extensive literature on migration indicates that social scientists have long recognized the importance of voluntary organizations in the life of immigrants. Their research documents the variety of functions of migrant organizations from preserving continuity in the members' social experience to serving as mechanisms for adaptation to new demands.[8] To perform such functions, however, organizations must be relatively stable; this has not been the case of Puerto Rican organizations in Maplewood. The inconstancy and unreliability of their groups deny the possibility of such stable functions and comprise a barrier to incorporating the migrant into city life. If groups such as the confederation could project their constituent minorities upward into decision-making circles and stabilize their influence in the broader political process, if the overarching institutions would be responsive to the voices they hear, then what the late Oscar Lewis defined as the culture of poverty would be eroded.[9] Thus, the confederation's history addresses a fundamental problem in urban America: the struggle of a disadvantaged minority to achieve solidarity, a sense of community and power, not by a gradual assimilative process but by means of organized collective action.

The second purpose of this book is to delineate social change in a small natural group, the confederation. The opportunity to study social change arose unexpectedly while I participated in the group. At first the confederation was locked in the dilemma of whether to take a direction inward toward the satisfaction of the expressive primary group wishes of the members or a direction outward toward the city's governmental and service agencies in control of the resources valuable to the total migrant community. The two basic incentives that made Maplewood a fertile place for the Puerto Ricans' organizational efforts converged in the life of the confederation and imposed upon the group difficult organizational problems. While in the throes of the dilemma, the group lost the support of American advisors, deposed its first president, and turned aside the brunt of an attempted political take-over. When it was on the verge of dissolution, an intelligent, determined leader emerged, established her own singular control, and took the group through the crisis and into rebirth.

Meanwhile, the confederation had begun to experience basic social change. As it reached out to pressure the city's officials, it exposed itself to intrusions from the outside and change took place: with the clarification of the group goal, norms emerged to regulate the conduct of the members and to change their traditional relationships; an attempt was made to develop an ideology supporting the direction of change. In addition a shift occurred in the composition of the membership whereby values and class-related experiences progressively favored the group's growing activism; docile and uncertain at first, they became more forceful, even militant, in their negotiations with city officials. Because Maplewood's Puerto Ricans had no solid precedent for the successful actions of an independent apolitical group, the confederation had to change itself socially as it attempted to achieve goals that had eluded other groups. Fortunately, but quite by accident, I was provided with the opportunity to do a detailed study of social change in this small, natural group. Such studies are rare in sociology.[10]

The city, the groups, and the persons in the narrative, with the exception of the researchers, have all been given pseudonyms to ensure anonymity. The pseudonyms of the confederation's members are common Puerto Rican names, but none is the real name of a person in the study.

NOTES

1. The findings of this study were published in Lloyd H. Rogler and August B. Hollingshead, *Trapped: Families and Schizophrenia* (New York: John Wiley & Sons, 1965).

2. See Nathan Glazer and Daniel Patrick Moynihan, *Beyond the Melting Pot: The Negroes, Puerto Ricans, Jews, Italians and Irish of New York City* (Cambridge, Mass.: The M.I.T. Press, 1963), pp. 107-108.

3. The statement on the unique characteristics of the Puerto Rican immigrants is taken from Joseph P. Fitzpatrick, "Puerto Ricans in Perspective: The Meaning of Migration to the Mainland," *The International Migration Review*, 11, no. 5 (Spring 1968): 8-9. Along with Fitzpatrick's thoughtful article, this entire issue is devoted to recent studies of Puerto Ricans and contains an annotated bibliography on the subject.

4. For example, see Milton M. Gordon, *Assimilation in American Life: The Role of Race, Religion, and National Origins* (New York: Oxford University Press, 1964), p. 76. According to Gordon's assimilation variables, the Puerto Ricans are the least assimilated minority.

5. Sociologists generally view societal differentiation as the factor which best accounts for the proliferation of voluntary associations in American society. For a succinct statement of this point, see David L. Sills, "A Sociologist Looks at Motivation," in Nathan E. Cohen, ed., *The Citizen Volunteer* (New York: Harper and Brothers, 1960), pp. 74-75. The rise of ethnic awareness among Puerto Ricans is a process which mediates between the new experience of marked social differentiation and the wish to form ethnic organizations.

6. Among these are: Nicholas Babchuk and C. Wayne Gordon, *The Voluntary Association in the Slum*, University of Nebraska Studies, New Series no. 27 (Lincoln: University of Nebraska, 1962); Basil G. Zimmer and Amos H. Hawley, "The Significance of Membership in Associations," *The American Journal of Sociology* 65 (September 1959): 196-201; Arnold M. Rose, "Attitudinal Correlates of Social Participation," *Social Forces*, 37 (March 1959): 202-206; Charles R. Wright and Herbert H. Hyman, "Voluntary Association Memberships of American Adults: Evidence from National Sample Surveys," *American Sociological Review*, 23 (June 1958): 284-294; Howard E. Freeman, Edwin Novak, and Leo G. Reeder, "Correlates of Membership in Voluntary Associations," *American Sociological Review*, 22 (October 1957): 528-533; Murry Hausknecht, *The Joiners: A Sociological Description of Voluntary Association Membership in the United States* (New York: The Bedminster Press, 1962); Richard F. Curtis, "Occupational Mobility and Membership in Formal Voluntary Associations: A Note on Research," *American Sociological Review*, 24, no. 6, (December 1959): 846-848; Wendell Bell and Maryanne T. Force, "Urban Neighborhood Types and Participation in Formal Associations," *American Sociological Review*, 21, no. 1, (February 1956): 25-34; William H. Glaser and David L. Sills, eds., *The Government of Associations* (Totowa, N. J.: The Bedminster Press, Inc., 1966); *Sociological Inquiry*, vol. 35, no. 2

(Spring 1965); Herbert Maccoby, "The Differential Political Activity of Participants in a Voluntary Association," *American Sociological Review,* 23 (October 1958): 524-532.

7. C. Wright Mills, Clarence Senior, and Rose Kohn Goldsen, *The Puerto Rican Journey* (New York: Harper and Brothers, 1950); Elena Padilla, *Up From Puerto Rico* (New York: Columbia University Press, 1958); Beatrice Bishop Berle, *80 Puerto Rican Families in New York City* (New York: Columbia University Press, 1958); for a systematic discussion of research studies on Puerto Ricans on the mainland and island see Joseph P. Fitzpatrick, *Puerto Rican Americans: The Meaning of Migration to the Mainland* (Englewood Cliffs, N. J.: Prentice-Hall, Inc., 1971).

8. See, for example, Kenneth Little, *West African Urbanization: A Study of Voluntary Associations in Social Change* (Cambridge, England: The Cambridge University Press, 1965); William P. Mangin, "The Role of Regional Associations in the Adaptation of Rural Migrants to Cities in Peru," in Dwight B. Heath and Richard N. Adams, eds., *Contemporary Cultures and Societies of Latin America* (New York: Random House, 1965).

9. Fitzpatrick, *op. cit.,* pp. 15-16, infers this point from Lewis's studies, *Five Families: Mexican Case Studies in the Culture of Poverty* (New York: Basic Books, 1959); and, *La Vida: A Puerto Rican Family in the Culture of Poverty, San Juan and New York* (New York: Random House, 1966). Fitzpatrick's analysis of the concept of the culture of poverty is, I believe, quite correct.

10. Wilbert E. Moore, *Social Change* (Englewood Cliffs, N. J.: Prentice-Hall, Inc., 1963), pp. 54-55.

PART II

The Birth of
the Hispanic
Confederation

2

From an Idea
to a Group
.

In its five-mile southward course, a street traverses the old and the new of metropolitan Maplewood, through enclaves of different ethnic groups and races, from comfortable suburban affluence at one end to an inner-core slum area of the city at the other. On one side of the street in this predominantly black neighborhood are small commercial establishments — grocery stores, laundries, liquor and pawn shops, and Catholic and Pentecostal churches. From early morning into the evening, the sidewalk is crowded with pedestrians and clusters of men standing about talking in doorways. On the other side of the street, flanked by the low- and high-rise brick apartment houses of a public housing project for low-income families, stands the elementary school.

The coordinator of a community school program in the elementary school, Frank Joyce, pondered the lack of participation of Puerto Rican residents in neighborhood organizations. One purpose of the community school program was to serve as a center for the organizational resources in the community to meet the needs of the neighborhood. Although 48 Puerto Rican families lived in the public housing development, Joyce realized few participated in the Parent-Teacher Association, the Citizens for Safety, the housing project's City Council, the Women's Club, or the committee in charge of writing a neighborhood newsletter. They were neither availing themselves of opportunities to learn, nor registering their opinions and complaints through the established organizations. Few even attended the elementary English classes of the city's adult education program given for persons deficient in the language.

Joyce knew that needs often had to be defined, for they were not always apparent to the persons who experienced them. Even "the old perennial problems," inadequate housing, unemployment, ethnic and racial discrimination, could be solved only by bringing them to the attention of the neighborhood through organized groups. Thus, Puerto Rican isolation from such groups had to be overcome.

Joyce was not disposed to attempt solutions until he first had made careful plans. A 33-year-old black, he had been born and raised in the Deep South and educated at a university there. He had an awareness of the importance of meaningful communication. Accordingly, it was in character that when Joyce became aware of the problem of the isolation of Puerto Ricans he thought carefully about how to proceed. First, he decided they should be encouraged to join the established organizations which, although predominantly black, reflected the racial composition of the neighborhood. By working together, he thought, the Puerto Ricans and the blacks would learn to relate to each other, and, since both shared the "problems" associated with minority groups, they had a common basis for group action. Joyce felt it was important that the Puerto Ricans *not* form their own ethnic group. This would only lead to further isolation and separation from the neighborhood.

His second assumption, stemming from experience in community action, was that it takes time for groups to become effective. He had no faith in the possibility of quick solutions to deal with obstinate problems of unemployment, discrimination, poor housing, and the lack of proficiency in English. Joyce's experience counseled patience. In addition, he believed that invoking a crisis was not an appropriate stimulus to group efforts. Although symbols with common, but deep, emotional meaning can be used to rally persons into immediate action, Joyce thought this tactic was wrong, because it would leave many serious problems unsolved. His philosophy was that the crux of the problem, ". . . is to develop something, a know-how, a skill within people that can both solve the problem and sustain the people. Something that can be carried from this situation to many other situations. This . . . is the important thing and it takes a bit longer to do this."

With these ideas in mind, Joyce turned to Mrs. Aida Quevedo, a Puerto Rican resident of the neighborhood, who had a son in elementary school. In several informal talks, he discussed with her the Puerto Ricans' isolation and how to overcome it. Mrs. Quevedo, however, was not a good choice to initiate action among the Puerto Ricans. Ever since migrating from San Juan to Maplewood 11 years before, Mrs. Quevedo had felt disgruntled with life. Born on a small farm outside of San Juan 40 years ago, of parents who barely had three years of formal education, she decided at an early age that she did not want to live on a farm all her life. She finished the second year of high school, and, subsequently, one year of secretarial training. At 14 years of age she took her first job, operating a sewing machine in a rug factory. She earned about $30 a month during the following three years, a substantial wage in the period of the Great Depression. She married and had five children within seven years. She started a small clothing and cosmetic shop which at times did over $400 per month in business, but her husband believed they would find greater economic opportunity in the United States. Although she did not want to leave the island, the family emigrated to Maplewood. Instead of moving ahead, however, they seemed to be regressing economically. Mr. Quevedo's "vices" — drinking and chasing women — became worse in Maplewood. Within a year of the move, Mrs. Quevedo divorced him. Shortly after this, a daughter not yet 15 years old, was raped by two black boys in the public housing project. The girl then eloped with a Puerto Rican boyfriend and went back to the island. Two older children were working in a factory and two younger children were still in school. Although Mrs. Quevedo received $273 a month from public welfare, which was supplemented by the earnings of almost $500 a month from her two employed children, she identified herself as a middle-class person, and public welfare payments were a source of embarrassment and humiliation to her. She felt socially and morally superior to her neighbors in the public housing project.

She said that in Maplewood white Americans despise blacks and think Puerto Ricans are blacks, so they treat both groups the same: "Americans consider us [the Puerto Ricans] to be the worst thing in the United States, and we have no opportunity to improve ourselves." On the other hand, she saw her Puerto Rican neighbors making no effort to push upward. Their sole response to discrimination was to call themselves Spaniards — Hispanos — to avoid being labeled black, a strategy betrayed by their own behavior: "Puerto Ricans are loud and improper when they get together. . . . The men chase prostitutes and get drunk. . . . They are so confused about morality, that they have forgotten entirely what is right and wrong. . . . Their parties always end in fist fights. . . . There is always one in the group who will report to a wife the infidelities of her husband." Mrs. Quevedo yearned to get away from her compatriots. Even more than the raw winters of Maplewood, even more than the lower-class neighbors who were Puerto Ricans, Mrs. Quevedo disliked blacks. She said they were "nasty and impolite, and their women, dishonest."

Thus, in reviewing her experiences, Mrs. Quevedo saw the move to Maplewood as an unfortunate one. On the island she had enjoyed a sense of satisfaction and well-being, but life in Maplewood had brought an acute rash of problems — her husband's increased drinking and philandering, the divorce, the raping of her daughter, and the humiliation of public-welfare payments.

At the time Joyce contacted her, Mrs. Quevedo was not a member of any of the organizations he wanted Puerto Ricans to join. However, he explained the problem to her and urged her to speak with her compatriots about it. Mrs. Quevedo told him she believed that, "Puerto Ricans do not like to be in groups," that when brought together they work at cross-purposes, each pursuing his own goals and selfish interests. Moreover to do as Joyce wished would have involved her in visits to persons she scorned as coarse and immoral. After three or four conversations with her, Joyce concluded that he was "really getting nowhere." He said, "She does have a very heavy accent in speaking English. I felt that while she might be very good working with the Puerto Rican population, that is, the Spanish-speaking population, her accent would prevent her from communicating adequately . . . that there would be a need for communicating both with English- and Spanish-speaking people . . . I had difficulty understanding her myself and could not picture her in a local group wherein . . . she would have difficulties in communicating her ideas to them."

Mrs. Quevedo did, however, advise Joyce to turn to a Catholic priest at a nearby church, who was known for his interest in the Puerto Rican community. The priest, Father Ryan, quickly convinced that there was such a need, volunteered his services and became the second link in the activities of the confederation. He suggested that Joyce speak to Mrs. Cristina Estebán, a devout and very active member of his church. Taking immediate action, Father Ryan telephoned Mrs. Estebán and made arrangements for her to meet with Joyce.

Mrs. Estebán was a marked exception among the Puerto Rican migrants. She had completed two years of college in Puerto Rico and, although her English was accented, she spoke it fluently. She was or had been chairman of both the Spanish mass and the Spanish catechism program, as well as president of the Legion of Mary. She had been a member of a neighborhood newsletter committee for the housing project in which she lived, of an advisory council associated with a community school program in the neighborhood grade school, and the Parent-Teacher Association. With three children to raise, a husband to serve, a household to manage, and a full-time job in a garment factory, Mrs. Estebán followed a crowded schedule from early morning to late at night, moving urgently from one responsibility to the next. Since she was widely known in the clubs, groups, neighborhood, and city agencies of Maplewood, where she had lived for 12 years, she was often called upon to serve as an interpreter for Puerto Ricans who did not know English. She had a large circle of friends, associates, and coparents she had acquired as a result of her many activities.

Unlike Mrs. Quevedo, Mrs. Estebán enjoyed a sense of well-being, did not feel her black and Puerto Rican neighbors were socially inferior, and found gratification in her involvement in community affairs. A sense of expansiveness, civic commitment, and self-importance infused her social relations with both Puerto Ricans and Americans in Maplewood. She said, "I have learned a lot and have come to be recognized. I am accepted and respected. I have good friends. Persons at the top in the community recognize me. They ask my opinion and advice about Puerto Ricans. . . . I can recommend persons for employment. . . ."

Mrs. Estebán was not surprised by the problem Joyce presented to her, for she also had observed that Puerto Ricans were not a part of the organized life of the neighborhood. On past occasions, other Americans had discussed the same situation with her. Joyce, however, unlike the others, proposed that something be done immediately. Mrs. Estebán said, "I told him that I could not speak for the Hispanic people. I told him that it would be better to write them a letter to invite them to a meeting. Then, what they said should be accepted."

The purpose of the meeting would be to discuss ways to induce Puerto Ricans to participate in organizations. Joyce followed the suggestion and drafted a letter of invitation which was then translated into Spanish and stenciled for mimeographing by Mrs. Esteban. The letter was delivered to the Puerto Rican residents of the neighborhood.

After seeing Joyce, Mrs. Esteban visited her neighbor and friend, Rafael Zayas, who also lived in the public housing project, to discuss the problem. Rafael Zayas was understanding and sympathetic and offered his active support. Mrs. Esteban reported, "He told me that if the persons refused to come [to the meeting], that he would accompany me in visits to all the persons in the housing project, that he would be with me to the last moment."

Although Rafael Zayas took his promise to help Mrs. Esteban and the confederation very seriously, he was never to have any official position in the group nor was he, in any sense of the word, to be a leader in the Hispanic Confederation. He was burdened with a physically and mentally retarded daughter whom he refused to have placed in an institution. When he came to meetings he was a reliable and quiet participant, but when he had to work overtime, was needed at home, or became overwhelmed with depression at his daughter's condition, he did not come to the evening meetings. Nonetheless, to have defaulted on his vow to Mrs. Esteban, he said, "would have made a liar of me."

In keeping with his vow to help Mrs. Esteban, Rafael Zayas telephoned his brother, Diego, to invite him to come to the first meeting. Diego Zayas was very different from his brother. As an amateur student of American history, he had often thought about groups in American life. He found it easy to understand why the Irish in the United States were accorded preferential treatment. They had earned what they had, he believed, by being a tightly knit and politically effective minority. President Kennedy, for whom he had named his youngest child — John Fitzgerald Zayas — was evidence of the power and affluence of the Irish in the United States. After the Irish, he said, the Italians came and, at first, paid the heavy price of being relegated to the bottom of the social heap. Through the Mafia they then thrust themselves upward into the higher levels of American power. Puerto Ricans not only had no Mafia, but they also labored under the stigma of the assassination attempt on President Truman and of gunshots in Congress in the early 1950s. Diego saw the Irish and the Italians as paramount examples of the Puerto Ricans' need for unification, but he realized that in Maplewood they were unorganized, rent by conflicting voices, and unable to develop strong, aggressive groups that would extract from American society what was rightfully theirs.

To get persons to come to the first meeting and, later, to join the confederation, Mrs. Estebán freely discussed with her friends and neighbors her own personal sacrifices as a devoted wife and mother who found time to help her compatriots even though she worked full time at a factory. She invoked the civic responsibilities of American citizenship, reminded her compatriots that they had no reason to complain about the treatment they received in Maplewood unless they made efforts to remedy problems, and pointed to the almost sacred obligation each Puerto Rican had to help his own kind. She believed enthusiastically in what she said.

One neighbor whom Mrs. Estebán visited was Mrs. Quevedo. She knew Mrs. Quevedo was already familiar with Joyce's concern about Puerto Ricans and that she was an energetic person. However, Mrs. Quevedo was discouraging. Mrs. Estebán said, "She told me of the many difficulties of working with Puerto Ricans and that recently she had made the sign of the cross invoking God to forgive her for washing her hands of the affair as Pontius Pilatus had once done . . . [she felt] nothing could be done with the Hispanos."

Mrs. Estebán was offended by this reaction, but she finally persuaded Mrs. Quevedo to cooperate as a personal favor. Mrs. Estebán told her, "Persons should come to meetings with a desire to work, not to please me . . . [I told her] that if she had tried before and not accomplished anything, she should not feel discouraged. When one cannot progress one way, one looks for another way in which to make the community [of Puerto Ricans] progress." Mrs. Quevedo attended ten meetings while her disgust with the group and her suspicion of Mrs. Estebán's motives mounted. Others at first refused to cooperate or dropped out after a short time. Fidel Amador, for example, told Mrs. Estebán that he wanted nothing to do with other Puerto Ricans because they were not responsible, even with persons trying to help them. Nevertheless, he made token efforts to participate, left the group for almost a year, returned, and was then elected vice-president against his wishes. He served briefly in this capacity, then quit the group. His wife, on the other hand, joined the group almost a year after it was formed, participated regularly, and contributed to meetings with great verve and energy.

Ten to 12 persons attended the first meeting which was held in the last week of November of that year. With the exception of the Christmas holidays, meetings were held every two weeks during the next four months. From the very beginning, however, the meetings took an unexpected turn. Joyce's idea had been to bring Puerto Ricans into already established groups in the community. This message had been transmitted by Joyce to Mrs. Estebán, to Rafael Zayas, and then on to Diego Zayas who took it as a call to organize Puerto Ricans into their own ethnic group.

The desire to form a new group dismayed Joyce, for he believed that an ethnically based organization would further isolate the Puerto Ricans from the community. It was just this isolation which had initially aroused his concern. In addition, at the first meetings, the group began to consider the exclusion of Spanish-speaking persons who were not Puerto Rican. This would leave out Mexican, Colombian, and Cuban families living in the neighborhood, although their problems were the same as those of the Puerto Ricans. They also planned to give first choice of jobs to unemployed Puerto Ricans if opportunities should be discovered. Though understandable to Joyce as a form of "natural loyalty to one's own people," these discussions nonetheless repelled him. They reminded him of the prosperous middle-class blacks in Los Angeles who had recently denounced the migration of southern blacks to their city because it undermined their social and economic gains. Joyce reported, "I was pretty angry and I so expressed myself. If this was what they wanted, if they were going to exclude other Spanish-speaking people who faced the same kind of problems they did because of language barriers, I could not in good conscience be a part of it." His plea was effective. The group decided to accept other Latin American nationalities. Although some members continued to believe that the group should be exclusively Puerto Rican, the issue of nationality was never again raised as a point of controversy.

As coordinator of the community school program, Joyce dealt only with residents of the immediate neighborhood. Puerto Ricans from different neighborhoods of the city, however, attended the first meetings. The residents of the immediate neighborhood felt it would have been indelicate, if not downright insulting, to have denied membership to a person from another neighborhood, particularly if this were done while he was at a meeting. Among Puerto Ricans there were no ingroup-outgroup sentiments dividing neighborhoods. They attached little or no feeling to living in one neighborhood instead of another. The migrants thought a place of residence reflected a geographical accident or a convenience, not a matter of importance. Thus, the group became citywide. In the same fashion, both Protestants and Catholics attended the early meetings, and it was decided that membership was not to be based upon religion. Joyce was concerned, nonetheless, that religious differences might introduce a divisive issue in the group, particularly since Father Ryan, who had first referred Joyce to Mrs. Estebán, served as a resource person at the early meetings. Neither Joyce nor the priest wanted the presence of a clerical collar to influence the group, but their apprehension was unfounded. The religious affiliation of the members was never an issue in the life of the group.

With the decision to form a citywide nonsectarian group available to all Latin Americans came an effort to gain the support of the migrant community. Led by Mrs. Estebán, three or four persons visited Catholic and Protestant churches with Spanish-speaking members, as well as Puerto Rican restaurants and grocery stores, to solicit signatures. A person's signature was taken as an indication of support for a citywide group, although no decision was made as to the total number of signatures that would be required to assume communitywide support. Afterwards, it was never clear how many signatures had been collected. Some of the priests and ministers, restaurant and grocery-store owners, who promised to solicit signatures, never returned the lists; and the members of the group never followed up on such contacts. The effort to assess and gain community support was carried out haphazardly and, as a result, failed to yield what it was supposed to: an exact number of persons who supported the development of the group. Because an effort, however erratic, had been made to gain community support and because those persons contacted greeted the representatives of the group cordially and with interest, the assumption was made that the group had the support of the migrant community. This, in turn, conferred legitimacy upon the efforts and proved to be consequential to the life of the confederation. It seemed to some members, particularly to Mrs. Estebán, that the migrant community had incurred a set of obligations to the group, some of which were formulated in a subsequent meeting at which a name was chosen.

Some persons believed that the adjective "Puerto Rican" should not be included in the name because the group was for all Spanish speakers. But other members objected to words such as "Latins," "Spanish-American," or "Pan-American," because these were names used previously by other groups that had disintegrated — their treasurers had allegedly stolen funds, the groups had been sold out to the local political interests, or the members cynically disregarded their promises to help the migrant community. Whatever the alleged causes of failure, the names of the groups had unpleasant connotations.

Rafael Zayas considered the choice of the name "Hispanic" to be politically unwise. The name would implant a stigma on the group and condemn it to failure because Americans viewed the Hispanic republics of South America as unstable and corrupt. He preferred "Puerto Rican" to be in the group's name, and the group would then be restricted to Puerto Ricans.

Mrs. Estebán argued on behalf of the name Hispanic Confederation. She thought the noun "confederation" was singularly appropriate because it meant a hierarchical arrangement of groups. It implied a citywide program of unifying all Spanish speakers into their own neighborhood groups. Each neighborhood group would, in turn, elect representatives to serve in a higher council, namely, the confederation. Thus, the members of the confederation would be the leaders of the neighborhood groups. Although the confederation was never to be this intricate an organization, nor did the members embark upon efforts to make it such, the name gave birth to the idea, and the idea embodied the loftiest wishes of how the migrant community ought to be organized. The members voted to name the group The Hispanic Confederation of Maplewood.

Despite its not being a true confederation, at least in organizational structure, the name of the group acquired symbolic meaning. To persons who eventually opposed the group, the name carried the unwarranted and insulting presumption that this was *the* Puerto Rican group of Maplewood, *the one and only group* representing the migrant community, which was precisely the way that Mrs. Esteban thought of the group. The point was further clarified by a comment her brother Alfonso Vilá made: "If any neighborhood wants to form a group, it must be done through and with the approval of the confederation, because the confederation is set up this way, and one cannot violate its law."

Mrs. Estebán was by far the most active person in organizing and directing the meetings. At Joyce's request, she assumed the responsibility for inviting persons to meetings, and when the group sought community support she led the effort. At meetings she tried to guide the discussion, but it was difficult for she also had to translate from Spanish to English for the benefit of the two resource persons, Joyce and Father Ryan. Joyce believed that Mrs. Estebán should be the official chairman of the group, and he announced this at a meeting. Some members recoiled at the suggestion; they did not want to be led by a woman. This provided an insight for Joyce into Latin culture — "that women do not take a front seat." He mentioned it to Mrs. Estebán who, at the next meeting, told the members that if her being chairman would detract from the group's effectiveness she did not want the position. Subsequently, elections were held. Diego Zayas became president of the confederation by a margin of one vote, Mrs. Estebán became vice-president, her brother Alfonso Vilá, the secretary, and Ema Batista became treasurer (although this last office was later eliminated).

Mrs. Estebán was not offended by this action. By this time she had begun to have serious doubts about the group's capacity to succeed, and she did not wish to be held responsible in case of failure. Also she feared the loss of popularity that might ensue if she had to take the side of one or another of the members during discussion at meetings. She willingly accepted Diego Zayas as president of the confederation.

The president, the vice-president, and the secretary comprised the *junta directiva* ("board of directors"), while Mr. Joyce and Father Ryan served in an extra-official capacity as resource persons. Although their role as a resource person was limited by the language problem, their presence was relevant to the group's development. Both of them viewed the role as a passive one, requiring that they take a "back seat" at meetings. Both agreed that they wanted to develop, not assume, leadership, that they would provide information to the group and impart decisions made by the group to persons in the city who could help solve the problem under discussion, that regardless of the decisions made they would help the group to define problems and aid the members to develop problem-solving skills, and that they would give the group support. Both viewed their participation as temporary, keeping in mind that once the group was established and functioning, "the need was to work ourselves out of a job."

Of the two, Joyce was the more important. It was Joyce who initiated the development of the group. It was Joyce who provided the meeting place at the elementary school in which he worked. It was Joyce's forceful statement of opinion that opened the confederation to all Spanish speakers in the city. Although it had not been Joyce's intention that a new group be formed, in his desire to see the Puerto Ricans become active in community life he adapted himself to the development of the confederation.

Joyce believed that if membership dues would exclude even one potential member or if the inability to pay would embarrass one person then there should be no dues. The members agreed quickly not to involve themselves in the management of funds, but it was not for Joyce's philosophical reasons. They were concerned with the failure of earlier groups after officers had been accused of squandering or making off with collected monies. They felt any group collecting money was open to charges of pilfering funds. This point even became the subject of humorous comment at a subsequent meeting at which there was a notably poor attendance. Diego Zayas said, "What happened was that we asked for no dues or donations. If we had, we would have a lot of Puerto Ricans here to see if we were using the money for our own personal use."

Joyce saw the confederation as a group of concerned citizens seeking solutions to the problems affecting the Spanish residents of Maplewood. He did not want the confederation to become a political pressure group or to engage in partisan politics. His personal temperament and philosophy ruled out noisy demonstrations. He had serious misgivings about the effectiveness of crisis-oriented groups, feeling that they tended to collapse once the emotions of an aroused membership were spent. He believed a group should proceed slowly, achieve limited goals, develop its inner resources and solidarity, and, eventually, as a self-sustaining enterprise, strive for more difficult goals.

Because of the language barrier, the Puerto Rican participants were not aware of the full range of Joyce's theories about groups. Their decision to stay out of partisan politics coincided with Joyce's views but not because they shared his elaborate assumptions about group development. They decided against political activity, much as they had decided not to handle money, by responding to unhappy memories of groups that had failed.

Thus, the Hispanic Confederation of Maplewood, a citywide, nonpolitical, nonfund-collecting organization of Spanish-speaking residents, resulted unexpectedly from the desire to lessen the isolation of the Puerto Ricans in one neighborhood of the city. Although some of the ideas of the members coincided with those of the resource person, they were, in fact, based not on his philosophy of group organization, but on the simple fear of failure. The processes intervening between the idea and the birth of the group clashed, intertwined, and merged to establish a modest but important foundation that set the pattern for the future.

3

Crisis in the Group

•

At this point in the narration of the life of the group it is essential that I introduce myself in my role as a member of the Hispanic Confederation. A sociologist
by profession and a Puerto Rican by birth and upbringing, I had become interested in studying the life of the Puerto Rican migrants in Maplewood while I was
teaching at the university there. I spent many hours in restaurants and grocery
stores owned and patronized by Puerto Ricans, lingered on the street corners of
the inner-city neighborhoods where they lived, attended religious services conducted in Spanish, visited families, and talked to agency officials who were in
touch with the migrants. Eventually, I learned of the English classes for Spanish
speakers sponsored by the Adult Education Department of the Maplewood
Board of Education. It was there that I met Fidel Amador.

Although Amador had declined Mrs. Estebán's invitation to participate
actively in the Hispanic Confederation and later dropped completely out of
the group, he felt concern about the Puerto Rican migrants in Maplewood. He
said, "Most of us do not know English at all; then, when we learn a few words,
we learn the worst ones. When people hear us, they form bad opinions of us.
One of the first things we learn to say in English is 'What the hell!' A policeman
stops us for a traffic violation and we say to him 'What the hell!' "

For this reason, Amador had joined an adult education English class. The
class was small — from three to 15 students — the room was quiet, and there
was an air of easy sociability, humor, and relaxation. After the teacher lectured
on vocabulary, grammar, and pronunciation, each student endeavored to master
the assignment on an individual basis with the assistance of volunteer teachers.

In March of that year, as part of my effort to learn more about the Puerto
Ricans in the city, I had become a part-time volunteer teacher in this program.
When the students turned to their individual assignments I found myself helping
Fidel Amador. As we worked on his pronunciation, we paused now and then to
talk, and he told me some of the problems of the migrants. He said that there
was not a single Puerto Rican policeman or fireman in Maplewood and hardly
any Puerto Ricans in local city, state, or federal agencies. To overcome this

23

problem, he said, Puerto Ricans had formed many organizations to represent their interests as an ethnic group, but they had all met with failure. Another such group, he told me, had recently been formed, but he had no desire to become a member for he had become disillusioned with groups in general. At this time, he could not recall the name of the group.

A few days after I spoke to Fidel Amador, a young woman who worked for the city's antipoverty agency gave me the name of the group which recently had been formed by Puerto Ricans — The Hispanic Confederation of Maplewood. She told me that the confederation was to have a meeting on the first of April and that I was welcome to attend. Representatives from the Commission on Equal Opportunities and the city's antipoverty agency were to speak at the meeting which had been advertised in a flyer. This meeting was the first I attended.

At that time the Hispanic Confederation was in the fifth month of its life and was known to many agencies and organizations in Maplewood. Word had spread from the elementary school where the group met and from the antipoverty agency, as well as through other channels, that a Puerto Rican group was working for the betterment of the Spanish-speaking community.

The program for the evening of April 1 was outlined in a flyer distributed widely in Puerto Rican neighborhoods. In addition to the date, time, and place of the meeting, the flyer contained a clear and relevant statement of policy: the group did not collect funds and did not engage in demonstrations, meaning that it sought to avoid street-side, pressure-group activities and partisan politics. The purpose of the organization was to improve the lot of the Puerto Rican by working with local agencies and institutions, modifying their services and developing new programs. At the meeting there would be four speakers — one from Maplewood's Commission on Equal Opportunities and three from the city's antipoverty agency. Each speaker would discuss the purpose of his agency, the services it provided, and ways that Spanish-speaking persons in the city could be helped by the agency. Comments and criticisms would be welcomed. Translators were available and refreshments would be served. At the bottom of the flyer in large letters was an invitation to attend the meeting to learn about and contribute to the Hispanic community of Maplewood.

The flyer clearly reflected the character of the group and the decisions made during prior meetings, and that the group was committed to the use of conventional means to achieve its objectives. If successful, the end result would be the development and extension of services for the benefit of Puerto Ricans, all taking place within the broader organizational life of the city.

About 35 persons came to the meeting and, including the speakers for the evening, at least one-third were Americans. The small tables in the library of the elementary school, where Joyce — the early catalyst of the group — worked, were brought together; chairs were carried in from other rooms, and, after some confusion because of different ideas about arranging the room, the participants were seated in a ring of chairs around the tables. The main speakers for the evening sat at the front of the tables on each side of Mrs. Estebán who, at the very last moment, discovered that Diego Zayas, the president, had not arrived; as vice-president the responsibility of chairing the meeting devolved upon her. She was angry and upset. Several months later she told me she had felt very nervous that night at having to sit in the front of the room facing the group flanked on each side by important guest speakers, having to introduce the speakers and the members of the group without preparation, having to regulate the question-and-answer period, and having to translate from English to Spanish and back.

In a barely audible voice, quivering with uncertainty, Mrs. Estebán welcomed the group, made introductions, and turned to the first speaker, the representative from the Commission on Equal Opportunities. The speaker explained the state government's recent enactment of laws prohibiting discrimination based upon race, religion, or nationality in housing, employment, and in relation to working conditions, salaries, and membership in labor unions. His agency, he said, would investigate all complaints of the violations of such laws and, if valid complaints were submitted within 90 days of occurrence, legal action would be taken against the guilty parties. He gave assurance that his agency would cooperate to eliminate discrimination and he repeated the address and telephone number of the office to which complaints should be reported.

Although Mrs. Estebán endeavored to translate, those who did not know English understood little of what the speaker said. Fearing to appear impolite, Mrs. Estebán was hesitant to interrupt the speaker to translate before she forgot what he had said. When she did interrupt to translate, the audience fragmented into small groups to discuss the statement. At other times, there was confusion at the discontinuity of listening to two speakers alternating between an unknown and a known language. Much of what the speaker said was lost.

As the first speaker concluded, Diego Zayas, the president, arrived and sat next to his brother, Rafael, who immediately directed an angry rebuttal at the speaker. How could it be, he inquired, that equality of treatment was a right when the municipal offices of the city discriminated against Puerto Ricans trying to register as voters. He illustrated his point by describing in detail an experience of his wife. This evoked angry comments from Puerto Ricans who had suffered similar indignities. Their daily experiences with discrimination contradicted the speaker's statements. The speaker then tried, through the translator, to clarify what he had said — discriminatory practices did exist, laws on equal opportunities were designed to eliminate such practices, and his office was responsible for investigating all complaints. Mrs. Estebán, uncertain of her role from the beginning, lost control of the meeting. A number of persons, all talking at the same time in

Spanish, recounted personal incidents of discrimination to whoever would listen.

When Mrs. Estebán was able to restore order, she repeated the address and telephone number of the office to which complaints should be reported. She then turned to the three speakers from the antipoverty agency each of whom addressed the group. Only one speaker, Carlos Otero, aroused any audience reaction. Otero prefaced his statement by saying that as a Puerto Rican he understood the hardships of a minority group with a different language and culture. However, he said, opportunities were available and Puerto Ricans should work hard to capitalize upon them. As a specialist in testing job applicants, he offered his help in referring persons to appropriate jobs. Although Otero was of Puerto Rican birth, he seemed to antagonize the audience. He had left the island as an infant and his Spanish was broken and he spoke it with an English accent. One person commented aloud, "I don't understand English, but I don't understand his Spanish either." Some persons attacked him bitterly. To them, testing meant unpleasant quizzes, interviews, and questionnaires. They charged that every visit to a local agency involved an endless round of questions, some personal. Otero attempted to explain in both languages the importance of testing, but the migrants could not understand the purpose of answering questions when what they wanted was a job. One man said, "I came to this city to work with my hands, not my mouth."

During the meeting, Mrs. Estebán noticed me. She said later that I seemed to be "very observant" and "was the only stranger there." She welcomed me to the meeting and expressed her pleasure at my being there. After the meeting she introduced me to her brother, Alfonso Vilá, and Frank Joyce, the advisor. Since she had chaired the meeting, I had assumed that she was the president of the group, but she explained that she was vice-president; she then introduced Diego Zayas as president. Zayas was distant and inquisitive. Unlike Mrs. Estebán who accepted me immediately, he questioned me in Spanish repeatedly, using the formal *usted* ("thou"). I told him my name, that my father was American and my mother, Puerto Rican, and that I had been born and raised in Puerto Rico. They commented that my maternal name, Canino, was really part of my name. There were more questions. I told them I was a teacher of sociology at Maplewood University. I had come to the meeting because I was interested in studying the life of the Hispanos in the city. They finally agreed that, since I spoke Spanish, had been born and raised on the island, had a Puerto Rican mother, and a surname such as Canino, I was a Puerto Rican. My identification as a member of the ethnic group proved to be essential to the study of the confederation.

The following week, Maplewood's Council of Churches invited me to a meeting at which the topic of discussion was the relevance of the ministry to Spanish-speaking people. On the agenda for the occasion were questions about the needs of the city's Spanish community and the availability of factual data on the Spanish population. It was reported that, among Puerto Ricans, one family in five was Protestant, one in three Catholic, and the remainder were "nonchurch related." Of importance was the listing of the Hispanic Confederation as one of eight possible sources of data on Puerto Ricans, the other seven being either official or quasi-official agencies of the city. Although the confederation did not have any such data, to be listed on an official agenda of Maplewood's Council of Churches was a sign of institutional recognition, as was the invitation to the meeting extended to two officers of the group — Diego Zayas and Alfonso Vilá.

After a brief prayer, the president of the Council of Churches began the meeting by posing the question of whether or not the Puerto Ricans intended to stay in Maplewood. The clergymen simply wanted to know if they were dealing with the needs of a stable or transient population, but the blunt and ambiguous question put Zayas on the defensive, making him feel that his commitment and loyalty to the host society were being tested. This was a touchy point for a first-generation migrant whose bonds of kinship and ethnicity still extended deep into the island and whose nostalgic memories of the homeland were still very much alive. Zayas turned to me after the question, his face flushed in anger, and shrugged his shoulders as if to say, "You see the problems we face!" He did not attempt to answer the question. After a short tense silence, he told the group that he got up every morning at three o'clock to go to work and from early afternoon, when he left work, until late at night, he visited Puerto Rican families — "my people" — to help them in whatever way he could.

The discussion then turned to the topic of leadership. One minister proposed that a meeting be held with all Puerto Rican leaders in the city to arrive at a better definition of the needs and problems of this population. Zayas became angrier. "Leaders?" he shouted in accented English, "Who are the leaders? I don't know a single leader." He went on to tell the group with bitterness in his voice that self-proclaimed leaders often appeared before elections when they visited families to persuade them to vote for a particular political party. After elections, he told the council, the "leaders" disappeared, not to be heard from again until the next election. "For this reason," he continued, "the Hispanic Confederation is not political, nor is it religious." Vilá joined Zayas in describing the difficulty of organizing and maintaining groups among Puerto Ricans because of a lack of unification in the migrant community, and he introduced the topic of discrimination against Puerto Ricans.

Zayas then took over again. Earlier he had spoken in English, but now he turned to me to say he wished me to translate from Spanish what he was about to say. He complained that Maplewood's general hospital had a policy prohibiting anyone from speaking Spanish. Several of those at the meeting disputed the existence of such a policy, but to clarify the matter the Council proposed an investigation of the complaint. After further comments about the plight of Puerto Ricans, the meeting was adjourned with a promise by the Council of Churches to give whatever help they could to the problems of the migrants.

A full year elapsed, however, before this group again invited representatives of the confederation to a meeting, again for the purpose of discussing the ministry and the Spanish-speaking people of the city. There were other such meetings sponsored by religious and civic groups; the inevitable conclusion of these meetings was that Puerto Ricans were in desperate need of help. The meetings ended and the groups faded into the background of the confederation's life, but no religious or civic group played a role in its drive to improve the lot of the Puerto Rican.

Diego Zayas and I left the meeting of the Council of Churches together. It was late and he had missed the last bus so I drove him to his home. He looked tired and tense. He told me he had been suffering from severe headaches; his wife had been sick, and her medications were expensive. He then asked me if I would serve as advisor to the confederation.

Zayas's invitation to me to join the group as advisor was made without consultation with the other group officers and members. He believed that as president it was his right to take independent action. Several months afterward, he told me that in addition to needing an advisor with brains he needed a translator, for although he knew enough English to "defend" himself at meetings with Americans he felt more comfortable speaking Spanish and there were times at meetings when, in a fit of anger, he reverted to his native tongue. Also, he said he was opposed to American advisors because he believed they could not make contributions to the group. He told me, "The problems of the Hispanos are of the Hispanos. If we, the Hispanos, cannot solve our problems, then a Frenchman cannot solve them. He (the Frenchman) might try, but he could not do it." Zayas's invitation indicated that he had accepted me as a compatriot, and it gave me a very welcome access to the group.

At Zayas's request, I had already served as translator at the Council of Churches' meeting. I decided I would serve as a translator for the group when asked, but I was not sure of what else I would do for them. What seemed important was that I respond only to the most minimal expectations essential to my continuing participation in the group. I had hoped such expectations would coincide with my desire to avoid activities which might strongly shape the course of meetings, the relations between members, their attitudes toward each other, the objectives of the group, and its contacts with persons, agencies, and organizations. I also decided that the data of the study should include my actions and feelings and the members' responses to them. The changes in the group and my own emotional involvement subsequently led me to modify my original stance as too narrow and constricting.

Four days after I had accepted the invitation to become an advisor, the confederation held a meeting. The officers of the group — president, vice-president, and secretary — and seven members were present. I was there as an advisor, as were Carlos Otero, the testing specialist for the antipoverty agency, and David Jordan, a young man who also worked for the antipoverty agency.

As the meeting began, Jordan showed the participants a letter he had drafted to the Commission on Equal Opportunities stating that in the near future the confederation would submit a list of specific incidents of discrimination against Puerto Ricans. With no further explanation, Jordan then began to ask each person present if he or she had registered as a voter. He spoke in broken Spanish and some of the members could not understand his question. With Mrs. Estebán's help, he let them know that he wanted the names of Puerto Ricans who were not registered voters, either among, or known to, those who were present. He and Otero planned to take such persons to register as voters and to assist them with the required test. Jordan said if the registration officials prevented the translators from helping or if registration was denied for any reason whatsoever this would be reported among the complaints to be submitted to the Commission on Equal Opportunities.

While Jordan was trying to explain the importance of the plan, Rafael Zayas again recounted the story he had told to the group at an earlier meeting about his wife's failing to pass the test although she was fluent in English. He claimed the registration official had been insolent, and then he raised a question about Puerto Rico's status: "If it is a commonwealth," he asked, "why is it not represented by a star in the American flag like the Commonwealth of Massachusetts?" The question precipitated an argument. Someone countered that Massachusetts was represented in the flag because it was a state of the union. "But how can it be a state," Rafael argued, "if it is a commonwealth?" Despite Jordan's exasperated efforts to focus the discussion on his plan to register voters, the issue of commonwealths and states dominated the group's attention. Jordan pleaded with them to take action on the voter registration, but only after their emotions were spent on the argument did the group return to his plan, and the arrangements were finally completed.

The need for more advisors to the confederation was taken up. Jordan recommended Rafael Zayas, and the president, Diego Zayas, agreed, but Rafael rejected the proposal. The two brothers began to argue; they withdrew to a corner of the room, still arguing. Several minutes later, Diego returned to the group, shrugged his shoulders, and reported that Rafael would not be an advisor. By this time the group was discussing Vicente de Serrano, the Puerto Rican political boss of Maplewood, who had been suggested in jest as an advisor. The members explained to me that to have Serrano associated with the confederation would be a disastrous mistake since he was a merchant in political influence, seeking to capitalize upon the problems of Puerto Ricans for his own personal benefit. Each election year, they said, he suddenly developed an interest in the welfare of his compatriots with the aim of delivering their votes to the Democratic candidates. In exchange, he personally reaped the benefits of patronage and political influence. Although it had not been a serious suggestion, Serrano's name was rejected unanimously and with grim finality. Diego Zayas then affirmed his determination to keep politics and religion out of the confederation and repeated the point he had made at the Council of Churches' meeting about the lack of leaders. Mrs. Estebán agreed. She said, "I have never heard a Puerto Rican say that Vicente de Serrano was a leader." There were nods of approval, as the meeting came to an end.

Two days later 12 Puerto Ricans went to the Hall of Records to register as voters. The difficulties anticipated failed to materialize, and all but one were registered successfully. The one exception, Justino Vilá, the father of Mrs. Estebán and Alfonso Vilá, was 69 years of age — the oldest member of the confederation and considered by many of his compatriots as an honored elder citizen. At meetings he was attentive, displaying a quiet dignity. Even when the group discussion was in English he showed interest, turning from one speaker to the next although he understood little of what was being said. His humor was sardonic, but his thoughts were sober and he believed strongly in doing the proper thing. He did not read, speak, or write English, so he was not offended at being denied registration as a voter. He said that the registration officials had been cordial with him and with the group.

Thus, the attempt to establish a claim of discrimination in the voter-registration procedure failed and with it the effort to compile a list of discriminating incidents to submit to the Commission on Equal Opportunities.

Diego Zayas had not gone along to the voter-registration office, but he had heard that while there Mrs. Estebán had been trying to persuade the new voters to register for her political party. The next night he opened the meeting with the statement: "There are things we must talk about. It is important to keep politics and religion out of the confederation; otherwise the group will be destroyed . . . ," and he immediately attacked Mrs. Estebán. She vehemently denied the accusation, explaining that she had turned to greet her father and brother in Spanish during the registration procedure and the Republican registrar, misunderstanding her action, had accused her of influencing people to register for the Democratic Party.

Zayas did not accept her explanation. He went on to tell the group that at earlier meetings, Mrs. Estebán had been overheard trying to persuade members of the confederation to join her church. Caught by surprise, Mrs. Estebán tried at first to defend herself but soon changed to a personal counterattack against Zayas. The exchange was bitter. Jordan tried to pacify them, failed, and in disgust left the room. He returned shortly, but seeing the argument still in full force, he left again. The other members listened with interest making no effort to arbitrate or contribute to the noisy encounter. Jordan returned again to the meeting and in a loud voice drowned out the argument proclaiming that it was entirely appropriate for the confederation to encourage registration of voters, for only 500 Puerto Ricans were registered in the city.

The argument over, Rafael Zayas began to tell the group a long story about one of his jobs which had involved janitorial work in the hospital. As he told the story, the other members talked about the meeting planned for the following night when the director of the Community School Office was to be the invited speaker. They tried to formulate questions to ask after the speech. Rafael then intervened to tell the group that his child had flunked kindergarten two years in a row and only after he had threatened the teacher and the principal was the child promoted to the first grade. His brother Diego remarked that Maplewood's educational system was distinctly inferior to that of Puerto Rico. Mrs. Estebán disagreed sharply, claiming that Maplewood had better schools than Puerto Rico. Quickly, another argument was under way, and several persons got up and left the meeting.

The following night, 11 persons came to the meeting to hear the director of the Community School Office report the results of a survey of Maplewood's public schools. There were 21,000 students in the public schools, he said, of whom 42 percent were nonwhite; 4 percent of all students were Puerto Rican. Because of their uneven residential pattern they were unevenly distributed in the city's 38 schools. Replying to questions, the speaker said that the Department of Education was aware of the language problem of Puerto Rican students. Some were being taught by bilingual teachers, and volunteer English teachers were being recruited.

This information was accepted passively until Rafael Zayas stirred the group with a question. I translated as he asked what the Department of Education proposed to do about supervising students who were participating in the controversial bussing program started at the beginning of the school year as a first step in correcting de facto residential segregation in the schools. The speaker reacted as if the general advantages and disadvantages of the program were under question, since this plan had been given much attention in the local press and had aroused in many people throughout the city a deep set of emotions and attitudes about racial segregation, education of children, political ideologies, and the American way of life. Rafael, however, was not interested in such philosophical evaluations, nor were the others who joined the discussion. Their expressions of concern about a very delicate subject prompted even those who were fluent in English to turn to me for a translation. I finally isolated the point of the discussion. They were concerned about the sexual advances made by black boys to

Puerto Rican girls on the buses. Rafael said, "The boys [Puerto Rican] can take care of themselves, but what about the girls?" The speaker, unaware of the Puerto Rican norm of sheltering young girls, took this as a general question about *all* students, affirmed the officials' concern, and promised closer supervision. The topic was thereby removed from the issue of black-Puerto Rican relations, but the speaker's assurances did little to still the apprehensions raised by the subject, for the casual talk following the meeting continued to center on fears for Puerto Rican girls who rode the school buses.

The next meeting four days later had hardly begun when Diego Zayas interrupted Mrs. Estebán to challenge her comment about the benefits of formal education. Years of schooling, he said, were not necessarily indicative of education. Persons with little schooling were well educated, indeed, if they achieved objectives through knowledge of the environment. Mrs. Estebán then agreed with this definition of education but countered that mastery over the environment is achieved primarily through schooling. The argument, which spread to the whole group, then evolved into a discussion of Puerto Rican problems in Maplewood beyond those of education. Diego Zayas said that employment was the worst problem and no help could be expected from the State Employment Service. The staff, he said, did not know Spanish and treated Puerto Ricans rudely, but what was more important, they always sent Puerto Ricans out to jobs as common field hands, keeping the factory jobs for preferred clients. The discussion ended in a proposal to invite the director of Maplewood's State Employment Office to speak to the group and to let him know the many complaints against his office. A date for the month ahead was set and plans were made to stimulate attendance at the meeting. At the group's request, I agreed to write a letter of invitation to the director of the employment service, provided it was dictated and signed by the appropriate official of the confederation.

At the next meeting two weeks later, the members were delighted to learn that the director of the State Employment Office had accepted their invitation to speak. After talking about the incidental events of the day Mrs. Estebán brought the meeting to order, insisting that preparations for the speaker's reception had to begin immediately. She urged her brother, Alfonso Vilá, to begin to write down what she told him for a flyer to be distributed in Puerto Rican neighborhoods. She no sooner began, however, than her thoughts strayed to her pressing problems: her husband had recently been ill; one of her brothers was in the hospital; there was a possibility that she would lose her job at the garment factory; and she was having trouble with the administrators of the housing project where she lived. Impatiently, Diego Zayas began to draft his own flyer. Mrs. Estebán then criticized what he was dictating, and another personal argument broke out.

Mrs. Estebán then asked who would introduce the speaker, but before anyone could answer she returned to her problems with the housing administrators. Rafael Zayas interrupted to tell about his income tax refund. Alfonso Vilá complained that the small clothing store he had just established was already nearly bankrupt. As the meeting deteriorated into a forum for expressing personal problems, no decision was made about the introduction of the speaker.

A week later as I drove through a public-housing project on my way to the group meeting I noticed two police cars parked in front of a high-rise building with a crowd around the door. Rafael Zayas, who was at the elementary school when I arrived, knew about the incident. Two of his compatriots had a fight, he told me, and one man battered the other with a baseball bat. Someone at the scene had wanted Rafael to call the police, but Rafael had refused. He said, "Then you have to give the police your name and address. You never know where such a thing is going to lead. Also, those two are both my friends and I knew why they were fighting. It was private and, as a friend of both, I could not violate their trust by divulging it to anyone."

Entering the room during this conversation, Mrs. Esteban overheard Rafael and proceeded to denounce him as typical of all unthinking Puerto Ricans who react violently to real or alleged provocations. It was imperative, she said, for Puerto Ricans to learn to control themselves. She told us that one night when she was awakened by a man who had broken into her apartment, her husband had wanted to load his revolver, but she had insisted on calling the police. The man was apprehended and taken away. "You see," she pointed out, "one can cope with a problem without resorting to violence."

"But," insisted Rafael, "you took a chance. That man could have been armed with a knife and slashed or even killed you before you would have known it. Any time anyone attacks me, I am ready to fight." He went on to tell another experience and Mrs. Esteban retorted heatedly with still another story. By this time the group had gathered for the meeting, but the argument continued for an hour. David Jordan's efforts to pacify the contenders were fruitless. Each continued to defend his views noisily. Jordan left the room, returned, listened a while, and finally shouted that the confederation needed to get down to business. Then, the argument subsided.

Jordan told the group that the director of the State Employment Service had accepted the invitation to speak to the confederation because a campaign was being planned to recruit agricultural workers for truck farms in the state. Pressure for the campaign came from the higher echelons of the federal government, and the director would undoubtedly use his appearance before the group to seek workers. Jordan warned the group that workers on the truck farms were a motley criminal crew who fought with knives or broken bottles and that Puerto Ricans hired for such work would first be subjected to insulting questions at the employment office and then required to work nine hours a day, six days a week, for $40; they would not be permitted to drink while they were working and their living quarters would be inadequate.

Jordan later confessed to a personal dislike for the director of the employment service and told me that the abysmal living conditions of Puerto Rican farm workers in the state made him angry. He said; "I guess I was being hostile, but I developed a dislike for him when I first met him. The first time I went to his office he was interviewing a job applicant and he said to me, 'I'll be with you as soon as I *get rid* of this applicant.'"

Since employment was such a problem for Puerto Ricans, the group agreed that the director was the most important speaker the confederation had ever invited. For this reason, insisted Mrs. Estebán, all preparations should be detailed and complete, and she reiterated that it was the president who should introduce the speaker, and chair the meeting. Since Diego Zayas had not come to the meeting, she said she would make it a point to instruct him about the procedures to be followed. She requested guidance on how to greet the speaker, introduce him, conduct the question-and-answer period, and bring the meeting to an end. She took copious notes in precise outline form. She also offered to distribute the 2,000 flyers Jordan had stenciled under the assumption that it would take this many to ensure an attendance of 100. In addition to the usual information on the date, time, and place of the meeting, the flyer stated that understanding of employment programs would improve the opportunities for the Hispanic community. Mrs. Estebán asked me, and I agreed, to assist her in delivering the flyers to their places of distribution.

Thus, one week later I found myself driving Mrs. Estebán to Puerto Rican neighborhoods to distribute the flyers. We were accompanied by her father, Justino Vilá, dressed in his best — a suit, vest, and hat, all in black, with a heavy gold watch fob and a medallion of the Virgin Mary dangling from his vest. When Mrs. Estebán had asked me to drive her around she had not mentioned her father, but as the afternoon progressed it became clear to me that not only did Don Justino find it an opportunity to see old friends but also he was acting as a chaperon — his presence protected his daughter's reputation.

We visited nine places — grocery stores, restaurants, a Catholic church, and the homes of two Puerto Rican lay ministers — and at each place Mrs. Estebán was greeted effusively and warmly, the women embracing and kissing her when she arrived and left; the conversation was mainly about relatives. As we drove from one place to the next, she told me about the persons being visited, their background on the island, when they had arrived in Maplewood, where they worked, and about their friends, enemies, and personal problems. She identified each person within the relevant network of blood and affinal relatives and described present and past linkages among families. She traced connections through the *compadrazgo* ("coparent relationship between godparent and the

34

parent of the baptized child"). When I tested her knowledge of this system of relationships by asking her about some person I had met, she not only knew the person but also could identify his blood, affinal, and coparent relationships and supplemented this knowledge with information about who his friends were. Now, while I carried the box of flyers and her father stood by lending respectability to the occasion, she explained the purpose of the visit to her friends, and brought her knowledge of the community's affairs up to date. Though brief, the visits were long enough for a rapid and intense exchange of information about relatives. No member of the confederation was as well informed as Mrs. Estebán about the details of migrant life.

The last stop of the afternoon was at the home of the Reverend Arturo Prieto from whom Mrs. Estebán requested cooperation in distributing the flyers. The Reverend regretted that he could not do much because he no longer had a congregation. Since working full time in the factory job Mrs. Estebán had helped him get, he had had to neglect his religious duties, and besides, he told us, his congregation had disbanded because they had no place to meet. He promised, however, that he would come to the meeting and would bring one of his disciples.

While Mrs. Prieto urged refreshments on us, the Reverend said that he meant no offense to me as a university professor, but knowing the gospel truth was of far greater importance than being well educated. He told us a long story of his conversion to the religious life, which his wife interrupted to affirm what a wretched, sinful person he had once been. Despite the religious medal hanging from his watch fob, Don Justino took offense when the Reverend began to attack Spiritualism as a pagan religion. Before the argument could proceed further, Mrs. Estebán ushered us out of the house, thanking the Prietos for their hospitality. As we walked to the car, Don Justino said to me, "I must apologize. I generally do not oppose persons or argue with them, but I had to set that man straight on Spiritualism." The visit to the Prietos' house brought to an end the confederation's more than month-long preparation for the meeting with the director of the State Employment Service.

Although 2,000 flyers had been distributed, attendance at the meeting fell far short of Jordan's estimate of 100 persons. At the social hour following the meeting I talked with those I had not met before and asked how they had heard about it and what had prompted them to come. Almost all had heard about it from relatives and friends and came with them, or they had already attended at least one meeting of the group. Not more than three or four persons had seen the flyer, so its effect upon attendance was, in all respects, negligible. Attendance was almost entirely a result of the network of associations extending from those persons who were active participants in the group. Including officers, advisors, the speaker, and some interested Americans, 36 persons attended the meeting.

Diego Zayas welcomed the group, announced that there would be a guest speaker, and asked the secretary to read the minutes of the last meeting. Vilá was surprised, for minutes usually were not taken or read, so he mumbled a few words about questions which had been asked the former speaker from the Community School Office. Zayas then turned the meeting over to Mrs. Estebán who, after a brief introduction of the speaker, said she would translate from English to Spanish for the benefit of the audience and I would translate from Spanish to English for the benefit of the speaker. This was an unexpected division of the work of translating, but equally unexpected was the fact that the meeting was being chaired by both Zayas and Mrs. Estebán, for Mrs. Estebán had vowed that this time the president would be in full charge.

The speaker began by displaying flyers advertising, in Spanish, jobs for Puerto Ricans. One of the flyers described the opportunities and attractions of agricultural work as part of the campaign to recruit farm workers. He explained that job counselors were available at the employment office and that there were a number of job-training programs. He realized, he said, that there was a language problem, but there were two or three persons at his office who could "fight their way through Spanish." He spoke for 20 minutes, a much shorter period than had been expected.

No sooner had he finished than Diego Zayas jumped up with the first question: "Why is it that Puerto Ricans who go to your office are immediately referred to agricultural work without being told of other employment opportunities?" Before the speaker could answer, Zayas told the group that in 1959, having just been discharged from the United States Army after the Korean War, he went to the employment office where they insisted upon referring him to a farm job. Since then he himself had helped many Puerto Ricans to get other kinds of jobs and he knew from personal experience that the employment office always sent Puerto Ricans to the farms. The speaker denied the accusation, arguing that the group had to understand how the employment system functioned and the limitations imposed upon the services offered by his office. Along with information on job vacancies, he told them, potential employers indicated qualifications that the applicants must have. He could not change qualifications that reflected the employer's judgment of the skills required for the job. Perhaps, he went on, Puerto Ricans were sometimes underclassified according to their level of skills, but again, this was a result of the language problem. Communication was impaired, and Puerto Ricans often hesitated to ask questions when they came to his office.

The meeting suddenly became tense as murmurs of disagreement spread throughout the audience, and several persons began to dispute the speaker's explanations. One insisted that no one at the employment office had sufficient mastery of Spanish to assist the Puerto Ricans. Another asked why they didn't employ a Puerto Rican with bilingual skills. The director said this was impossible because he had to select employees from a list submitted to him by the central office in the state capital. He explained the bureaucratic regulations under which he worked, and he repeated that if an employer required the job applicant to be fluent in English he had to consider this requirement in recommending applicants for the job. Factories did not want to employ workers, he said, who did not know English because they would then have to hire another person as a translator to give instructions in Spanish. Diego Zayas responded with the contention that to withhold employment because of inadequate English was to deny Puerto Ricans the opportunity to learn the language on the job. Several others argued with the speaker who responded by reiterating the rules and regulations governing his office. Although he was director, he said he had no control over the services that were provided, and he cited regulations making each request impossible within the limitations of his office's budget.

Diego Zayas began to shout at the speaker and wave his fist. "Budgets! Budgets! Budgets! That is all we hear from you people. We cannot do this and we cannot do that because of budgets for this and budgets for that. But I bet if someone were to take a close look at your budget he would discover expenditures of far less value than what we are proposing to you."

Mrs. Estebán looked at Diego disapprovingly. No one was mediating the discussion. Indeed, Diego was leading the attack with his caustic comments, and the others were following, all criticizing the employment office at the same time. At first controlled, the speaker began to flush in anger. "Let me ask you a question," he demanded. "That's only fair since you have asked me so many. I would like to know why you hold these meetings in Spanish?"

While Mrs. Estebán translated, several persons looked astonished at the question. The first to erupt was Diego Zayas who bypassed me as translator and talked directly to the speaker in English. "Look, Mr. Director," he said. "Let me ask you a question. If you lived in Puerto Rico and were trying to form a confederation of Americans, just what language would *you* speak?"

The speaker gave no answer, but instead requested the privilege of asking another question: "Who has to adjust to whom?" Employers, he said, were not going to modify the qualifications. It was the person looking for work who had to adapt himself to the requirements defined by the employer. Diego immediately took up this point. "Look here! I am familiar with the qualifications you talk about. I have had personal experience with them. I once took a civil-service examination at the post office and scored 85. I was told that to be employed I had to score 90, but I know that if I had scored 90 the requirements would have been raised to 95. Had I scored 100 they would have demanded 200."

The point, Diego went on, was that job qualifications were flexible and did not have to be taken as dictated. Often, he said, the alleged requirements were increased to rule out Puerto Rican applicants. Requirements, he insisted, were

37

just a guise to cover the practice of discrimination. He then tried to bring the meeting to an end, but Mrs. Aida Quevedo, the woman to whom Joyce had first turned in an effort to bring Puerto Ricans into community organizations, insisted on being heard. She requested that I translate her question which turned out to be a long passionate speech about the need for cooperation between Puerto Ricans and Americans. She finished by calling attention to the warmth and hospitality accorded to Americans living on the island and to the inferior treatment given to Puerto Ricans by Americans in the United States. Unity between the two was impossible as long as Americans benefited at the expense of Puerto Ricans, she said.

While I translated, several persons interrupted to ask what, in fact, Mrs. Quevedo's question was. She insisted that she *did* have a question and she *would* be heard. "I would like the speaker to tell me his reasons for asking insulting questions," she said. I translated the question, but the speaker did not answer. This time the meeting was completely out of control and came to an unannounced end.

In response to the specific issue of qualifications for jobs, the director of the employment office had raised the question — who should adjust to whom? Although he was concerned only with the problems of employment, the question had a much broader meaning to the audience. The answer, obviously, was to be understood as "It is you, the Puerto Ricans, who must adapt to us, the Americans — to rules we established before you arrived." This point touched upon emotionally sensitive facets of the migrants' adaptation to the American environment with its apparently unyielding discriminatory standards. It invited agonizing comparisons between the dominant and subordinate cultures, sometimes leading to the painful conclusion that what Puerto Ricans are — *nuestra manera de ser* — is of little consequence when matched against the hard requisites of the industrially advanced and prosperous American society. During the meeting the speaker had become a symbol to the Puerto Ricans of the opportunities being denied them, of the rigid rules which, when applied, inevitably worked to their disadvantage, and of their reduced self-esteem.

In the heated exchange between audience and speaker, Mrs. Estebán, noticeably upset, withdrew from the group. She went to the back of the room to arrange the cookies, donuts, and soft drinks which were to be served as refreshments. After the meeting she wasted little time before reprimanding Diego Zayas. "What a way to behave! President of the confederation and you insulted our guest of honor. You were hostile, angry, and belligerent. It was clear to everyone. Such behavior is not proper for you or for anybody else, but particularly for you because you are president. You comported yourself badly."

Even those who had also attacked the speaker nodded in agreement. Such a breach of etiquette, they felt, was unjustified, regardless of how wrong the speaker had been. But as we walked together to the parking lot Diego was unrepentant. He confessed that he had had an urge to punch the speaker. His brother Rafael said to me, "Mr. Canino, you see the kinds of things we have to put up with. I think you understand them now."

A week later Mrs. Estebán telephoned me, still upset about the meeting. Attendance had been poor, she said, because those we visited that afternoon had not cooperated by distributing the flyers. They were being influenced by some Puerto Ricans who, envious of the confederation, were spreading rumors about the group. Several months later, she told me that the main problem at that time had been Diego Zayas's lack of leadership. Although his uncontrollable outbursts were unpleasant, she said, he was not a "bad" person; he was simply wrong not to plan the meetings. He claimed that planning was unnecessary since he carried the agenda in his head, yet often when starting a meeting, he said, "Well, what are we going to discuss tonight?" Mrs. Estebán told me indignantly that he disregarded her advice to have minutes taken and read at each meeting, believing that as president all decisions should be solely his own. Moreover, she complained, his beliefs were as wrong as his actions, since he thought the American advisors were "cheating us ... taking us to be stupid ... and not willing to do anything to help us." She reported that she could not dissuade him from suspecting the American advisors.

By this time there had been changes in the advisors to the group. Father Ryan, the priest who had first served as an advisor along with Frank Joyce, had discontinued coming to meetings. Joyce, too, had stopped attending regularly. Unlike David Jordan, Joyce viewed his role as a passive one. When arguments at the meetings reverberated through the halls of the elementary school, where he had arranged for them to meet, he came in for brief moments, usually in a vain effort to arbitrate conflicts and quiet the group. The lack of organized procedure at the meetings made him impatient. He told me: "They ramble on and on. The tendency is to beat one point to death. We introduce the question of employment and 30 persons at the meeting have to relate some 15-minute experience they had in trying to get a job without really offering any constructive ideas. This group needs to learn how to take an idea and follow through."

A year later, Joyce told me he had left the group because he felt it was a firmly established, going enterprise although no one else in the confederation shared this optimistic view. Unfortunately, his departure was not interpreted in the way he meant it. Word got around to the members and outsiders that Joyce wanted to dissociate himself from the group because nothing had been or could be accomplished. Whatever his reasons for leaving, Joyce never returned to the group. Summer vacation started at the school and the room was no longer available as a meeting place. Without any discussion of this fact, the group never again met in the elementary school where Joyce worked.

The principal American advisor at this time, David Jordan, urged the group repeatedly to take action about the discrimination to which Puerto Ricans were being subjected. He attempted to organize group feeling against an environment he viewed as hostile, but he failed to arouse in the membership an emotional fervor to right the wrongs he felt so deeply. His growing dissatisfaction with the group was markedly noticeable in his frequent pleas that much needed to be done and time was being wasted in irrelevant discussions and personal arguments. He came to only one more meeting before he, too, abandoned the group.

Even the members were becoming disillusioned with the confederation. Ironically, the very ones who most often expressed their own personal problems at the meetings and at first had found the experiences of the others interesting began to grow weary of the procedure. One said, "Why listen to their problems? My family and relatives have enough problems. I could be listening to theirs." Meetings became progressively more disorganized as each person's problems stimulated the others to tell their own. Even the feeling of relief (*desahogarse*) — to "undrown" oneself by talking about one's personal problems — was seldom complete, for soon one person interrupted, followed by another; these digressions pushed the members into a circle of further and more extensive self-revelations and, at the same time, frustrated each person's desire to be heard. During this period several members withdrew from the group. One of them, Pepe Batista, explained to me: "They are always arguing and discussing personal problems. They were so confused that they discussed two or three topics at the same time and never reached a conclusion."

The actual structure of the meetings invited dissatisfaction. They began from one-half hour to a full hour late, and often it was not certain if they had actually begun or if they were waiting for other members to arrive. Even though most persons who came were known to the others in the group, the meetings usually began with a time-consuming round of introductions: the name of each person was stated and his address in Maplewood, his hometown on the island, other places he had lived, the year of his arrival in Maplewood, and where he was presently employed; occasionally, further identification was noted by mentioning blood and affinal relatives and coparents. These introductions activated the communal bonds among the Puerto Ricans and set the tone of the meeting. The presence of relatives — mainly Mrs. Estebán's father and brother, and Diego Zayas's brother — reinforced this procedure.

Although problems discussed at the meetings were often relevant to the goals of the confederation in that they demonstrated instances of general conditions among Puerto Rican migrants in Maplewood in need of improvement, the group was unable to weld individual complaints into common issues and then formulate plans for remedial action. Occasionally, when a step was taken in this direction, the effort would be frustrated as interaction between members again became diffuse, because the topic lacked clear focus and the level of discussion turned personal and conflict-ridden. Energies were dissipated, and the participants became discouraged by the frequent arguments, particularly those between the Zayas brothers and Mrs. Estebán.

Despite the services of translators, most information presented by speakers from local agencies remained unassimilated and unused because coherent internal procedures were lacking. When a speaker was sufficiently well understood so that his attitudes became symbolic of the humiliating experiences in the new environment, the members would strike at him verbally; having spent their emotions, however, they could not develop or sustain action either against him or against the source of discontent he represented. The attention of the group was riveted upon the situation of the meeting, not upon distant goals. They were not able to defer gratification, no matter how transient and incomplete, until some future date.

Thus, during this period, the first phase in the life of the confederation, the group was in an organizational limbo. Unable to create satisfaction among the members, continuity in the pursuit of external objectives, or effective internal procedures leading from one decision to the next, the confederation could not provide its members with either the pleasures of intimate, warm primary associations or the feelings of accomplishment, importance, and recognition that come from participation in an effective action group. Consequently, in the eighth month of its life, after 28 meetings, the group was in crisis. The Hispanic Confederation was on the verge of reproducing the failures of other Puerto Rican groups in Maplewood.

4

The Political
Assault

•

Mrs. Estebán was strongly committed to the confederation and fearful that it would break up. She went about urging friends and relatives to join the group, and she often turned to me as group-advisor. She telephoned and visited my university office to discuss rumors about the confederation, the difficulty of organizing Puerto Ricans, and her plans for the group. Having taught school in Puerto Rico, she also was interested in educational problems and enjoyed talking to me as a fellow professional. But regardless of how often the topics strayed to her other interests, she always came back to the confederation. As a result of the group crisis, our friendship grew, and she began to make me her confidant.

When the members were denied the use of the regular meeting place (the elementary school where Frank Joyce worked), the confederation's problems increased. During the first summer of the group's life, meetings were held in different places: a church, an office in the city's antipoverty agency, and once, when the recreation room of a Catholic parish was unexpectedly locked, on the front steps and sidewalk of the church. One evening the group could find no place to meet. At my suggestion we went to the university building that housed my office and used a medium-sized seminar room. The building was centrally located, the room was soundproof and air-conditioned and, with little effort, could be arranged for meetings. Mrs. Estebán asked if all future meetings could be held there. I had serious reservations about her request, as I did not want the group to seem to be connected with the university. She pressed me on this point, however, and I finally agreed, with the understanding that there was no obligation on either side.

Mrs. Estebán began to assume the mantle of leadership. Without consulting the members, she arranged for the meeting place. To bolster her point, she explained that the confederation was, after all, a citywide organization and should be accessible to all Hispanos regardless of neighborhood. Undoubtedly, her decision was also based upon the prestige of meeting at the university, a point she did not hesitate to mention when recruiting new members.

Along with recruiting members and ensuring that the group had a convenient

meeting place, Mrs. Estebán turned her attention to the need for organized procedures at meetings. Although her own contributions often were unrelated or
incidental to the topics being discussed, she complained at practically every
meeting about the lack of organization. One evening she announced that members should not discuss personal problems at meetings. She said that people were
tired of hearing about personal problems and such recitations consumed time
and created confusion. There was no vote on this rule, nor were its advantages
or disadvantages discussed. As vice-president Mrs. Estebán had no official authority to control group discussion, but occasionally she began to use the rule, de-
claring persons "out of order" when they failed to comply. Although she, herself,
often violated the rule, this inconsistency was never discussed by the other
members. These changes resulted largely from Mrs. Estebán's attempts at stabili-
zation and guidance through a critical period.

In contrast to Mrs. Estebán's public and widely known efforts to cope with
the confederation's difficulties, little was seen of Diego Zayas during the five
weeks that followed the meeting with the director of the city's State Employment Office. Nor did he attend the following two meetings. Rumors circulated
that he would soon have an ambitious plan to rescue the group and make it successful. He told some members that he was consulting with a friend — a lawyer
in New York City — who had experience in the development of Puerto Rican
action-groups.

The truth was, however, that Zayas's secret moves were designed to hide his
plans that had resulted from a chance meeting with Vicente de Serrano, the
Puerto Rican political boss of Maplewood.

To understand the political system as a source of influence on groups such as
the confederation, it is necessary to examine the role of the political boss. This
role is central to the dissemination of political influence in the migrant community and perhaps is best studied by describing the actions of the political boss
and their meaning for the migrant and for the political structure of the city. Because a political rally brings together many of the relevant actors in the scene —
candidates for office, established and aspiring politicians, migrants, the political
boss and his aides — it reveals the public, ceremonial features of the political boss's
role. The rally also reveals the pressures on the political boss and how the person
in that role, in this case Vicente de Serrano, copes with such pressures.

Shortly before a municipal election, in the fall after the founding of the confederation, Serrano organized a political rally. The flyer advertising the rally
stated that the honorable mayor would present solutions to housing, employment, and civil rights problems of Puerto Ricans, that a dance would be held
afterward, and drinks would be served, all at no charge. The flyer was signed by
Serrano and one of his aides. Of the candidates in the coming election, the
mayor was the central figure and would be the ranking dignitary at the rally.

Although scheduled for 7:00 P.M., this turned out to be "Puerto Rican time." During the usual delay, the audience was entertained by a Puerto Rican band which also played at the dance afterwards. Finally taking the microphone, Serrano opened the rally by announcing that many of the speeches would be in English but, since the attending Puerto Ricans knew English, Americans should be aware that this fact presented no problem. (Of course, many in the audience did not know English.) He introduced the Democratic town chairman and the candidates for office — probate-court judge, city treasurer, city clerk, and sheriff — pronouncing their names in Spanish. As each candidate was introduced, he stood to be recognized, then went to a table where he sat facing the audience. Serrano's political aides hovered around him, whispering in his ear. At almost nine o'clock the mayor had not yet arrived, but Serrano assured the audience that he would come soon. Finally, the mayor arrived. There was a perfunctory round of applause as he came forward to sit with the other candidates.

Serrano then spoke, explaining that Puerto Ricans had a more valid right than most Americans to march in the Columbus Day parade, soon to take place, because Columbus *had* discovered Puerto Rico, whereas there was some doubt as to who had actually discovered the United States. The mayor then spoke briefly. He said he would be proud to lead the Puerto Rican contingent in the Columbus Day parade and that Puerto Ricans would be given equal employment opportunities if they had equal skills. (This was the extent of the announced plan to solve the Puerto Ricans' problems.) The mayor looked tired and drawn. He took pride in his ability to communicate with ethnic minorities, but he had been ill and felt ineffective that night. Each candidate then spoke for a few minutes, emphasizing the importance of voting. Some tried a few words in Spanish, their mispronunciations evoking subdued ripples of laughter from the audience; others recounted anecdotes of their visits to Puerto Rico — the hospitality of the people, the warmth of the climate. The mayor's assistant told the group that the mayor was the Puerto Ricans' good friend and that Serrano was often at city hall seeking favors for his compatriots. Serrano then permitted each of his aides to say a few words as he stood nearby dominating the whole procedure with his commanding presence. None of the speakers matched his talent for oratory.

Before the short speeches, between, and afterwards, Serrano was in full control of the situation. He talked about a variety of subjects. Americans, he said, had to get over the idea that Puerto Ricans were "bandits"; they were first-class citizens, he asserted, having fought courageously in two world wars; they were people of honor and dignity, the heirs of true democracy, for among them, he said, "the blackest person is white." He referred to himself as one who could pass for any nationality but was proud to be Puerto Rican. He recounted his years of self-sacrifice for his compatriots and told the audience that he welcomed the rise of leadership among them and the development of ethnic organizations, that he would cooperate with all groups and all leaders, and would continue to work on behalf of the Puerto Rican community as a translator in court.

Then, turning to the candidates but still speaking to the audience, he told them that during the election four years previously he had bolted the Democratic Party and gone to work for the Republicans because, "at that time I did not think the Democrats were doing enough for the Puerto Ricans." He soon recognized, he went on, that this had been an error because, "it is the Democrats who help the Puerto Ricans." The mayor, he said gesturing toward him, was a friend of the Puerto Ricans, and he, Vicente, was free to go to city hall at any time in the interests of his countrymen.

At the end of his speech, he struck a new and ominous note:

> I know you have all heard bad things about me. I know everything that goes on. You will hear bad things about me when this rally is over. Let me tell you that Vicente has had many knives stuck in his back, but the blades bend and the knives fall to the ground.

When the rally was over, dancing started, free beer was served, and Serrano mingled with the crowd, speaking to almost every person there. To one, he complained that he had wanted to hang a Puerto Rican flag in the building as a decoration for the rally but, he said, "They steal everything." To another he boasted, "The Puerto Ricans are under my control. They will do anything I say."

In response to a later question, Serrano said that at least 200 persons had attended the rally. By my count there were 97. Perhaps one-half of these were under voting age, the majority of them teen-aged boys who had come for the entertainment. While the ceremonies were under way, most of the audience ignored the speakers and talked to each other. Some were not even aware that the mayor had spoken and they knew little about the candidates or the offices.

As a political ritual reenacted before elections, the rally did little to convert voters to the party or to stimulate them to vote. Intended or not, the real result of the rally was to validate Serrano's importance as political boss. While most of the audience had come to meet friends and have fun at the dance, all realized that Serrano was in command as host. In his speech he had managed to convey to the Democratic candidates his loyalty to them and his importance in getting votes for them. At the same time he had shown the Puerto Ricans his importance to *them* through his influence at city hall and his friendship with these men in power. He had also presented a picture of his own indestructibility. The whole performance, including his exaggerated estimate of the turnout was intended to impress both sides with his qualities of dynamic leadership. It was a remarkable demonstration of the political boss's role, but in order to maintain his standing with the Democratic bosses, it was necessary to bring and keep Puerto Rican groups under his control. For this reason Serrano planned to take over the confederation by forcing a merger with the recently formed Pan-American Association.

The Pan-American Association had grown out of the Legal Assistance Office established in the spring of that year and located on the other side of the city's business core from where the elementary school in which the confederation began was situated. The neighborhood was a racially mixed slum — the city's largest — and had the greatest concentration of Puerto Ricans in Maplewood. The Legal Assistance Office was part of a nonprofit corporation supported by public and private funds. Its purpose was to give local minorities legal aid and representation both in civil and criminal problems and in their contacts with the police, landlords, the business community, and schools. In addition to providing free legal service, another purpose of the Legal Assistance Office was to organize the financially deprived of the neighborhood into associations of tenants, parents, and action groups.

In a very short time, the Legal Assistance Office developed a large clientele and became the informal meeting place of interested Puerto Ricans. Of the professionals working there, the Puerto Ricans were most attracted to James Finn, a personable, 26-year-old lawyer who had a zest for dancing to Puerto Rican music and a general interest in Latin American culture. Late in the afternoon and in the early evening, Finn and his Puerto Rican friends would carry chairs from the office to the sidewalk in front of the pool hall next door. There they would sit and talk about the girls walking by, the baseball scores of the day, the police's unfair treatment of slum dwellers, and the availability of small-business loans for poor persons. Out of these conversations came the idea that the Puerto Ricans were in desperate need of an organization to represent their interests. They dismissed the confederation as unimportant. Encouraged by Finn's enthusiasm and promises of cooperation, the Puerto Ricans in this congenial sidewalk group decided to form the Pan-American Association of Maplewood.

The association was more ambitious, intricate in organization, and formally planned than the confederation. The procedures for the election of officers and the conduct of meetings were explicitly stated and defined. The group's objectives were to inform members of their legal rights, duties, and obligations as citizens, to provide protection within the law, to aid in the pursuit of favorable economic status, and to improve living, working, and housing conditions. The group acquired legal status through state incorporation as a nonprofit organization. A large hall was rented for $300 a month, with dance floor, billiard tables, a stage, and a bar. The members numbered about 100 and each paid monthly dues of $2. To get additional funds, admission fees were collected at dances, and raffles were held, the prize being a round-trip airplane ticket to San Juan. They paid $40 for a black-and-white banner containing the American and Puerto

Rican flags, which became the emblem of the association and was carried proudly in parades. To advertise the dances and recruit new members, a loud-speaker mounted on a car was rented, and members drove about the Puerto Rican neighborhoods broadcasting their messages in blaring Spanish. Legally incorporated, with a written constitution, a clubhouse, banner, uniforms for members to wear in parades, and a lawyer (James Finn), the association was an organizational landmark in the history of Puerto Ricans in Maplewood. Its members had considerable justification to look down upon the confederation as a failure.

Not the least of the association's many advantages were the qualifications of its president, Antonio Tejada, a 42-year-old, tall, balding man of aristocratic bearing and quiet but sure dignity. A high-school graduate, Tejada was fluent in English. He had travelled the world as an Army sergeant and been wounded in the Korean War. In Maplewood, Tejada worked for the Adult Education Program recruiting Puerto Ricans for the English classes. He had often suffered from discrimination but still thought that there were many opportunities for Puerto Ricans in the United States.

Tejada felt a strong pride in his Puerto Rican identity. He believed that Puerto Ricans had a moral obligation to develop their own groups, not only because of the practical benefits to the migrant but also because it was through groups that the "inner spirit and beauty of the Puerto Rican race" could be revealed to Americans.

Tejada had been invited to join the confederation by his *comadre* ("co-parent") Mrs. Estebán and attended two meetings, but he thought the bonds of ritual kinship did not compensate for the disorder and confusion, the lack of respect for authority, the persons seeking selfish gains and solutions to their own personal problems, which he observed at the meetings. He vowed to his wife that he would never return to the group. What he saw at the confederation meetings, he said, contradicted the noble traditions Puerto Ricans should be trying to express to Americans. In addition, he was not persuaded that the confederation was an authentic organization because it did not have funds or a clubhouse. When Tejada met James Finn, he was impressed, joined in the development of the association, and was elected its president.

James Finn and the officers of the association did not want the group to be part of a political party or to be officially linked with one, but at the start they did not prohibit political activities as the confederation had done. On the other hand, they *did* agree that Vicente de Serrano had to be kept out of the group, just as the members of the confederation had done. The agreement to exclude Serrano was unanimous and seemingly resolute. Thus, it was surprising to James Finn that, when he arrived at the association's inaugural dance, Serrano was there to greet him and his guests. The ubiquitous political boss issued orders to his aides about the arrangement of tables and chairs for *abogado* ("lawyer") Finn and his honored guests. The same incident was repeated at subsequent dances. Finn said later:

> As soon as I arrived at a dance he would come charging across the floor, embrace me, and talk my ear off. He wouldn't let me get away, talking all the time and introducing me to people. Whenever I was able to break away from him, people would come up to me and say, "You know about that guy, don't you? Don't let that guy con you." There was a great deal of fear [of him].

The officers of the association had taken the usual precaution at the inaugural dance of hiring four policemen to supervise the crowd of between 400 and 500 persons. Serrano, however, arrived early and dismissed the policemen, telling them that their services were not needed. The guests Finn had brought to the dance were persons whom he thought could be of future help to the members of the association — factory owners, the head of the Legal Assistance Office, and a man in charge of a new city project through which persons who had been arrested were to be released without posting bail. After the guests were seated, Serrano took the microphone to tell the Puerto Ricans about them. He went on to say that he had dispensed with police supervision in order to demonstrate to the guests that "We are decent people, not dirty and disorderly." Maria Porrata, sitting in the audience, said later that she felt insulted by Serrano's words, and she heard hostile comments from others who were angry that the Americans were being treated with such deference.

The inaugural crowd began to dance only to be interrupted by Serrano inviting the American guests to say a few words over the microphone. Sullen and angry, the crowd listened, then went back to dancing. Soon, a fight broke out. Bottles crashed against walls, chairs and tables were overturned, and knives were drawn. The officers of the association hastened to evict the troublemakers and quiet the disturbance, but Romero Ponce, the treasurer, had his head gashed by a broken bottle. Many of those the officers had been planning to recruit as new members left the dance, as did most of the married couples. (Maria Porrata who was entrusted to safekeep a bottle of whiskey took it home at this point and sold it later for $2.) Serrano was enraged and reportedly vowed to "find those little bastards who started the fight and fix them by getting the police to arrest them." According to Finn, he said afterwards, "That's the way these lower-class Puerto Ricans are." Despite the agreement to exclude him, Serrano had managed to intrude into the association's affairs.

Unlike the confederation, the association was very active, continually involved in a variety of plans and arrangements. They gave dances, sponsored a baseball team, participated in parades, recruited members, collected dues, and maintained a bank account. Finn said later on:

> People were acting on their own. One officer would plan a dance, then others would hear about it when he lined up a band. The executive meetings consisted of three of them getting together, or even two of them, over a few beers; then they would call the other two [officers] and tell them what they had decided. If they wanted something, they would write a check without consulting the others or they would run out and buy something.

Finn considered such disorganization to be the group's central problem, and he tried to solve it by implanting a semblance of formal procedures at meetings. He said:

> I was coaching from the side, prompting. I used to write out what Tejada should say, how to ask for motions, how to get a vote. It was funny; the first time he did this, he asked if anyone wanted to make a motion but they kept quiet. So then I showed the officers and members how to make motions but no one would ... they preferred to shout and holler, or to make impassioned speeches rather than to do things in an orderly way.

Finn also tried to get the members to take notes so that afterwards there would be a record of the decisions made. To facilitate this task, he even brought his own tape recorder, but he said later, "They just would not have an orderly meeting. They just would not do it."

To the officers, organized procedures at meetings presented impediments to restrict and delay their plans for the group. Such procedures were contrary to their habitual individualistic way of decision making. Finn's opinion was that this attitude stemmed from their status as a minority, with rules and regulations not of their own making imposed upon them by society to their disadvantage. But whatever the source of resistance, his attempt to have the group run on an orderly basis failed.

Disorganization in the executive body created problems which reverberated throughout the group. Some members raised questions about irregularities in the treasury. Maria Porrata's comment was, "They always have the same $150 in the treasury. It never increases and it never decreases. They are always running dances and more dances, yet the amount remains the same. I don't know what they do with the money, but the $150 never increases."

Management of money had been a cause of trouble in other Puerto Rican groups, and the association proved to be no exception. Suspicion eroded the members' confidence in the officers. Tejada, having once participated in a group in which the funds allegedly disappeared, became concerned. He recalled that this incident destroyed the organization, for the members then refused to pay dues or come to meetings. Now, he even incurred personal debts to support some of the association's activities, but the pattern of impatient and erratic spending continued, and rumors flew about the Puerto Rican neighborhoods that funds were being pilfered.

Because decisions were not shared or made in an orderly fashion, the officers found much to quarrel about. They argued bitterly over the frequency and the elaborateness of the dances they sponsored, about which band should be hired, even about which beer should be sold. Contrary to Finn's advice, they attempted to sell liquor at the dances, an illegal activity which brought on police raids. With each activity sponsored by the association, the officers became more and more entangled in a round of seemingly irreconcilable differences.

James Finn's original enthusiasm gradually changed to weariness and frustration over the demands made on him. The officers were proud to have him as an official consultant who gave free professional advice to the members and signed the membership cards as an attorney-at-law. (Hearing that the association had a lawyer the members of the confederation even became fearful of legal prosecution.) But to Finn, affiliation with the association came to mean almost full-time work, undisciplined and unpleasant meetings, and subjection to telephone calls at all hours of the night from members seeking legal advice on matters which he did not consider urgent. Although his work involved assistance to all poor residents of the neighborhood, the officers of the association made claims that his services were only for the association. When it was rumored also that he was being paid by the association, Finn was upset, for his salary came from the Legal Assistance Office. A final-but-bitter experience was Romero Ponce's allegation that Finn had refused legal counsel to a Puerto Rican client. The young lawyer felt the accusation betrayed his efforts and was an insult to his pride and professional ethics.

Meanwhile, Serrano kept in touch with the group at dances and through Romero Ponce, the treasurer of the association. When the officers decided to exclude the political boss, Ponce agreed, but he had reservations. His friendship with Serrano extended back 16 years. Ponce had come to the United States at the age of 19 to earn enough money to return to Puerto Rico and marry a girl there. His first job in the United States was as an itinerant laborer on a truck farm outside of Maplewood. There he met Serrano who was trying to help Puerto Ricans escape from very bad conditions on the farms. In Maplewood, Serrano got him a job through the Democratic town chairman, working for the city as a refuse collector. Ponce was proud that over the years his wages had increased from $1.17 to $2.25 an hour, and that he had been able to bring his family from Puerto Rico to Maplewood where he bought them a house. Ponce was sometimes resentful of Serrano for calling him *"el Negro Ponce,"* ("Ponce the Black") a label he would not have accepted from anyone else, but most of the time he felt indebted to the political boss: "Serrano has been almost a father to me," he said.

50

By means of such loyalty Serrano planned to use Ponce in his take-over of the confederation. He told Ponce that two groups would divide the community, that there should be only one voice speaking for the migrant, that of the Pan-American Association. He insisted that by naming itself the Hispanic Confederation, its members were making false claims of representing other groups, and a retaliatory move was justified. By no means the least persuasive argument was the need to politicize all Puerto Rican groups. Implicit in the arguments, of course, was Serrano's plan eventually to bring the association under his control. Ponce, however, was not worried because he also believed that politics were necessary for success. He said:

> Everything has to be linked with politics. If one does not embrace politics, one gets nowhere ... because these people [the politicians] are the ones who control the city and the state. We [Puerto Ricans] don't control anyone. They can throw us out of here whenever they feel like it and send us somewhere else. If you are here, you have to be with them. This is the way it has to be.

Ironically, while the take-over of the confederation was underway, the association was not linked to the Democratic Party and, according to James Finn and Antonio Tejada, certainly not under Serrano's control. The political boss was present in the group only during ceremonial occasions such as dances. Yet, even though both groups had determined to exclude him from membership, he was able to use the association as a backdrop from which to attack the confederation.

In their talks, Serrano told Ponce he blamed the association's difficulties on Tejada, alleging that the president could not be trusted because he was a drunkard and a dictator. He lavished praise on Ponce as a person with "good ideas" and, at the same time, presented himself as the one person who could rescue the group from its difficulties. When Tejada and Finn saw the group drifting toward politics, their opposition hardened. To overcome this, Serrano first got Ponce to approve of any plan he had; he then would turn to the next officer to tell him Ponce approved and so on. By the time Tejada heard about it, the officers were all in favor of the plan and any opposition from Tejada would lead to his being labelled a dictator. This "snowball" tactic generated pressures among the officers to go along with whatever Serrano had in mind. It was difficult, if not impossible, for Tejada and Finn to counter the boss's maneuvers in so disorganized a group, torn with personal antagonisms and in which decisions had always been made individually or in ad hoc fashion.

The issue that brought the situation to its climax was politics. Tejada feared that partisan politics within the association would further weaken the group. He said, "If you want to see Puerto Ricans united, don't talk to them about politics. The Puerto Rican who comes here comes to see his friends, to get a job, to live religiously. Those who come here with the idea of politics are in a minority."

51

Tejada also voiced an opinion on leadership: "I have more confidence in a person who has education than in one who is a politician of any kind. A person with a good education can guide and teach those who are in need of learning something, but political groups have leaders without the qualities of leaders. A leader only because he knows the mayor and others? This is a leader?"

The officers' personal animosities toward each other provided Serrano with an incident which opened the way for deposing Tejada. At one meeting of the group, Tejada became very angry with the unruly participants. He believed strongly that a leader should be respected by his followers. When he was unable to control the meeting, he lost his temper. What followed varies according to the teller: One version is that he said even the lower forms of the animal kingdom follow their leader. Others said he called them pigs. The rumor spread quickly that Tejada had called all Puerto Ricans pigs. Serrano then demanded Tejada's resignation as president. He had no official authority, of course, to make such a demand, but he based it upon his presumption that he represented the moral integrity of Maplewood's Puerto Rican community.

Tejada replied that he would sue Serrano for defamation of character. He told an intermediary, "This is a democracy, not South America." Serrano, however, called the Democratic town chairman insisting that Tejada had to go. The town chairman put through a call to James Finn concerning the incident.

Later, Tejada came to view his resignation as a result of the intrigues of the political boss who was "first for himself, second for himself, and third for himself." James Finn left the group, concluding philosophically, "the cards had already been dealt from the beginning by Serrano. He was a terrific strategist." The association then became the Hispanic Democratic Club of Maplewood with Romero Ponce as president and Serrano as "coordinator." Serrano accomplished this change in slightly more than one year.

The Pan-American Association was not able to weather Serrano's political assault, but the confederation had better luck. When Diego Zayas told Serrano the confederation's problems, Serrano proposed that the group be disbanded and merged with the recently formed Pan-American Association. Although he was not an official member at that time, Serrano's self-interest would best be served in this way. He convinced Zayas that it also was in the interest of the Puerto Rican community that there be a link between city hall and the confederation. To demonstrate that his claim of influence with the city's governing officials was not an idle boast, Serrano quickly arranged an appointment for Zayas to see the mayor.

Several weeks after this appointment, Mrs. Estebán became aware of Zayas's political intrigues. One evening her husband, Eduardo Estebán, who had once served as Serrano's bodyguard, was visited by Romero Ponce. In keeping with the sex division in Puerto Rican culture that church matters concern women and politics concern men, the visit was to persuade Eduardo that the confederation should be merged with the association even though Eduardo rarely attended the confederation's meetings and it was Mrs. Estebán, not Eduardo, who was interested in the group. Mrs. Estebán intervened, to protest on the grounds that from the very beginning the confederation had been sponsored by the Catholic church. (She was referring to Father Ryan who had first put her in touch with Mr. Joyce and had served the group briefly as advisor.) Actually the confederation had had no official or unofficial ties to the church, Father Ryan, himself, having insisted upon a sharp separation between the two. Mrs. Estebán, however, had no hesitation about invoking the group's religious obligations, and Romero Ponce was silenced for the time being.

Mrs. Estebán's suspicions proved true when Diego Zayas informed her of his political plans. She told him that the confederation always followed democratic procedures and that he was free to present his plan at the next meeting. Meanwhile she formulated her own counterproposal, that of disbanding the executive committee, composed of the president, vice-president, and secretary, and appointing a new interim committee to guide the group until the holding of elections in the near future.

Encouraged by his private appointment with the mayor and the talks with Serrano, Zayas went to the next meeting certain he could change the nonpolitical character of the confederation. To assure victory, Serrano ordered Romero Ponce and another aide to attend the meeting to help Zayas. Before the 12 participants even began discussing politics, however, Zayas and Ponce got into an argument over the inclusion of Americans in the confederation. Diego had always believed the group should be entirely Puerto Rican and Americans should be admitted only as "observers." Ponce disagreed heatedly because, he said, "everything Puerto Ricans are or have they owe to Americans." By the time the issue of politics was raised Zayas was already under attack, and the proposal he had conspired and labored to prepare began to fall by the wayside.

In explaining the details of the proposal, Zayas was at a disadvantage. He did not want the group to be a part of the Democratic party or of any political party, for he did not want to surrender control of the confederation to Serrano. Nonetheless, he had come to believe that partisan politics were necessary if the group was to achieve its objective of helping the Puerto Ricans in Maplewood. What he wanted for the confederation was to follow a strategy of independent political action in which parties and candidates would receive the group's support according to the best interest of the Puerto Rican community, or in the vernacular to be for *candidatura* ("candidates"), or to pursue the "politics of an empty stomach." This position assumed that before each election the confederation would agree on the best candidates or party and then, although party lines might have to be crossed to support individual candidates, all would obey the group's decision in a disciplined and unified way. If any member's political preferences were different from that of the group, they would have to be suppressed. Efforts to develop such groups had never succeeded in Maplewood, and Zayas's plan was assuming a level of efficient organization far removed from the realities of the confederation.

Thus, the plan was inherently complicated and difficult for Zayas to explain at a confused and agitated meeting where he had lost control from the beginning. The promises of support from Serrano's aides did not materialize, for they proved to be almost incoherent in their speeches. Later, Zayas regretted the entire episode, including his collusion with Serrano. He told me that the political boss had attempted to destroy the confederation by instructing his aides to create disorder at the meetings.

Mrs. Estebán led the opposition to Zayas by requesting an endorsement of her plan to establish an interim committee to guide the group until the prospective elections took place. In her drive to recruit new members she had personally invited most of those in attendance, and her strategy worked. Zayas told the group they should follow his wishes as president, but Mrs. Estebán circulated a sheet of paper and explained that by signing it the members were voting for the interim committee. So confused was the meeting and so bewildered were the participants that even Serrano's aides signed the paper. When the votes were tallied and Mrs. Estebán's plan won, Zayas resigned.

One week later, Mrs. Estebán held a meeting to which Zayas did not come. After the usual round of introductions, she narrated the nine-month history of the confederation, beginning with the observation that Puerto Ricans were not participating in Maplewood's organizations and concluding with a discussion of the last meeting at which the president had resigned. She announced the rules of the confederation: that it took no part in politics or religion, that it did not collect dues, and that *it did not try to solve personal problems at meetings.* Mrs. Estebán then implied that Zayas's plan to make the group political had been a betrayal of this legacy and indicated sarcastically that on numerous occasions he himself had inveighed against politics and against Serrano. Nonetheless, she continued, the members should have an opportunity to express themselves on this point, especially because the last meeting had been stormy and confusing and minutes had not been taken (as already mentioned, minutes were seldom taken at meetings).

Each member then took a turn condemning the former president. Feelings which had been suppressed were now aired openly. The criticisms were repetitious and not restricted to Zayas's betrayal of the group. Their accusations covered a range of inconsiderate and irresponsible behavior that all claimed to have felt. The collective pronoun *nosotros* ("we") was used in the assault against him. "Nosotros" stood together opposed to Zayas who represented all the things gone wrong with the confederation. By eliminating Zayas, the group was purging itself of all maladies, and a feeling of purification came over the membership. Never before had they experienced such unity of feeling. At the height of the emotional purge Mrs. Estebán repeated the regulations of the group, and all seemed in agreement.

At this point, Romero Ponce arrived with another of Serrano's political aides and tried again to persuade the members to merge with the Pan-American Association. They took turns presenting arguments until Romero Ponce presented what he considered the final appeal: if the groups merged the members would be bound into "brotherhood" so that, he claimed, "when you are in need I help you, and when I am in need, you help me." Mrs. Estebán quickly jumped in to rule the proposal out of order because the confederation "by law does not address itself to the personal problems of its members." This reply so befuddled the persuaders that no further word came from them. The feeling of nosotros still very much present, the other members presented a solid front against the "invaders."

Thus, the final defense was not the confederation's rule prohibiting political involvement but rather the newly emerged norm prohibiting attention to personal problems. At first advanced as a means of coping with the problems of unrestrained discussion at meetings, the rule proved useful in protecting the confederation from political take-over.

There was more to come, however. At midmorning four days later as I worked in my office at the university, there was a heavy authoritative knock on the door. I immediately recognized the person who entered as Vicente de Serrano, for his picture had appeared recently in the local newspaper along with an article commending him for many years of leadership among Puerto Ricans. Serrano was white-haired, in his late 50s, slightly under six feet tall, large of body, and had strong, distinguished Roman features. His bearing was that of a man accustomed to command. Having identified me as Rogler-Canino, he introduced himself, sat on a chair, and began pounding on my desk with his fist announcing that he had been trying to get in touch with me. This opening maneuver apparently was intended to intimidate me. He said:

> Let us get right down to business. I sent two of my aides to the confederation to turn it into a political organization. They were rejected by the group. The confederation is not really a confederation, for in Spanish the word means a group which represents a number of organizations. The confederation represents no one. *I* represent the Puerto Ricans in Maplewood. *I* brought them here. The confederation has not done one damned thing for them. It must merge with the Pan-American Association. It must be political.

If need be, Serrano continued, pressure would be brought to bear by the mayor, the Democratic town chairman, lawyers, judges, and even the governor of the state. All of these persons knew him by his first name, he said.

Serrano's claims to control the organizational life of the Puerto Ricans were based upon his many years of self-sacrifice. Thirty-two years of hard personal work justified the power he now enjoyed, he told me. Even now, he said, he was working on behalf of Puerto Ricans accused of crimes, serving as interpreter in court. He often spent more than the fee he received taking the judge and the lawyers out to lunch. At nights, he informed me, he was a "superintendent" at a local factory where he also had been instrumental in getting jobs for Puerto Ricans. Serrano continued:

> Why do I sacrifice myself? My wife, a nice Italian lady, is always asking me that question. She says the Puerto Ricans don't appreciate it. I don't know why I do it. Look at me. I don't look like a Puerto Rican. I could pass for any nationality, but I am proud to be a Puerto Rican. I speak Puerto Rican Spanish, not that fake sing-song Mexican Spanish some Puerto Ricans imitate. I identify myself as Puerto Rican wherever I go.

There were compelling reasons for the confederation to become political, Serrano said. Everything accomplished in the city, he explained, was a result of political influence and if Puerto Rican groups were to be effective they had to be incorporated into the Democratic party. He said, "How can one work against such an overwhelming political machine? See what happens even to the Republicans? Where do they end up? Hired by the Democrats to work in all these city agencies, that's where. I once bolted the Democratic party to work for the Republicans, but I realized this was an error. You can't fight the machine."

Serrano then pulled his chair close to mine and launched an attack against the "worthless" confederation. He accused Mrs. Estebán of discrimination against blacks and of feeling superior among Puerto Ricans "because she thinks she has a better education." He knew all this, he said, ". . . because I know everything that goes on in that group. In fact, I know everything that goes on in the Puerto Rican community. No matter what it is, it ends up in Vicente's ear, even a letter about Puerto Ricans sent to the mayor."

Serrano had identified me as the person in control of the group, despite my attempt to maintain neutrality on the issues before the confederation, in particular not to participate in the discussion about Diego Zayas and the political takeover. He knew, he said, a group had to have a ruler and I appeared to be the logical candidate. After all, he had reasoned, the group met at the university where I was a professor, and I had been going to its meetings for several months. I felt it was essential to dispel his idea of my control of the group and to explain my position to him. At the same time, I wanted to get to know him better. I told him that, although the group met at the university, it was not sponsored by the university or by me. It was free to meet wherever it chose and free to decide whatever it wanted on any issue, including the proposed merger. I insisted that I

was making determined efforts not to interfere in the decisions of the confederation and that my purpose was to study the life of the Puerto Ricans in Maplewood. I said that since he was very knowledgeable about the life of our compatriots I would welcome his cooperation with the study.

Serrano was incredulous at my response, for he had expected resistance or
refusal to cooperate. He looked me over carefully and his initially belligerent
attitude changed to one of graciousness. "So you are going to write a book about
Puerto Ricans," he said. "Vicente knows more about this than anyone else. I will
introduce you to the boys so you can see what it is all about."

A year later, during a series of intensive interviews with him (see Chapter 5),
I directed his attention to our first meeting. His answer was subdued and apologetic:

> They [his aides] had said the group had a Puerto Rican professor. I was in-
> terested and wanted to find out about this so I could put him wise to what
> was going on ... They said the confederation took orders from Rogler-
> Canino, so I said to myself, "I better go and find out what the story is because
> he must be crazy to give them [the Puerto Ricans] orders. They don't even
> know how to take orders."

Nothing in this retrospective account indicates the determined effort he had
made that day in my office to cajole me into permitting the merger to take place.
A year had elapsed and there had been many changes in the organizational life
of the Puerto Rican community. He no longer felt that I was a member of the
outgroup intruding into his domain. He had come to accept me as an observer
and, although a professor, sublimely ignorant of things he knew so intimately.

Serrano's successful maneuvers to take over the association and his assault on
the confederation were aimed at imposing political binds on the two groups. By
taking over the two organizations, Serrano planned to reinforce the security of
his own political life. This politician's view of his role as political boss and his
description of his background, thoughts, desires, and ambitions are an interesting
facet of the development of migrant leadership. Serrano's first-person narrative
discussion of these subjects is reported in the next chapter.

5

Vicente de Serrano: The Puerto Rican Political Boss Speaks

•

Before I tell you how I first got involved in politics, let me make it clear that politics is behind everything in this country. This government is based on politics and the president of the United States was put there by politicians and has to do what the politicians want. Politics is a transaction in which one hand always watches what the other is doing. That's all it is. You give the politician votes and he in return will back you up in housing and jobs. Today, it is not what you know but *who* you know and how you approach people. By knowing the politician, one manipulates to get jobs. If he likes you, you are made, but if he doesn't, then nothing! It's not how smart you are, it's the contacts you have. In Maplewood, nothing can be successful without political backing, because it's a machine no one can beat.

When I came to the United States in 1926, 90 percent of the Puerto Ricans were young men who came here to live with their families. They had more education and came here to stay. Now we have this group — the $45 group. [$45 is the minimal one-way fare between New York and San Juan.] This group creates the problems we're having with Puerto Ricans in the United States and is spoiling everything. Of the 5,000 Puerto Ricans in Maplewood, 500 are in the $45 group, and they are the ones who end up in court. You always see the same faces, the same group in trouble all the time. Anybody who does not want to work in Puerto Rico, who likes to fool around, play the numbers, and shoot dice, comes to the United States for $45. Then they say to themselves, "If we can't work, we'll go on relief." At one time Puerto Ricans were not on relief, but now they have gotten into the habit. Yes, that is the attitude, not of all of them, but of the younger generation coming now. It's disgraceful! Take, for instance, the six of them I have working for me in the factory making $2 an hour. They don't save money to get married. Imagine, I have to tell them to please not make trouble, but all they have in mind is to play around, roll dice, and buy a race car. But most of this is the young kids. The older Puerto Ricans who have been here a long time, who have settled here, do not get into trouble like the ones coming now. A family with children in school or at work will not be heard from. Now the problem is the 17- or 18-year-old bums. They are rough people, chronic criminals who don't believe in anything.

Out on the street corners is where you find the $45 Puerto Ricans, fooling around, gambling, driving cars without a license, not working. They come to this country and want to get rich overnight. Yet, the only way you can make money quickly is the way that will put you in jail. By gambling, selling liquor without a license, the rackets — by breaking the law — you can make money easily. I'm not talking about those who have been here a long time, have jobs, are settled with their families. It is those who come to make a couple of thousand dollars, then put the money in their pockets and return to the island to show off. There is the trouble.

If I were an official in the Puerto Rican government, I would never let them leave the island unless they had some identification card with fingerprints, because they are taking advantage of this country. With my very own eyes, I have seen Puerto Ricans change their names in court. They change so often you don't know who the person is. They use both their father's name and their mother's name as they do in Puerto Rico, only one day their name is Juan José López, and next day it is Juan López José. You don't see colored people changing their names, but the Puerto Ricans do it even though they know they will get caught and it will be bad for all the others. It's not just the names. They also use different social security numbers to collect unemployment. They work with one name and a number in a job, then a different name and number in another job. But you can't beat the government. Sooner or later it catches up with them, and then they cuss me in court.

I keep telling these guys that they have all the rights of the American citizen, but they have to do what every citizen does, fill out an income-tax return. But hundreds and hundreds don't believe that because they themselves lie so much. At one time, the government allowed stubs from money orders [money sent to dependents in Puerto Rico] to be used as evidence of dependents. So one family would borrow stubs from another family, and so on. But the government got wise to this. Eventually, they catch you. Once an American fellow, a wise guy, told me, "Those dependents in Puerto Rico must be living very well with all the money their relatives are sending them from here." He was just a wise guy, but it is true that Puerto Ricans know all the tricks.

In fact, there should be a law that Puerto Ricans must pass an English examination to become American citizens, just the same as other foreigners. But no, it is not that way, and we take advantage of it. We have the privilege of doing whatever we want. Because we see Americans driving in Puerto Rico we think we don't need a driver's license here. Believe me, you go to them and tell them to study to get a license and they reply, "Who needs it?" But when they are caught and have to pay $25, they get mad. Everybody who drives without a license gets charged $25, but they say the judge has it in for them. See what I mean? Puerto Ricans have things in their mind that are not true.

I'm always reminding the Puerto Ricans that they have never seen me yelling or fighting with a policeman. I talk to him nicely because someday I might need his help and he is here to protect me too. But the Puerto Ricans who come here don't understand that. It is because they are ignorant.

Just the other day we fixed one in court so that he won't get into trouble again. He got five years. In Puerto Rico three or four months ago, he got into a fight and cut up his wife and concubine into little pieces. They put $3,000 bail on him and he jumped bail, got a $45 ticket, and came to the United States. Here in Maplewood they locked him up on a charge of vagrancy. When the police and I talked to him he said he wanted to be sent back to Puerto Rico. We called up the Puerto Rican government and the FBI on the island, but they did not want him back. Imagine! They wanted us to keep the problem here. If they want Puerto Rico to gain the respect of the United States then they should have taken this criminal back to the island and put him in jail.

It's the same way with the Italians. All the bad ones came to the United States because their government sent them here. For that reason, the Italians have a bad name, but the Puerto Ricans are as bad as the Mafia. Many have harmed and killed in Puerto Rico, and they are here today. They won't listen to reason because they know everything, particularly the younger ones. The older ones will listen and accept advice. When I talk to the younger ones, I tell them that I only wish someone had talked to me when I came to the United States, but they won't listen.

Take the men on Thursday or Friday nights, when they get paid and hit the bars. Right away they get high, and they are big fellows, strong and afraid of no one. They get out of line, and right away they forget what you have done for them. They tell you they'll fix you if you tell them anything. They'd rather take orders from someone who is not one of them, who will treat them like a dog, than from one of their own kind. Many resent taking orders from a Puerto Rican who has the authority to give them orders. When these drunks are in court I'm a good guy, but when they are drunk on Friday night, I'm no good. You see? They do not want to listen to anyone and for that reason they resent the higher group [of Puerto Ricans]. They think because I speak English, I am a show-off. Maybe that's because Puerto Ricans don't get along with each other and are jealous of each other. As a nationality, they are fickle, but once they join together to believe the right thing all this nonsense will stop of one being higher and one being lower. That is the story of the Puerto Ricans here.

When I came to this country I had no trouble with English. In fact, people thought I was an Englishman because I spoke such grammatical English. So I am always telling the Puerto Ricans that here we are a minority, that in Rome do as the Romans do, but it is hard to get them interested in bettering themselves because they come with the idea that they will be here today and gone tomorrow. As soon as they get a little money they go back to the island. That's something big for them, but not for me. I have been here a long time. I have my family here. I make good money. I don't think I will go home; for a visit, maybe yes, but not to stay.

Here, everybody treats me right. In fact, no one thinks I'm a Puerto Rican. They think I'm a different nationality, but that is one thing I will never do, deny that I am a Puerto Rican. Discrimination has no room in my beliefs. You see me mixing with all Puerto Ricans, colored or not. I don't care. As I told you, if they are colored and treat me right, then things are all right. But if they don't treat me right, then I don't mix with them. You see, I figure at my age all I can do is preach what I have learned to the rest of the people. There is nowhere higher to go. I am a plant manager [foreman] and that is an honor. I have Americans working for me and I am consulted. That makes me proud because I am a Puerto Rican.

There are Puerto Ricans, you see, who through their own efforts learn to speak a little English by going to school or by mixing with people of their own level. These people want to live a little more decently. You have to give them credit. They are doing a wonderful thing for the Puerto Rican community, but they are not willing to mix with the $45 crowd who have been in jail for robbery, who are in the courts every day on a charge of breach of the peace, or who are in the streets drunk. The people who are elevating the Puerto Rican name are not going to mix with a crowd of knife-carrying hoodlums. The high group is hard-working, married people who don't go from house to house carrying stories, hanging around poolrooms, or staying out in the street. They go to church, try to raise their families the best way they know how, and mind their own business. They do what any decent American citizen does — obey the law. Anyone who resents them is either crazy or jealous because he himself could be in that category if he behaved the way they do. If I got drunk all the time, were arrested every week, got into fights, then of course people would resent me.

The ones with education are no trouble at all. They know what they are doing. They have common sense. But it is the other ones, the $45 class, that makes the trouble.

It all boils down to one point I have mentioned to the mayor and to other important people. Many persons don't know why we come to this country. Many think we are foreigners and don't even know where Puerto Rico is. A lot can be done if they give out pamphlets wherever Puerto Ricans live in the United States to tell people about the Puerto Ricans' habits, customs, and all the reasons why they come to this country.

Actually, Americans treat the Puerto Ricans better than they treat blacks, and the colored people resent Puerto Ricans for being hard-working and because they think that coming from farms, the Puerto Ricans will work for less money. But that is not true; there is a law that everyone has to be paid a minimum wage. Yet if the Puerto Ricans get started on that civil rights thing – publishing their complaints in the newspaper – they would be treated the same as the colored. Opportunities in Maplewood are the same for all, but if Puerto Ricans act like blacks, they will be treated as such. It is only now that I have begun to hear about discrimination against Puerto Ricans. There was none before.

I first got interested in politics as a child because my stepfather was president of the Socialist party of San Sebastian, my hometown. My stepfather came from Spain – he was tall and fair-skinned – and he was a professional cigar-maker by trade and a good businessman. He was called the "father of the poor" because when a poor person died my stepfather always delivered the eulogy, telling everybody how good the dead person had been. No matter what time of the day or night, my stepfather would dress up to go to the cemetery. Everybody in town liked him, and he could have been mayor but he refused because he said he was too honest. He wanted to earn his money the hard way and help the poor. I am the very same way.

Years ago in the New York airport I saw Puerto Ricans being brought from the island with numbers on them just like slaves. And there would be a man waiting to load them into a truck to take them to farms. For this he got $50 a head. Afterwards I went to 129 farms where they worked for 51¢ an hour without toilet facilities and had nothing. I would sneak into the fields and tell them, "You are American citizens and you are supposed to be treated like one, not like pigs." I spoke with a man from the Commonwealth Government of Puerto Rico and he agreed that action was needed, that the government had to look out for the welfare of the Puerto Ricans migrating to the farms here. We got tough about it and demanded that Puerto Ricans have adequate places to sleep and to take showers. The wages were raised and now they live better.

Anyway, I went to the farms and raided them. I used to bring the Puerto Ricans away from the farms and into Maplewood. On one raid, I brought Eduardo Estebán [Mrs. Estebán's husband] to town, got him a job at the factory where I worked, helped him get settled, and ever since, he has been a good friend of mine, a nice fellow who always follows me. Another time, I stole five Puerto Ricans from a farmer who was going to shoot me. Romero Ponce [Serrano's political aide who led the assault on the confederation] was one of them and he can tell you how the farmer was looking to kill me.

Also, when Puerto Ricans in town got into trouble, I would go to court and interpret for them, all for free. Then when the court began to pay an interpreter I took his job away because he was not doing it right. Now, when I go to court to help, I send Puerto Ricans to all of the lawyers so that everyone can get a piece of the business, not just one lawyer.

I also visited my friends throughout the state to help them in politics. Then, when people in companies and factories asked me about hiring Puerto Ricans, I always told them, "Don't get guys from New York because they are wise guys. I will tell you people who really want to work and you can hire them." You see, that way I got jobs for my friends and for this I never charged anyone anything. I have never done anything wrong. Then, one day, I was called from Democratic headquarters and they said, "Vicente, let's get the Puerto Ricans to vote." This was of interest to me because at that time I knew some Puerto Ricans who wanted some favors. After I went into politics I got a lot of people jobs in the city. That's how it started.

Right now, I could go up to the mayor's office and if he is busy he will ask me to come in and have a seat. He wouldn't do that for just anyone, but he always listens to me, never sending me away. That night at the rally I gave, he had to get out of bed sick to come, but he is a good friend of mine and he came. I don't know why but he thinks a lot of me, at least that's what I have always heard. Anytime I want to see him, he sees me.

The mayor knows the Puerto Ricans' problems and he knows also that we keep them under control by talking to them. He takes it for granted that Puerto Ricans will listen to me and that they won't cause trouble. He knows we play ball with him. Take the time when this so-called Puerto Rican leader who is from a town with no more than 25 Puerto Ricans asked me if I would picket the state capital for the Puerto Ricans. "Me?" I said, "not me! The people of Maplewood have nothing to picket about. When we want something we go to the mayor and the mayor listens. That's a party [Democratic] that plays fair with us. Why should we picket?" I told the mayor not to worry about Maplewood Puerto Ricans picketing. As a result, I got nice letters from the governor and the mayor. This so-called Puerto Rican leader got nothing. Listen, you can't jump in the river and swim against the current. The governor once said, "Fellows, bring me a list of all Puerto Ricans who are available, reliable, and capable of working in state jobs and I will see to it personally that they are taken care of." No one had ever done such a thing for us before, so why should I picket? If we had given the governor such a list and he did not give them jobs, then I would be the first to picket.

And John Maranelli — the Democratic town chairman — is a good friend of mine. His office is always open to us just like the mayor's. I can go down and say,

"John, I need $500 to throw a party for the Puerto Ricans," and he will give it to me. Who else can do that but me? That's the reason I don't cry if the confederation won't invite me to its meetings. Anything I ask for downtown, if I'm right, John helps me. Anything I need for my boys he's with me 100 percent. He's a wonderful man and likes to help Puerto Ricans. One time he told me that as an Italian he always tried to do a lot for his own people. Guys like that you have to respect. He thinks a lot of me because I am trying to do the same thing for my own people. He admires me. He's my ace-in-the-hole.

But in 1960 it was not this way. I got mad and turned to the Republicans. They named me president of the Puerto Rican Republican party in the state. This happened because of Bill, "the Dominican." He is not really a Dominican; that is just what they call him. He is a Polish Jew who left Poland when the Jews were thrown out and lived in the Dominican Republic and learned Spanish. Then, they made him court interpreter, and he was making money off the Puerto Ricans and thought he could get them to do what he wanted. He wanted to lead them. Also he owned a business and tried to control those who owed him money. To him, business is business because he is a Jew, but for me it is quite different because Puerto Ricans are my people. I help from the heart. So then I had it out with "the Dominican" and told him what I thought. You see, if I can talk for a man in court and save him money, I will, but not "the Dominican." He was in politics because he wanted to build a store on land belonging to the city and he wanted the city to give it to him — he was a political leader out of convenience.

Then the mayor asked "the Dominican" to organize a political rally, but he was lost without me because he does not know how to talk to people. My people had begun to ask me why they should follow "the Dominican" as their leader. I told "the Dominican" that Puerto Ricans are free people and he cannot tell them what to do. I got mad and told John Maranelli, the Democratic town chairman, "you'll see who's the boss around here. You'll see who controls the Puerto Ricans." I did it to show them who the leader really is.

You see, I was angry also because one of my boys, Cabrera, had passed the examination to become a policeman but they did not make him one. That did it! Right away, I formed the Puerto Rican Republican party of Maplewood and made Cabrera the president. I told the people to turn from the Democrats to the Republicans and held a rally to which 1,700 Puerto Ricans came. When they came, when they followed me, I knew they believed in me and that I was their leader. All of this with but one purpose — to show city hall that Puerto Ricans have only one leader, me! It was to prove that if anything was done wrong or that I did not like I could turn the Puerto Ricans away from them.

I had the Democrats scared and was damaging them because I made Republicans out of Puerto Ricans who had never been Republican before. While Maranelli was at voter registration I would bring in Puerto Ricans for the Republicans and shout to him, "John, five more for the Republicans." And John would reply, "I know Vicente, you don't have to tell me. I know who the leader is."

Anyway, "the Dominican" sent out a couple of guys to gather up the drunks from the bars because he couldn't get anyone else to come to the rally. I sent some of my boys to the rally to see what was going on and there were only 25 persons there, mostly kids. But that dope Cabrera — "the Dominican" called him up and said, "Hey come to our rally and interpret for the mayor and we'll pay you $25." And that Cabrera went! My assistant, you see, had turned against me, even though I had made him president of the Republicans. How could a man like this be a leader? Cabrera is cool, cool as the devil, but you see how stupid he is. Anyway, that year the mayor almost lost the election. He won by only 3,000 votes. They found "the Dominican" can't compete against me. They sent me a blank check and told me to fill it out for whatever amount I wanted. I still have it at home. Afterwards, Maranelli and I talked it over and I returned to the Democrats.

Right now, I'm the guy the mayor and Maranelli recognize as the leader. Nothing can be done with the Puerto Ricans unless they consult me first. That was the agreement I made with them to get me back to the Democrats. If "the Dominican" wants to put in his two cents, that's all right, but I'm the one who makes the decisions. I have no problems with the mayor or Maranelli. The Puerto Ricans are the ones who give me problems because they don't believe in the principles of democracy and this is wrong. If only they'd do as Americans do and help build a democracy.

Take voting. If no one in this country would vote there would be no government. The American people as soon as they are 21 run to vote. And you would be surprised by the Italian people who came here. The first thing they did was apply for citizenship papers so they could vote and it was a pleasure because they knew they were contributing to the government. But the Puerto Ricans are used to Puerto Rico where they get $5 to vote. I have to work hard to get them to register because they resent being told what to do. They think if they vote the city should give them a job right away. Do they think there are 80 million jobs in the government, one for each voter?

It is difficult to get Puerto Ricans to register, so most of the time, when they owe me favors, I tell them to go and register. One fellow I loaned $30 to get out of jail. He didn't have the money to pay me back so I said, "do me a favor — go and register." He couldn't say no. When I get a guy a job or I get another one out of trouble for driving without a license, I say, "Hey listen, you'd better register because anytime you need any more help, the door is always open." You see, that's the way I set them up. By doing it this way, things change. A few years ago, the mayor thought the Puerto Ricans were not a political force. Now he does because lately with the number we are registering he's getting more votes.

Last year in two days we registered 300. Now we plan to register even more.

I hardly ever go to see the mayor or Maranelli, not unless I really need to see them. Men in their position have a lot on their minds so the less you bother them the more you get out of them. If you are a pest they give you little things just to get rid of you, but if you don't bother them, save things up and then put them in their hands, then you get action. For instance, the other day I told the mayor that there should be Puerto Ricans on the Board of Police Review and he said, "Vicente, that is a good idea because Puerto Ricans are a minority group. If resignations come through, I will keep that in mind." I also told the mayor that Puerto Ricans should be working in the antipoverty agency. Before, they had mostly colored people working there. Now Puerto Ricans work at the antipoverty agency and I don't have to tell them that I was the one who put them there.

The same way with Maranelli. I don't go to him unless it's something important. The less you see him, the better, but once in a while you have to make sure he sees you around and won't forget you. That's why I tell the fellows not to bother Maranelli because he's only going to ask, "Where's Vicente?" They tell me their troubles and if they are worthwhile, I myself will go see him.

You see, I don't want to be the main cheese. I only do the dirty work for them [the mayor and Maranelli]. I'm always in the background. My way of doing things is never to be at the head of anything. I figure that by sitting in the background I can see, watch, hear more, and even help more than if I sit in front. I could be president of all these groups [Puerto Rican], but I let the boys be the big shots as long as I control them from behind. They can name whoever they want as president for there are some who always want to be president. I myself never work for a title because, as I have told my friends, "What's the use of being a general plant manager if they only pay you $50 a week. I would much rather be a foreman and earn $150 a week. With money you eat." The same way with groups and clubs. If I were in front everybody would be jumping up and down to see me and I am too busy for that. I have too many things on my mind. Not being president I can go to the club [Pan-American Association] when I want, sit back and chat, and not be responsible for the problems and programs of the group. I'm there just watching what's going on, sitting in the background, observing. When I don't like something I tell them, "That's no good!" If I were mixing it up with everyone and in everything, I wouldn't know what's going on. It's the same way with Maranelli; you don't see him around. He's always in the background. It pays to do it his way and that is what I do.

I'm very clever about it; no? No one in Maplewood can hurt me. There is a lot of jealousy of me, but I have a solid reputation. No one can say, "Vicente took $5 from me to get me a job. Vicente is a crook. Vicente has double-crossed me." If there is anything that can hurt me, I stay out of it. Take that club, The Pan-American Association. I'm the head of it but when I go to a dance I pay at the entrance so that no one can talk about me. They all know that it is my club.

You see, the reason I build clubs and organizations is to work through them. I build them with a political idea and I back them up. I couldn't do all the politics by myself as I once did. With a club you draw people to a meeting place, and you talk to them and get more votes. You can use the club to register voters or as headquarters on election day. The more Puerto Ricans go to the club, the more favors you can do for them. When the fellows want to have a party or a dance they are on their own, but if anything happens, they come to me. I'm the guy who tells them what's going to be done. And if dances is what they want, that's good for them. A lot of people go to dances, you see, and when you need them on election day, they are right there. You don't have to go out to look for them.

And it is through groups that Puerto Ricans gain political recognition. That is the reason we have rallies, to be recognized, as are the Italians and the Greeks. Why do you think colored people are now in a position to demand? Through politics. That's why! Otherwise they would be nobodies. Social activities don't mean anything in this city. They [the politicians] don't care how many dances you have. You can't get a job by going to a dance. You get it through politics. Politics is the only thing.

Do you know how the Pan-American Association started? Well, you see Romero Ponce and the fellows came to me to ask me what to do. I replied that I didn't want to get mixed up into any more clubs. "I'm getting fed up with you people," I told them, "because you won't listen to me. I'm getting old and tired and I'm not looking for more work for myself. I have done all I can and am known all around. My friends are all made. I want to get away from it all." But they insisted, so I said, "Okay, I will help and back you up, but don't tell anyone that I'm going to back you up. I will be in the background." That's how the Pan-American Association started.

But the group did not work very well. At first, I thought that James Finn being a lawyer could do a few legal things for them. He worked for Legal Aid in a Puerto Rican neighborhood, most of his cases were Puerto Ricans, and he was always around. But his point of view was different from mine, and he was using the Puerto Ricans to build himself up. He's not a bad fellow, but I didn't see eye to eye with him. I have found that Irish people always believe different from me. They always want to dominate others. Nobody dominates Vicente!

Finn was an opportunist. Take an article he put in the newspaper. I read it very carefully. All there was in that article was Finn, Finn, Finn. Not one word about Romero Ponce. If you are going to back up an organization, do something for the organization, then you mention the people who are working with you. So I called Romero and some of the boys in to ask them if this guy Finn was using them. "Be careful," I said, "I am too old for this kind of thing, but I know the game."

One day, I went to the Pan-American Association and said, "This club is not going the way it should. The association should be a political club." I told the boys it had to be political and if not I wanted nothing to do with it. You see, Finn made a grab for power but I knew the fellows would have to come to see me, and they did.

Then a guy named Tejada who came here only two years ago named himself president of the group. Only two years here and he got the idea he was a dictator, issuing orders at the club. Tejada wanted to be a big one. You can't go to a new place where nobody knows you and right away want this and that. At every meeting Tejada called the Puerto Ricans pigs; he said that they were just like animals. Many people resented that. And Tejada was with Finn here and Finn there. Tejada drinks a lot, never works with anyone, and never goes home. So one day I told him, "What the hell? Act like a human being!" Just because I said that to him, he said, "Be careful, Vicente, accidents might happen." That's right! He threatened me. All that even though I had gotten him a job working for the Department of Education. "Enough of that," I said, "I've been here 40 years and no one has ever threatened me before." I turned Republican against John Maranelli, against the toughest of all of the Italian gangs, and they could have gotten me bumped off many times because I did a lot of damage politically. But they respect me, and here is Tejada threatening me. "Hey," I said to myself, "What is this? Get him out of here."

Tejada always had a bunch of kids hanging around him. "I'll get them to take care of you," he said.

"Go ahead," I replied. Then, I said to Finn, "Look, before I get mad, get this guy Tejada out of here. Out!"

Tejada said, "Nobody can throw me out. I am the president."

I told him, "You elected yourself president."

I went to that club only once in a while, but when I saw things like that going on, I said to myself, "That's all!" Afterwards at a big meeting, Finn said he held me responsible for what was going on in the association. I told him that I was responsible and that I was going downtown to change the name of the group from the Pan-American Association to the Hispanic Democratic Club. I then went to see John Maranelli and he called up James Finn and said, "Look, I want those boys to have a club because I need them and I want you to talk to Vicente because he's my boy." That's all that happened, but Finn did not like it. He never came to the group anymore. He wanted Tejada there, not me, so he could do as he wanted. So, that's how I broke up the group and gave it a different name.

Tejada afterwards saw that he was wrong and was afraid he would lose his job. He talked to "the Dominican," who took him to see John Maranelli. I was invited but did not go. "The Dominican" told Maranelli that Tejada had not meant to threaten me. Maranelli replied, "I don't want to hear about it. It's all up to Vicente." Then "the Dominican" sent word to me that Tejada wanted to shake my hand; but I didn't answer. One night when Tejada was drunk he came to shake my hand and tell me that it was all a joke. "That was no joke," I said.

Now that the president has been thrown out, the group is moving effectively. We are trying our best, for no small minority can get anywhere if it does not know the people in the city government. If the city government won't recognize you, then you are licked, no matter who you are. For that reason, you see, I take the boys from the club to talk to the big officials in the city. By using the name of Hispanic Democratic Club, the group will get the backing of the Democratic party. In Maplewood, the party is just like a machine. And, like my old man used to say, "one must go with the tide." So I have told the club, "Fellows, this is a political club and when I want to do politics I am going to. Otherwise I don't want the club and I'll close it tomorrow." They agreed. I am going to get them a charter and a license to sell beer. That is the way you do business around here.

Puerto Ricans, you see, don't really want to represent their interests in the city. The whole problem comes from the island where people in one town think they are better than the others. This is exactly what happens among the Puerto Ricans here. They are not unified and the groups they form do not work as a whole. They do not realize that they are here, not there, and to forget Puerto Rico. There are people in groups here who only think of themselves, and the groups fail on account of some wise guy.

The main problem is that most Puerto Ricans don't have an education or very little of it. Then there are those who have been in the army or around, and who have met people, have a little education or a better job, and they think of themselves as better than the rest. The one with education thinks he is a mighty king; he gets on his throne and no one can tell him anything. This creates friction. Then the groups and associations fail. Politics is the only way because then you treat everyone the same way — drunks, bums, everyone. You can never have a perfect club, at least not here on earth. But there are guys who don't think that way. They are particular and want to have their own group — like the confederation.

When I first heard about the confederation I was surprised because I was not asked what I thought, nor was I invited. Everybody invites Vicente, but they did not. Maybe they were afraid I would take over. And I am the kind of fellow who if not invited I don't go. I didn't feel hurt about it. I thought that maybe there was somebody else better prepared than me to represent the Puerto Ricans. I'm getting old and I want somebody to fill my shoes, but among those I know very few can. Some think that because I am here in the thick of things, they should be too. But if you are a newcomer, you have to show you can step into the boss's shoes and this you are not going to do by degrading him. No, that will never get you anywhere. But if you show interest, intelligence, and are willing to cooperate you can always do better. The confederation was formed to knock me out of power. They called me a dictator because if something is bad I say it is bad and if something is good I say it is good. I don't care what the confederation says about me. The important thing is what the mayor says about me. They should know that Vicente is a tree that has had roots for 30 years. The confederation has not hurt me and never will be able to. No one can. I'm a made man and I did it without help and I don't need a thing from anyone. The confederation has never done a thing. I know this because everything that happens in Maplewood concerning the Puerto Ricans I know five minutes after it happens.

An organization should have principles and laws to follow and obey, some goals that it is pursuing. But the confederation — I don't know what it is. A couple of people get together and say, "We don't like the way the mayor is running the city." Then they drink a couple of beers and that's all they do. That's a confederation? That's nothing! You see in Spanish the word confederation means a society of groups, all united. If they are going to use the Spanish language, they should use it right. They have no confederation. To have that you get a group of reliable Puerto Ricans, married, with families, well-known in religion, a couple from the business world, a few who own grocery stores, people who deal with people, and then you get a few politicians because nothing gets done without politicians. Instead, they fight about this and that, some of them going to meetings only to talk about other people. It was like a family affair, women fighting with women.

I wanted the confederation to become part of the association, but they said they did not want politics. They don't understand that in Maplewood you can't do anything without politics. Diego Zayas wanted the group to go into politics and so I took him to the mayor so that he could see what it is all about. The mayor thought the group should be political and told Zayas. I told him the mayor recognizes Vicente as the leader and I get things done, but the others in the group did not want politics and so they threw Zayas out.

Diego Zayas is no leader. He's a Castro. And if you take everything to heart you cannot be a leader. This reminds me of what I told the governor. "I'm with the Democratic party because the Democrats do things for us, but if the Communist party ever should come into power and I think they can do something for the Puerto Ricans, I would be a Communist." I turn to the leader, not to the principles of the party or to the party because I like it. I play for the man at the head of the party because he's the guy who is going to do something for you. I could be a Socialist, a Democrat, a Republican, or a Communist. What I promise my people is what I look for in the party.

Mrs. Estebán is a nice lady and a good friend of mine, but she has taken the attitude that she is not being given a chance. She thinks they are against her and she has it in her mind that she wants to get even. She has her nerve! If you think people are against you, you cannot be a leader. She would be a good leader if she would forget that stuff that people resent her and then start anew. She should learn that to be a leader you have to take it as well as dish it out. But a lot of people don't want to take it. They just want to dish it out. They want it on a platter.

In other words, my idea of the confederation is that it's a group that wants to get even with someone it thinks has wronged them. They should forget that. What's done is done and you cannot wash it out. Let's start anew and form a group. That way the confederation could get somewhere but not by criticizing. For instance, before I turned Republican, I did not go to the mayor and say that "the Dominican" was no good. Had I done that the mayor would have said to himself, "You talk that way about him, you must talk the same way about me." No, I just told the mayor I was going to show him who the leader of the Puerto Ricans was and, had I not proven my leadership, I would have stayed away.

If I could talk to the members of the confederation, I would first ask them what they are after. Then I would put them in the right direction so that they could get something from the city, if that is what they want. I've been around long enough to know what they can get, but what can I do when they didn't ask me, they didn't tell me, they didn't consult with anyone? They just went ahead and formed a confederation.

If you want to lead, you can't have a chip on your shoulder as they do. To be a leader you have to do it the way I do. Some try to be leaders by being know-it-alls, by showing off their importance. There are some who have never been to school and go out and buy a ring to show that they have been to high school, but look at me. I don't even wear my high-school ring. I don't throw my weight around because I am a foreman. When people insult me, I don't pay attention. Some have told me, "With all your education how do you let them insult you?" Another person trying to build himself up as a leader would get mad and say, "I'll get even with him; I'll get someone to beat him up." That's no leader. That's a racketeer!

To be a leader you have to prove what is inside of your head and know how to express yourself. Romero Ponce, you see, wants to be a leader but he has nothing inside his head. To be a leader you cannot ignore the ones who are down and out because they are of your own kind. They are the ones you will help and live with.

I would tell an up-and-coming leader not to blow his top, to do things smoothly, politely, so that no one knows what you are doing. Be a good listener and, before you talk, get people's advice because they may know what they are talking about. Call them up and ask, "What do you think of this and that?" Then put the advice together and say what you have to say. That's what I do. Nobody has to know where you get your ideas from.

To convince people you have to have a line. When you are with intelligent people — people who are in a category above you and can teach you something — and they ask your opinion, you say something real fast — some bullshit thing. Then you pick out the one in the group who is the biggest and smartest and you ask him, "Am I right or wrong?" Now, he's not going to say in front of the others in the group that he was not smart enough to catch what you said. He will reply, "Yes, that is right." He'll agree with you because you have confused him. He's not going to lower himself in his own group by saying he did not understand you. That is why I talk fast and in a confusing manner. I know how to confuse others and for that reason I am not afraid to meet anyone.

I could have been a racketeer and made money off the Puerto Ricans. I know all the big Italians in the Italian lottery and they trust me. But I don't want to do anything against the law. When I go downtown I don't want to worry about some policeman or detective looking for me. The important thing is that if the Puerto Ricans don't like what I am doing, they can say, "to hell with you," because they don't owe me money. If I had a business they could never say that. For instance, 90 percent of the Puerto Ricans here buy everything on credit, spending their paychecks before they get them, so the guy who owns the store, gives them credit, and lends them money becomes their leader. Because they are in debt to him he has a hold over them. But you see, I don't have a business. I am a poor working man and no one can say I live off the Puerto Ricans. I am not that kind of leader. I have never made money from Puerto Ricans although I could have and today I would be a rich man. In fact, Puerto Ricans have cost me money. You know that most political leaders in Puerto Rico are broke. When Muñoz Rivera [the father of Muñoz Marín, the former governor of Puerto Rico] died he was a poor man.

I came to the United States because I wanted to be somebody. I wanted to show that we are as intelligent as any other nationality and should be respected too. And it has turned out, for a lot of people have great respect for me. I might blow my top and say things but I would never hurt anybody. My only aspiration is to be known for helping people and that I stand for the rights of every American citizen to be treated like a human being.

I am satisfied because I am what I wanted to be and nobody gave me a hand. I am afraid of no one. And when I quit, the Puerto Ricans will fight among themselves to see who is going to take over. There will be trouble and violence. A bunch of Puerto Rican racketeers will take over. The guy you now see playing the horses, building up $2,000, $5,000, or $10,000, who wants power, that is the guy who will take over. At least I can control the Puerto Ricans. Through me they get jobs. I get them out of trouble in the courts. I know people who will do favors for them, but none of the others can do this. You can't trust them.

I wish there was someone honest and decent who would play ball with me. I would push him up. I wish this because I am tired. It took me 25 to 30 years to do what I have done. These things you cannot do from today to tomorrow. It takes years of hard work, taking chances, a lot of headaches. I want to retire. Instead of political rallies and running here and there, up and down, I want to take care of my grass and flowers, but there is no one to take my place.

I love all the Puerto Ricans. They are a lot of headaches, but I love the headaches too. That is the story of the Puerto Ricans in Maplewood. Now that you have heard it, let me invite you to come to my farm; that is what we call our home. It will have to be some Sunday evening because that is the only time I am there. We can relax and have a beer. My wife will cook for us and we will eat in the patio. My patio is screened-in and has electrical plugs. We can look at my neighbor's swimming pool. We could use it but I don't know how to swim. We could sit and talk for a couple of hours. It's not a rich man's home, but it is nice there.

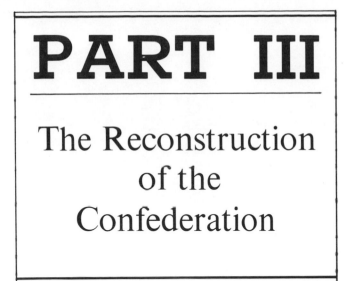

PART III

The Reconstruction of the Confederation

6

Rebirth of the Group

•

The bewildering events of the first summer — the crisis within the group, the chaotic meetings, the withdrawal of Joyce and Jordan as advisors, the successful efforts of Mrs. Esteban to counter the political take-over, and the stormy resignation of Diego Zayas — confused the members. Although Mrs. Esteban's attempts to cope with the group's problems and maintain its continuity made her the leader, there was no official president.

In our frequent talks, Mrs. Esteban told me she enjoyed the role of leader and wanted to continue it. When she asked me about Zayas's resignation, I replied that usually, in such cases, the vice-president becomes president. She knew this; indeed, she wanted to be president, but she believed the members should have the freedom of choosing their officers and she felt elections should be held without further delay.

Thus, two weeks after Serrano's aides failed to subvert the confederation, Mrs. Esteban convened a meeting to elect a new president and vice-president. Among those present at the meeting, three were her blood relatives, one her co-parent, and the remaining four her close friends. In an atmosphere of friendly approval, she opened the meeting with comments on the need for Puerto Ricans to organize themselves despite the vicissitudes the confederation had faced. Before she could finish these remarks, her brother Alfonso Vilá, who was also the group's secretary, rose to nominate Mrs. Esteban for the presidency. He explained briefly that her years of experience in Maplewood and her deep commitment to the Puerto Ricans and the confederation qualified her as the best candidate for the office. Quickly Justino Vilá, the father of both Alfonso and Mrs. Esteban, seconded the nomination. There were no other candidates for the office. Although Mrs. Esteban had assured her election by inviting to the meeting only friends and relatives, she thought the procedure was too hasty, perhaps appearing to have been contrived. She asked her brother to explain more fully why she would be a good president, and he did so. After this, Mrs. Esteban was elected unanimously.

The election of the vice-president proved to be more difficult. Justino Vilá nominated Fidel Amador who declined regretfully, explaining that after a nine-hour working day he had to be at his second-hand furniture store at night. Then Amador nominated Alejandro Rico, but Rico disqualified himself with the plea that he lacked the necessary education, preparation, and experience for the office. Amador and Rico then argued in behalf of each other's nomination and each respectfully countered the other. Annoyed by the exchange, Mrs. Estebán began to remind them of her own self-sacrifice, the hours, days, and months she had devoted to the Puerto Ricans, and her desire to continue such work. The vice-president, she added, had little to do other than observe meetings and officiate when the president was absent. Amador said that ruled him out: "I would be as nervous as a succulent cockroach trapped in a chicken coop of hungry hens." His pleas were ignored and group pressure continued until he agreed in a barely audible mumble. There was no vote, and a new and reluctant vice-president was acquired. Subsequently, Amador hardly ever attended meetings. His obligation to participate in the group devolved on his wife, Irma, as part of her marital responsibility. Mrs. Amador was a close friend of the new president and attended meetings regularly.

The elections over, the official meeting came to an end, but the members remained seated and, again, broke into a spontaneous round of condemnation of Diego Zayas. By attributing to Zayas the group's failures and blaming him for the unpleasant feelings associated with participation at meetings, the members shared strong bonds of mutual identification. The feeling of group solidarity, of being nosotros, was recreated, although the criticisms of Zayas were exactly the same as before. Having been enacted at the last meeting, the procedure now had an almost ritual character. Diego Zayas unwittingly was serving the cause of group cohesion. Very shortly, he returned as a regular member, but never again was he an officer of the confederation.

During the summer, Mrs. Estebán's activities as the informal leader, then her election as president, extended the range of the group's contacts into the city's political and bureaucratic structure and more deeply into the migrant community. As president, she redoubled her efforts to recruit members, and the confederation entered a phase of intensified activities.[1] A committee was appointed to study the educational problems of Puerto Rican children in Maplewood and to report recommendations to the group. A representative of the local antipoverty agency, APA, was invited to discuss plans for the formation of a consumer's cooperative of Puerto Rican families to purchase food at wholesale prices. A half-page flyer in Spanish was distributed in the community requesting Puerto Ricans to report to Mrs. Estebán or to APA all complaints of illegal or unscrupulous business practices by local merchants. Authorization was given for the collection and publication in a neighborhood newsletter, circulated in Mrs. Estebán's neighborhood, of stories about the confederation and the Puerto

Rican community. The possibility of a television program and a series of public lectures about Puerto Rican culture was considered. Plans were made to visit Puerto Rican families to invite them to participate in the confederation.

These activities centered directly upon Mrs. Estebán who projected herself forcefully into the presidency. Her civic work, however, went beyond this role. With a byline but without identification as the confederation's president, she wrote an article in Spanish for the neighborhood's newsletter, urging Puerto Ricans to attend adult education classes in English, to change their attitudes, and to cease rejecting their responsibilities. She repeated this theme at the confederation's meetings, emphasizing the need to be punctual, responsible and disciplined.

Urged on by the exhortations of the vigorous president, the group turned to a proposal made earlier in the spring of that year to confer with the mayor of Maplewood. The plan had been forgotten during the group crisis and political assault. Although the confederation had decided against involvement in partisan politics, the members agreed that power and influence in the city were organized according to a hierarchy and that all important decisions were made through city hall. The earlier plan had been to invite the mayor to speak at a meeting, but now they decided the group would go to him. During the visit, they would try to impress upon him that he could not evade their requests. If he did not cooperate, they would go again and again.

Briefly, the group's requests were for better supervision on school busses transporting Puerto Rican students, reduction of costs of transportation to school and of school lunches, and establishment of scholarships for adult Puerto Ricans who wished to improve their formal education.

Through its antipoverty agency, Maplewood had many programs for its economically poor people, but an additional proposition of the confederation went far beyond what any program had offered: this was the request that the municipal government establish and staff an office to serve the needs of the Puerto Rican population. The office would be recognized as belonging to the Hispanic Confederation of Maplewood and would deal only with the problems of the Spanish speakers in the community as the most disadvantaged minority in the city. A bilingual person with an intimate knowledge of Puerto Rican culture would direct the office. An adequate budget would provide support for whatever assistants were necessary and the office would function as a referral center, orienting the migrants and directing them to the appropriate city agencies.

Along with the desire to extract such promises from the mayor, Mrs. Estebán had a personal reason for wanting to lead the group to city hall. Once before, when she had met the mayor, he had asked if her work with the Puerto Ricans was in collaboration with Vicente de Serrano. Mrs. Estebán had taken the question as a deliberate insult. Now, she wanted to counter the insult by leading the confederation to city hall and by demonstrating that she was a leader in her own right. Accordingly, she came to my office to discuss her letter to the mayor, which I wrote and she signed as president of the Hispanic Confederation. The letter, mailed early in October of that year, requested an appointment with the mayor on either one of two dates, two or three weeks later. The appointment, however, was not made for three-and-one-half months, and the struggle that followed involved the rebirth of the confederation.

The letter gave rise to a sequence of events which affected the group. It began when the mayor, busy campaigning for the elections to be held the following month, forwarded the letter to Arthur McCall, the director of the city's anti-poverty agency. McCall, then, wrote to Mrs. Esteban asking her to telephone his secretary to make arrangements for a meeting with him and other interested persons. The letter conveyed the mayor's interest in "having the ideas in the letter fully discussed and followed up with practical suggestions." This assurance, however, did little to lessen the members' angry response. They felt that having sought an appointment with "the first magnate of the city" it was demeaning to be referred not even to the mayor's secretary but to McCall's secretary. What was perhaps usual procedure for the mayor and the director of APA was taken as an insult by the group.

Mrs. Esteban thought the affront was indicative of a plot to subvert the confederation. She remembered that a representative of APA had spoken at a meeting of the group about organizing a consumer's cooperative among Puerto Ricans. Few, if any, of the members understood the plans for such a cooperative, and now, as they recalled the plan, it conjured up ideas of mysterious arrangements and doings. Mrs. Esteban also alluded to clandestine efforts by the Pan-American Association to prevent the confederation from seeing the mayor. Other unidentified enemies also were working against the group she claimed. When I asked her who they were, she replied ominously, "I cannot tell you *now* what it is all about."

The members did not know what to do until, finally, Diego Zayas proposed that McCall's letter be disregarded and the group, once again, write directly to the mayor. The others agreed but stipulated that a copy be sent to McCall and that he be invited to attend the meeting with the mayor. This letter also was not answered. The election was over, and the mayor, having just finished an arduous political campaign, had gone on vacation. By the time his failure to answer the letter was realized, however, a new situation had come about which swept away the confederation's concern about the mayor.

Copies of the first letter had been duplicated and distributed widely among the personnel of APA, and as a result the confederation, and particularly Mrs. Esteban, were receiving unprecedented attention. Several of the APA personnel volunteered to serve as an intermediary between the group, on the one hand, and the agency and the mayor, on the other. The most concerned person was Roger

Davis, the assistant coordinator of the APA program for Mrs. Esteban's neighborhood. He visited her repeatedly, urging a meeting of the confederation to discuss the letter to the mayor. At first reluctant because of doubts about her authority to call a meeting with such official overtones, Mrs. Esteban finally agreed. The confederation and APA were to be formally introduced to each other: the agency, to the conduct of the group; the group, to the politics of the city's anti-poverty programs.

Twenty-eight persons came to the meeting, an unusually large attendance, but, indicative of APA's sudden interest in the group, six were employees of the agency. Following protocol, Mrs. Esteban opened the meeting by asking each person to introduce himself. She added that each should feel free to comment on what the group should be doing. Some persons spoke briefly; others made speeches. The Reverend Arturo Prieto stood up, cleared his throat, waited for silence, and then delivered a sermon on brotherhood. When Justino Vilá's turn came he also stood to address the group. With trembling voice and oratorical zest, he described the history of Puerto Rican-American relations, reading aloud from an article in a Spanish newspaper. There were ripples of laughter from the audience, but some were beginning to grow impatient at the long self-introductions.

Mrs. Esteban attempted in vain to still her father, but he continued, oblivious to her efforts. When he finally sat down, a motion was presented that the self-introductions be discontinued. Some members opposed it on the grounds that those who had not yet spoken should not be denied the opportunity given to the others. Arguments broke out. The motion was brought to a vote and was defeated, so the introductions went on. The last person to speak was a young man who had come to only one other meeting several months before. He was there now, he explained, because he wanted to hear what all the APA people were going to do for the Puerto Ricans. He concluded sardonically, "I, myself, am a person of great intellect, knowledge, and wisdom, as much as that of any doctor, but lately I have been washing dishes for a living."

Not understanding Spanish and unaccustomed to such doings at a meeting, the APA employees were befuddled. When Roger Davis's turn came, he explained the agency's programs in seven selected inner-city neighborhoods. Then he brought out a copy of the confederation's first letter to the mayor and discussed it in detail. If the group wanted to see the mayor, he said, he would cooperate in making the appointment since APA's concern was to help the Puerto Ricans. Most of the members had begun whispering among themselves, still caught in the informal mood created by the earlier part of the meeting, but Diego Zayas's attention never wavered from Roger Davis's face. He jumped up to ask: "If your agency is so concerned about us, why haven't you, as coordinator in a neighborhood with 75 Puerto Rican families, given a job to a single one of us?" An uproar followed, during which even those members who had been socializing took part in an attack upon APA. Davis promised to consider the criticisms; the meeting came to an end.

APA's pursuit of the confederation continued. The members could not understand the sudden interest and found it difficult to attribute honest motives to the agency after what was, from their viewpoint, the neglect of the Puerto Ricans in the city. When Davis, in an informal conversation, told Mrs. Estebán that the group should not bother the mayor (although at the meeting he had volunteered to make the appointment), the members became more and more suspicious.

Confusion soon became widespread as Davis, assuming that the Puerto Ricans should speak with one voice, attempted to join together the Hispanic Confederation and the Pan-American Association. He volunteered to arrange a meeting between Mrs. Estebán and Antonio Tejada, the two presidents. At this time, the Pan-American Association was not *openly* controlled by Serrano, but the members of the confederation, most of all Mrs. Estebán, were aware that the political boss was the dominant person behind the association. They had just barely escaped his plan to politicize the confederation under the guise of merging the two groups. In addition, Mrs. Estebán considered Tejada, her coparent, a traitor for he had quit the confederation to organize the rival Pan-American Association. Mrs. Estebán went to the meeting arranged by Davis, however, and reported furiously to me that she had been stood up. "They are treating me like a fool," she said. "It upsets me. It makes me even angrier because I know all of this is being initiated by a Puerto Rican [Tejada]." Mrs. Estebán was also apprehensive because she had been told that the association was being legally incorporated in the state. Not certain of what this meant, she had a vague idea that it meant the rival group's acquisition of official control over the organizational life of Puerto Ricans in Maplewood. Then she heard that the mayor was going to give *his* support to the association.

Mrs. Estebán's fear grew that these were not random occurrences. Over the summer the linkages between the mayor and Serrano and between Serrano and the association had been well demonstrated. The chain of connection was even longer now: Davis's attempt to dissuade her from visiting the mayor and his efforts to combine the two groups; Tejada's betrayal and his apparently clandestine attempt to merge the groups; the indignity of being stood up at a meeting she had not wanted to attend in the first place; the association's prestige in being represented by a lawyer and its legal incorporation; the mayor's forwarding the confederation's request to the director of the antipoverty agency; and APA's sudden interest in the confederation — the whole chain of events appeared to be organized to impede the group's progress, and Mrs. Estebán concluded that there was a conspiracy against her and against the confederation.

The growing problems of the confederation were further increased by criticisms from Frank Joyce, the coordinator of the Community School Program, whose initial efforts to bring Puerto Ricans into the established organizations of the neighborhood unexpectedly gave birth to the confederation. Joyce felt the group had left too many things undone and had failed to follow up on the initial contacts made with agencies and responsible persons. He believed the confederation should drop its city-wide organization and return to the concept of neighborhood group. This advice upset Mrs. Estebán. She admired Joyce as a person in an authoritative position, but his recommendation went counter to the tide of events that had been sweeping the group since the early summer. There had been too many changes for the confederation to revert to its original status.

Doubt-ridden yet anxious to lead the group forward, Mrs. Estebán continued to search for guidance until Carlos Otero approached her. Otero, a Puerto Rican who had been brought up in New York City, was now a testing specialist and vocational counselor for APA. He had seen the confederation's first letter to the mayor and had found it interesting, for he, also, was troubled by the fact that APA's programs had been aimed almost exclusively at blacks and were not reaching Puerto Ricans.

Otero had been struggling to persuade APA officials to develop special programs for the Puerto Ricans. To this end he had recently submitted to them a written proposal to form a small, bilingual "indigenous" group of "bridge people" to carry out recruitment, interviewing, testing, counseling, follow-up, and a host of additional supportive services to bring the Puerto Ricans into APA's training and employment programs. Despite his belief in the proposal's fundamental importance, it had received only perfunctory consideration, and there was little hope of its implementation. The confederation's letter to the mayor had suggested to Otero that working through this group with which he had long been out of touch he could pressure APA into accepting his proposal. The first step, he decided, was to show the confederation that their proposals, as stated in the letter to the mayor, were wrong and his idea was right. Mrs. Estebán was impressed with Otero's plan. They turned to me for support, but I reiterated my neutral stand in such decisions. Finally, a meeting of the confederation was called so that Otero could present his plan to the group.

Few, if any, of the members were able to recall their proposals in the letter to the mayor, but they knew they were opposed to Otero. The antagonistic questions came thick and fast at the meeting: Why his sudden interest in the Confederation? Why hadn't he attended other meetings? Why was it that when Puerto Ricans went to APA for help he didn't identify himself as one of them? Was it true he had identified himself as a Cuban?

Otero had an unfortunate habit of starting sentences in Spanish and completing them in English. This did little to still the members' suspicion of him. He was aware of this problem and told me subsequently in an interview, "I had to pick up middle-class [American] culture in order to be successful at college. It kills me that I have to be two different persons for two different groups."

More opposed to Otero than to his proposals, the members rejected his plan. As the meeting came to an end, Otero commented in an aside, "It's going to be funny seeing these people with the mayor."

The rejection of the plan further confused Mrs. Estebán. If she trusted Davis's advice, the confederation would be forced into a union with the Pan-American Association. If she trusted Joyce's advice, the group would return to the neighborhood where it originated and in effect would undo what it had accomplished. Other persons gave other kinds of advice freely, but the recommendations of Otero, Davis, and Joyce, she felt, were not to be taken lightly for each had a responsible position and could claim expertise in the problems confronting the group. Although Mrs. Estebán alluded privately to conspiratorial plots against her and the group, this did not appear to diminish her great respect for these three men who spoke with competence and authority and who were urging her to pursue mutually exclusive courses of action.

Discussions at the meeting were of little help in guiding Mrs. Estebán or the confederation to the choice of an alternative. When she recounted the variety of advice given to her, she went into great detail, from one minute fact to another, including her personal problems. The members were passive, withdrawing even more when confused, but occasionally they sallied forth to attack speakers invited to meetings such as Davis and Otero. They were overwhelmed by Mrs. Estebán's stories of her conversations with those in authority, and often did not even understand who had said what to her; yet, they seldom stopped her to ask for clarification or for a summary statement, nor was there an upsurge of sustained criticism of her. However confused or confusing were the accounts of her numerous public activities and problems, they were ostensibly relevant to the group. Most of her experiences away from meetings were related to group concerns, thus the norm prohibiting members from speaking about personal problems had an unequal effect upon participation and justified Mrs. Estebán's almost absolute dominance of group discussion. The situation favored the talkative leader and added to the disparity between her and the inert followers. Consequently, meeting after meeting was taken up by talk, and no proper course of action was planned.

Mrs. Estebán's growing indecision was exacerbated by the members. The group seldom attempted to analyze the contradictory advice it received. Rarely did they seek to weigh advice given against decisions already made. Decisions relevant to the group's goals *had* been made, and their conclusions had been stated as proposals in the first letter to the mayor, yet when Davis read the letter out loud at the meeting, some members who had contributed to the proposals in the letter wondered why such proposals had been made. Officially, the secretary of the organization should have been taking notes and reading minutes at each meeting, but Alfonso Vilá, the secretary, approached his task with little concern and great lassitude. When Mrs. Estebán reprimanded him for being derelict in his duties, the members dismissed the incident humorously as a case of sibling rivalry. Thus, even when the records of prior decisions were available, such as the letter to the mayor, they contributed little to the resolution of the issues facing the group.

Although the members could recall little about the letter to the mayor, they had not forgotten their request for an appointment. Two months had elapsed since the first letter was mailed and no appointment had yet been arranged. They became restive and impatient. The source of their unrest, however, was different from what it had been before. Previously, the members had felt frustrated, listening to the repeated personal complaints of other participants without being able to relieve themselves fully of their own personal grievances. Now dissatisfaction arose because of the tacit application of a new functional standard — whether or not a specified objective had been attained. Not having seen the mayor, the objective had not been attained, and this caused a new kind of unrest formed not by objection to hearing personal problems but by group concerns. To the members the person most immediately responsible for the delay was the president, and occasionally Mrs. Estebán became the target of sporadic unorganized criticism.

Along with her presidency of the confederation, Mrs. Estebán participated in many other civic and religious activities, had the obligations of a mother, wife, sister, and daughter in a large extended family, and was enrolled at a local college. Her performance as a student began to deteriorate. She said, "I cannot remember a thing. I cannot concentrate on the books I read. I have no idea of what is going on in class." In addition, she worried about her husband, his constant drinking, and ill health. She finally reacted to her persistent anxieties by developing a stomach disorder and insomnia.

In considering her many activities, Mrs. Estebán decided that she was involved in too many things and she would have to quit college. When she explained her decision to a college official, he could not understand her decision. She told me later the official said, "Why should the Puerto Ricans be so demanding of you? They should learn to work as we [Americans] do, learn to sacrifice themselves." Mrs. Estebán thought this comment devalued the Puerto Ricans as well as her own devotion to her compatriots. She was deeply disturbed by this incident.

Having made the decision that she would not leave the confederation, Mrs. Estebán then began to worry that her nervousness would be detected by others. Her close friends in the confederation did observe changes in her behavior and commented on her agitation and her rambling at the meetings, but, if annoyed at the confusion she created, they understood that she was under stress. In contrast to their attitude toward Diego Zayas, they did not feel condemnatory toward Mrs. Estebán. They remembered how often she had helped them through their own personal tribulations and knew she would always be ready to help again. Gratitude bound them to her and respect for her sacrifices on their behalf. Consequently, when they occasionally disagreed with her at meetings, they did so gently and when this failed to curb her incoherent rambling, they withdrew into passivity.

One exception to this pattern was David Alemán who had recently moved to Maplewood. Because he was a newcomer, he was not bound to Mrs. Estebán either by prior friendship or debts of gratitude, nor was he well known by the other members. Thus, he focused upon the issues confronting the group as if they were completely separate from the interpersonal relations between the leader and the followers. Alemán was a carpenter by trade, but his greatest interest was in composing music and poetry, and he was exceptionally articulate in both Spanish and English. He did not express himself in sudden bursts of unrelated ideas, as most of the members tended to do. A methodical thinker, Alemán decided the time had come to take action. Thus, at a meeting he attempted to summarize the group's problems. Two months before, he said, the confederation had decided to see the mayor and had written a letter to him. The mayor was busy and delegated the responsibility of seeing the group to APA. The members of the confederation, however, had rejected this plan. On the other hand, APA was preventing the group from seeing the mayor because it did not want the mayor to know that APA had neglected the Puerto Ricans. Moreover, the intrusions of Davis, Otero, and the others who had suddenly acquired an interest in the group had confused them. It was of utmost importance, Alemán went on, that they now reaffirm their original objective of visiting the mayor. He concluded with the reminder that it was the president's responsibility to carry out the group's decisions.

By now, Mrs. Estebán was doubtful of even serving as the group's spokesman at the mayor's office. She had been told by an APA employee that a man should act in this capacity because a man carries more authority. To make matters worse she was beginning to experience spells of laryngitis and feared this would occur at the mayor's office. After Alemán's pointed comments, Mrs. Estebán confessed her anxieties to the group and wondered out loud what she would tell the mayor and how she would answer his questions.

Suddenly, of their own accord, the members began to rehearse the visit, one person, then another, playing the role of the mayor. The acting mayor always took a tough officious attitude. When Mrs. Estebán's introductory comments turned into a long confusing discourse on the confederation's history, the "mayor" reminded her that his time was too valuable to be wasted on irrelevant detail. The "mayor" said things to Mrs. Estebán which the members had often felt but never expressed. The other members laughed, and the "mayor" moved to the attack: "What do the Puerto Ricans really want? Why should the confederation have its own office? Why didn't you go to the director of APA as I asked you to do?" Whenever Mrs. Estebán used the phrase "In my opinion," Alemán corrected her: "You are not expressing your own opinions. You are representing this group." But the discussion of appropriate answers did not appear to improve the organization of Mrs. Estebán's thoughts. Alfonso Vilá, her brother, commented that the problem was her habit of talking too much. David Alemán said the solution was for her to prepare an outline "down to the last detail" of what she was going to tell the mayor and how she was going to answer his questions. "Oh, Virgin of mine! My mother!," cried Mrs. Estebán, "What am I going to do?"

But a few days later, when informed by Davis that a date for the appointment still had not been set, Mrs. Estebán erupted in anger at him. She told him, "If the appointment is not made immediately, I, as president of the Hispanic Confederation, will telegraph the mayor for an appointment."

The very next day, a letter with the official letterhead of APA and the signature of Roger Davis was mailed to Mrs. Estebán. It was an invitation to a meeting between the confederation and the mayor of Maplewood to be held in a week.

NOTES

1. At this point in the group's life, Miss Carmen Sylvia García joined the confederation as my assistant. For further information on this point, see Chapter 12.

7

Visit to the Mayor and the Rebellious Aftermath

•

After three and one-half months of preparation, nine members of the confederation — five men and four women — gathered together in the mayor's waiting room at city hall. They were well dressed, elated but restrained, and somewhat uneasy about what was to come. Arthur McCall, the director of APA, arrived with four subordinate officials, among them Roger Davis and Carlos Otero. A top official of the city's Urban Redevelopment Agency arrived also. As they were ushered into the main office Mrs. Estebán stood near the mayor and introduced us by name. Each of us shook hands with him. (Afterwards, some members said they wished they would never have to wash their hands again so as not to "wash away the good luck.") The nine of us were seated at a large conference table with the mayor at the head and Mrs. Estebán next to him; behind us, in a row of chairs at the mayor's right, sat the city and APA officials. The confederation had center stage for the conference.

Mrs. Estebán then began again to introduce each member. Gently, the mayor reminded her that he had just met each of us, but, conforming to the confederation's ritual introductions and to her own plan, she was not dissuaded. Around the table she went, stating each person's name and address, and occasionally throwing in anecdotal information. Accepting the procedure, the mayor commented that he had been born in one of the neighborhoods mentioned and his father in another. Mrs. Abelando, the last person introduced, complained to the mayor that although she was a trained nurse she had to work in Maplewood as a nurse's aide because the state would not give her certification. The mayor directed his secretary to make a note of the problem to see what could be done. He did the same when Mrs. Estebán said that she herself was a qualified teacher but not certified by the state. Some members looked surprised at this discussion of personal problems.

Mrs. Estebán then spoke about the confederation as a citywide organization of leaders of Hispanic groups in Maplewood. In this, she was referring to the original plan of the confederation, not to what it had become. She asked the mayor to make a public announcement recognizing the confederation as *the* official Puerto Rican organization in Maplewood. The mayor, in an attempt at levity, inquired if the name of the group was the Hispanic *Democratic* Confederation. One member retorted that the confederation was not political, ". . . but you treat us right and the Puerto Ricans will give you 50 votes." The mayor asked if anyone knew a "big, strong, white-haired fellow active in Puerto Rican affairs" whose name he could not recall. It was my impression that the mayor was pretending to have forgotten the name (Serrano) in order to discover the group's attitude toward the political boss; an able politician, in office for 13 years, the mayor was known to have an exceptional memory for names and faces, and it was unlikely that he could not remember the name of the man who was the primary force mobilizing Puerto Rican support for the Democratic party. Mrs. Estebán hastened to identify Serrano and tell the mayor that the Puerto Ricans neither liked nor supported him.

Presently, what the members had feared began to occur: departing from the points on which she had been rehearsed, Mrs. Estebán began a long, rambling commentary about the city's Puerto Ricans. Along the way, she interjected the view that, unlike other Latin Americans, Puerto Ricans in Maplewood did *not* have problems because they were citizens. Some members again looked surprised at what she was saying, for the purpose of this long-awaited meeting was to dramatize the Puerto Ricans' problems and the help they needed. I felt she had not meant to say what she had said, but that, somewhat tense and increasingly agitated at speaking for the group in such a solemn, official, and important meeting, she was trying to narrow the separation between the Puerto Ricans and Americans in the room. When the mayor interrupted to ask if she had an agenda, she replied that she did not. "But Mrs. Estebán," David Alemán exclaimed, "The letter, the letter!"

A copy of the original letter to the mayor was brought out and reviewed quickly by the mayor, McCall, and Mrs. Estebán. The letter urged the municipal government to create and staff an office which would serve as a referral center for Puerto Ricans. McCall informed us that the facilities the confederation wanted were either already available or could easily be expanded to meet their requests. APA, he continued, was well aware of the Puerto Ricans' problems, for it employed two Puerto Ricans, one being Carlos Otero to whom he pointed. David Alemán's repeated attempts to speak were waved aside by Mrs. Estebán until, disregarding her, he broke into the discussion emphasizing the need for an office for Puerto Ricans. McCall took this as a request for a meeting room for the confederation and said office space and a telephone could be made available. No

one corrected him on this point, and thus the group's most important proposal
was bypassed in the discussion which followed. Finally, the mayor stood to de-
liver an impassioned attack against the city's slumlords who victimized minority
groups and "profited from people's miseries" through the "greedy and unscrupulous collection of usurious rents." He vowed to prosecute them for housing
infractions regardless of their race or creed. And, suddenly, the meeting was
over!

Afterwards, the members congregated on the front steps of city hall to talk.
Mrs. Amador lost no time in attacking Mrs. Estebán for saying that the Catholic
church did not speak on behalf of the Puerto Ricans; she insisted her own church
did. "Do you bear me ill will?" asked Mrs. Estebán. "Pay no attention to my
sister," Alfonso Vilá said, "because she recites errors and she thinks one thing
and says another." He was indignant because Mrs. Estebán had not allowed him
to speak at the meeting. David Alemán criticized her for not dealing with the
important issues and for not extracting definite promises from the mayor. Mrs.
Pomales stated that the meeting was "all politics and, knowing politics as I do, I
know they say one thing and do another." On the other hand, Mrs. Abelando
thought the meeting was "fantastic," not because the group's requests would be
met — she did not know about that — but because, ". . . they thought we would
come like *jibaritos* ("hillbillies") impoverished and poorly dressed, but we were
well dressed; we were *gente* ("persons commanding respect")!" Justino Vilá expressed no opinion because he knew no English and did not understand what had
been said at the meeting. Although Carmen Sylvia García — my research assistant
— and I did not voice our opinions, we felt that Mrs. Estebán, having strayed
from the main points, had failed to impress upon the mayor the importance of
the group's proposals. The only person who believed the group had been ably
represented was Mrs. Estebán herself. She was confident that the mayor would
be moved to act favorably upon their requests.

In an interview with the mayor six months later, I asked his thoughts about
the meeting, and he remembered it clearly. During his 13 years in office, he said,
he had rarely been visited by an independent ethnic association with requests
such as those presented by the confederation. Referring to other Puerto Rican
groups, he said:

> Let me put it rather delicately. There have been other groups who have come
> to me on a political basis. . . . The kind of thing the confederation requested
> from me was on a much higher level and was concerned with the more funda-
> mental questions of leadership and education; opportunities for training
> people; need for greater recognition on the part of city hall. . . . The other
> attempts to approach me have been on a completely political basis!

If the confederation's requests were on a "higher level" than those involving the usual bid for political favors, then really unusual was the *way* in which the group had established contact with him. He went on:

> The . . . interesting thing about the Latin American group (the confederation) is that they scorn the powerbrokers who attempt to represent them politically, and instead prefer to negotiate with city hall on the basis of what they feel the community should do for these people, not in terms of . . . political patronage, but in terms of assisting these people in adjusting to urban life. This is a totally different approach, as you know from the old concept. When the Irish first came to America, they were greeted at the docks of Boston with their citizenship papers in one hand and a certificate to go to work for the city in the other. This was a political venture and nothing else. But today, the Latin American confederation is here for different purposes.

The mayor emphatically denied knowledge of efforts to convert the confederation into a political organization. I pursued the point further by asking him how the group would have fared if it had become political. He answered:

> It doesn't make any difference. I've watched many ethnic groups go through this convulsion (political). The blacks have tried to organize on a political basis, and the Jews tried it 15 years ago when I first began to run for mayor. Actually what happens is that the average voter is far more sophisticated than anybody realizes. They understand what candidates stand for and what their programs mean. Frankly speaking, I have never had the problem of communicating with any of these groups. I think if we organize on the basis of what is needed in the community, the political benefits become obvious.

The mayor had clearly accepted the group's apolitical character. This identification was not affected by Mrs. Abelando's and Mrs. Estebán's comments on their individual problems of certification, for the mayor understood that the confederation was not seeking personal favors for its members. His reaction was quick and favorable: after the meeting he instructed the officials of APA, the Urban Redevelopment Agency, and the city Department of Education to cooperate with the group.

Although not one member of the confederation knew the meeting had been successful, Mrs. Estebán was firmly convinced she had met the test of spokesman with great success. Unsure of herself before the meeting, she now felt a renewed sense of confidence in herself and her ability to lead the group.

Only seven persons were present at the next meeting after the visit to the mayor — mostly those who had gone to city hall — because Mrs. Estebán wanted the immediate participants to be the first to discuss the visit before others were informed. She knew there had been criticism of what she had said at city hall, and I felt she wanted to contain the criticism to the small inner group. The visit to the mayor had sparked excitement among the members, but surprisingly at the start of the meeting, no one wanted to be the first to speak. Finally, David

Alemán volunteered the comment: "The doors are open, but we are still outside," referring to the still unmet promises of the mayor. Mrs. Estebán agreed, although she added: "Don't you have trust or faith that we will achieve good things, faith that we will be successful?"

Optimistically, Mrs. Estebán wanted to define the terms of the discussion to avoid unfavorable criticism of her spokesmanship. She said, "If I am going to get advice, let it be for the future, not the past." The issue, however, was what she *had* done as spokesman and, finally, it came to the surface when David Alemán averred: "We went to see the mayor about our problems, the many problems we have, as Hispanos, but you told the mayor that we did not have problems. When you said this, McCall's eyes opened wide."

Mrs. Estebán replied, "That is interesting."

Alebán went on: "Yes, his eyes opened wide indicating that if the Puerto Ricans do not have problems, they do not face a grave situation."

Mrs. Estebán asked him sarcastically, "You saw that? Are you a psychologist that you know how to observe such points?"

Alemán was not to be diverted. "Why did you tell him that?"

Mrs. Estebán took a deep breath: "Why did I say that? Do you want me to start talking now? If I start now you will all listen to me. I am not going to say things in a minute or two. I have to start . . . from the first things the confederation did. . . ."

Having issued a warning, the president spoke for 20 minutes about the history of the group — how it started, was named, became a citywide organization, the early program of speakers, the political assault, the difficulty of making an appointment with the mayor. At one moment she stopped to recall the exact date on which Alemán came to his first meeting. In the context of the narrative she was slowly making the point that, as a recent newcomer, Alemán had not yet earned the right to ask the question he had posed. Her experience included the totality of the group's life; his was very limited. She finished with generous compliments to the members for behaving well at the mayor's office.

Alemán's question remained unanswered, but Mrs. Estebán's long (and evasive) speech turned the members' attention toward their shared experiences, the importance of the group's efforts, and the breadth and constancy of Mrs. Estebán's contributions to the group. When the question was raised again, this time by her brother, it had lost its original sting. Her speech had dissipated the hostile tone of the meeting. Now she replied directly that, because Puerto Ricans were American citizens, they had fewer problems than other Latin Americans in Maplewood; it was wrong always, she claimed, to portray Puerto Ricans as a problem-ridden group. Emphasis should be given, she said, to their dignity and honor.

To some members, Mrs. Estebán's and Mrs. Abelando's discussion of their problems of certification at the mayor's office was an infraction of the rule not to mention personal problems. Immediately after leaving city hall, both had been roundly chastized; now, at the meeting, although the infraction was brought up again, criticisms of Mrs. Estebán were mild and restrained. Yet, for the first time in the group's life, members other than the president had used the rule as a basis for criticism, and, ironically, one of the targets was Mrs. Estebán who had been the first to state the rule, emphasize its importance, and employ it as a defense against the political assault. Thus, the norm was filtering into the group's system of sanctions and becoming their common property. Even its originator was not exempt.

Carlos Otero then brought out another facet of the rule's importance. Not familiar with its origin as a means for controlling unrestrained personal revelations, he saw it as the way in which the confederation established contacts with city officials. He said personal problems ought not to be brought up in public, official situations because: "To do otherwise would be to do it the way Vicente de Serrano does it — you help me, I help you." An exchange of personal favors, he continued, carried the stigma of political deals, and this would be both unseemly and ineffective. By keeping conferences with city officials on a high and impersonal level, the members could never be accused of selfish motives and city officials would be impressed with the group's objective of improving life for all Puerto Ricans as compared with the desire for personal gains for individuals.

As I discovered later, the personal character of the two women's complaints about certification was hardly noticed by the mayor, but he had been impressed by the "higher level" of the confederation's requests. His reaction corresponded exactly to the advice Otero was giving the group. Thus, the rule had double relevance for the confederation — to its internal affairs, and to its relationships with outside organizations — and an in-group virtue was shown to have out-group merit. By emphasizing the connection between the two, Otero introduced a new dimension into the confederation's developing norms.

As he talked to the members, it became clear that Otero was, at least tacitly, taking their viewpoint, speaking *with* them, not *at* them. At first, interested in the confederation as a means for developing his own Puerto Rican manpower project within APA, Otero was now identifying with the members and aligning himself with the group's goals. In turn, he was beginning to be accepted by the group. No longer were suspicious questions raised about his loyalty to the ethnic in-group as they had been when he started coming to meetings regularly several weeks before.

Having attended the meeting with the mayor as a representative of APA, he had stayed in the mayor's office with the other officials after the confederation members left. Now, the members asked him what had been said later. Otero told them that the group's requests were discussed seriously, and the mayor wanted the Department of Education, the Urban Redevelopment Agency, and APA to consult with the group.

At the same time that Otero's new identification was becoming apparent, the meeting revealed Mrs. Estebán's growing involvement with APA. Shortly before, she had been elected to APA's Neighborhood Advisory Board, a group consisting of 21 elected members, three from each of Maplewood's inner-city neighborhoods selected for poverty programs by APA. The board was the instrument through which the economically poor residents of the inner city were to be given "maximum feasible participation" in the development of antipoverty programs, according to the stipulations of the congressional law establishing the Office of Economic Opportunity. All applications for the development of specific antipoverty programs in the city were reviewed and voted upon by this board which, in turn, submitted its recommendations to the highest group governing the APA.

Proud to be the *first* and *only* Puerto Rican on the board, Mrs. Estebán looked upon her election as another way to help her compatriots and the confederation, but her ties to APA were now formal and her voice official. She had come to see APA as a vast, intricate, and powerful enterprise and she stood in awe of it. She approved deeply of APA, not the least reason being her new status as an intermediary with the Puerto Rican community. The APA officials told her of job opportunities available to Puerto Ricans and she, in turn, conveyed this information to her relatives, friends, and members of the confederation. Her reputation as a leader was thus enhanced, both in APA and among her compatriots. At the confederation meeting she told the members: "The person who speaks badly about the agency [APA] simply does not understand and does not want to understand. I am very satisfied with what they have done for me. They have offered me what I want."

Then she recommended that officials of the agency be invited to the next meeting to discuss how the Puerto Ricans were to be helped. David Alemán immediately opposed her, but it was Justino Vilá, her own father, who argued most forcefully against such invitations. He insisted no outsider should be invited because the meetings were disorderly and minutes were not kept. Outsiders would be appalled at the disorder of their meetings, he said, and added, "All we do here is spill a lot of words." When Mrs. Estebán continued to press for the invitations, Alemán moved that they not be sent, and the motion was carried.

Mrs. Estebán was unable to come to the next meeting of the confederation a week later because she had to be at a meeting of the Neighborhood Advisory Board. Accordingly, she called upon the long-absent vice-president, Fidel Amador, to direct the meeting and left instructions for the group to discuss the meeting with the mayor again and to take up the issue of inviting officials of APA. (Although this proposal had been rejected, she was insisting upon it.) Amador was not familiar with the confederation's recent doings and was apologetic about being chairman. He asked the secretary to read the minutes of the last meeting. Alfonso Vilá began: "On February 2, 1919, the Hispanic Confederation of Maplewood met to. . . ." One of the 14 participants corrected the secretary, for no meeting had been held in 1919, almost half a century before. Admitting the error, the secretary turned to another set of minutes, but again no one in the group could recall the meeting which he seemed to be reporting. This procedure was repeated several times, until amidst waves of laughter the secretary gave up, saying that minutes were not important in any case. This was typical of the confusion over minutes at other meetings of the confederation.

The discussion of the visit to the mayor had barely begun when Diego Zayas declared it to have been an absolute failure because the mayor had surrounded himself with APA and Urban Redevelopment officials, thereby relieving himself of the responsibility of acting upon the confederation's requests. Zayas said: "It is much like a man who wants to marry a girl but sends someone else to speak on his behalf. If the man does that, it means he does not really want to get married. He wants to stay at home." Other persons countered with the opinion that it was common practice for the mayor, as the city's top executive, to delegate responsibility to agency officials. Zayas, however, was adamant. "In other words," he said, "they swallowed us up like so much spaghetti. . . . Their promises hang in the air."

After his deposition as president, Diego Zayas had returned to the group but he always picked a chair away from the conference table where the others sat. This put him out of the inner circle of discussion and reflected accurately his marginal status in the group. He knew the group had rejected him, but never in private or in public had he expressed anger toward the individual members or toward Mrs. Estebán who had been his main antagonist. He felt that if the confederation had failed during his presidency, it still continued to be a failure. At meetings he was not hesitant to emphasize current disappointments, along with warnings to the members to be alert to the deceptions of officials. Now his explosively critical comments provoked David Alemán to intervene: "I suggest that, since it has been so long since you have come to these meetings, you listen more and talk less. Excuse the offense, but that is the truth."

Zayas replied: "I don't get offended so easily, *compadre* ('friend')."

Alemán went on: "It now depends on us. There [at city hall] they said, 'Come and ask and we will consider what we can do for you.' But if we continue doing what we are doing here, namely nothing, then we are going to get nothing. It is up to us this time. There is nothing more to say."

Having silenced Zayas, Alemán then urged that McCall be visited as soon as possible with the plan for developing the Hispanic Office to serve as a referral center for Puerto Ricans. His proposal was quickly endorsed, but when asked by Amador to represent the group as spokesman, Alemán refused, arguing that the president should be the spokesman for the group. Nonetheless, the vice-president felt it was necessary to select a spokesman immediately and since Mrs. Estebán was not present she could not be appointed. Alemán finally acceded, and the group had a new spokesman.

Alemán's reluctance to represent the confederation indicated the conflict in the members' feelings; on the one hand they wanted to move ahead — "Go while the matter is still hot," as one member put it; on the other hand, they thought it improper to proceed without the president. Tension and indecision were evident in the repeated expression of this point. For example, Mrs. Amador said at first, "We must be directed by one person [Mrs. Estebán] so that she can control us." Shortly after, she said, "We must demonstrate to the president that if, for one reason or another, she cannot come to a meeting, we *can* have a meeting anyhow. We should demonstrate to her that she can have confidence in us at these meetings." Mrs. Amador's comments showed respect for the president but a bid for independence from her. By the conclusion of the meeting, independence had won out.

When Mrs. Estebán heard about the decisions made at this meeting, she was outraged. She told me: "Well, they appointed a committee, but I have decided to ignore that. They can't do that. . . . I have other plans for the group. . . . I am not going to consider the task of that committee. I will stop all that."

After letting the members wait for two weeks, she finally convened a meeting. She began by congratulating them for having met in her absence and lavished praise upon the vice-president for chairing the meeting. Referrring indirectly to Amador's record of absenteeism, she emphasized the importance of an active vice-president. She then stated that the group now had urgent business in the form of a letter from the mayor to the superintendent of schools requesting him to consult the confederation about the educational problems of Puerto Rican students. Because the mayor's letter needed to be followed up immediately, Mrs. Estebán announced that, with the aid of two APA officials, she had written to the superintendent for an appointment to meet with the confederation. She did not mention the group's decision to visit McCall.

But this time, Mrs. Estebán's diversionary tactics did not achieve the intended result. The two-week period which had given her time to prepare had also given the others sufficient time to find out that she was bent upon thwarting the group's plan. Without further delay, and this time with no hesitation, Fidel Amador began the attack: "If we continue meeting here, we are not going to do anything. We are the ones who need help. Those people [in APA] are not going to come to us; we have to go to them. For this reason a committee was designated to go to them. Now, I ask you, why didn't they go? Why? We are all in agreement on this, no? Why?" Mrs. Estebán replied, "It is because they [the committee] had one objective and I another."

Diego Zayas interrupted: "We *jibaros* ["hillbillies"] complain we are hungry but we don't go to ask for food."

Taken aback by this attack, Mrs. Estebán attempted to introduce a different topic, a brief article reporting the confederation's visit to the mayor which was to be published in her neighborhood's *Newsletter*. When the members discovered that she had written the article in collaboration with an APA employee, they rejected it outright. They wanted no one from APA to report the confederation's activities. Moreover, the article implied that soon the mayor would develop programs to aid Puerto Ricans. Diego Zayas claimed Mrs. Estebán was making unwarranted promises and the Puerto Ricans were already saturated with, and cynical about, fake promises. When Mrs. Estebán replied that customarily one begins by making promises, Zayas questioned: "In other words, we are just beginning?"

"Yes," said Mrs. Estebán, "we are just beginning. At some place there has to be a beginning. If there is no beginning, there is no end. Right?"

Mrs. Amador put in: "But why announce the birth of a baby before it is born?"

No matter what topic was discussed, the members chose to disagree with the president. The issue provoking them to anger remained unresolved, and soon they returned to it: Fidel Amador said, "At that meeting the members cried out for action. The voting was unanimous!" Mrs. Estebán replied, "I like obedience. By obedience I mean that if I start one objective, one purpose, I want to follow the steps that will lead me there."

This exchange laid bare the issue. Mrs. Estebán believed she could, as president, command the obedience of the members. It had been this way since the time she had successfully countered the political assault, but the members were learning democratic procedures and valued their independent action. Now in the face of mounting opposition, Mrs. Estebán softened her attitude and confided to them information she had learned from her APA sources that the mayor had instructed the superintendent of schools to respond favorably to the confederation's proposals. For the group to take any other course of action, she said, would be to defy the mayor. By implication, she let them know that the decision to visit McCall represented the wrong target. (At the time it was my impression that Mrs. Estebán wanted to divert the group from pressuring the director of APA, an organization with which she had rapidly become identified, but her access to inside information failed to persuade the members.)

In the heated exchange that followed Diego Zayas shouted at Mrs. Estebán, "As president, you are completely and entirely out of order!" Momentarily the group was silenced by the officious tone of the charge. Having drawn everyone's attention, Zayas explained that a motion once made, discussed, voted upon, and approved could not be reversed by the president or anyone else.

Never before had anyone defended a decision of the group because it had been made according to parliamentary procedure (although Justino Vilá repeatedly talked about the need for such procedures). So justified, the decision seemed to be something more than the result of group discussion — almost a mysterious legacy of somewhat divine rules. The participants were duly impressed.

At other meetings, the president had been subjected to sporadic, unorganized criticism, but now she was the target of a sustained and relentless attack and no one moved to her defense. She seemed abandoned and unable to move the members in the direction she wanted. Finally, she seemed to relent, but she was tough and unyielding. What appeared, at first, to be a gesture of conciliation turned out to be a veiled threat. She said:

> If you think the office [Hispanic] is more important than going to the superintendent, as the mayor suggested, then we will do it that way. . . . I don't have anything at stake in this. If you want the committee to go to the agency [APA] without my going to represent you, then go! If they [APA] call me and ask me about it, I will say, "Well, I don't know. . . ."

Mrs. Estebán's comment indicated that she was offended by not having been chosen as group spokesman, and it was to this that Mrs. Amador responded:

> We want to work with you, to cooperate in everything. . . . We want you to have confidence in us, that we shall work united with you. We want you to have confidence that, if you cannot be at a meeting, we are not going to betray you. We don't want to divide ourselves into factions. We want to do something, to go someplace, to see how people are going to help us, to confront them. We want action! Do you understand?

The attempt to create a feeling of solidarity brought a few minutes of peace to the meeting but there was another sudden eruption when Mrs. Esteban announced her intention to invite APA officials to the next meeting. Again, this proposal aroused violent opposition. Alfonso Vilá, trying to identify the source of the problem, said to his sister: "It can be seen that you come here with plans already made. I have observed that you then defend the plans and confuse the members."

Mrs. Esteban replied, "I confuse the members? . . . Now tell me, do you want everything to be put as a motion to be voted upon? If you want it that way, that is how it will be. . . . I don't come here to command."

When another member presented a motion, but phrased it in garbled terms, Alfonso Vilá complained that he did not understand it. Mrs. Esteban was still angry at her brother for joining the attack against her. She told him sarcastically, "A secretary is supposed to request clarification if a motion is not clear. Do you understand?" The motion was then clarified and accepted without opposition, and the hectic meeting came to an end.

Once before in the group's life there had been a clear split between the president and the members, and it had led to the deposition of Diego Zayas. At that time the divisive issue involved the abandonment of the policy not to engage in partisan politics, but at this time no issue of policy was at stake. The deadlock between Mrs. Estebán and the others was, at least on the surface, a matter of opposing views about what the group should do. There was neither an issue of policy nor a point of logic at stake. Logically, there was no contradiction between the two views, as there had been when the group confronted politicization; nothing would have prevented the group's members from acting on both proposals, but now the bitter debate between the president and her opponents had led the participants to view the two proposals as mutually exclusive alternatives. It was a clash between an older form of group organization and a new one straining to emerge. The old form involved a dominant monolithic leader and passive followers; the new form involved more active and forceful participation on the part of the other members. Mrs. Estebán had acquired almost authoritarian dominance over the members, but if her actions had contributed strongly to the old form of organization, she had also unwittingly planted the seeds of change now blooming into rebellion. She had outlawed personal discussions, thus focusing the group's energies on external objectives. More than anyone else she had insisted upon objectives involving the collective welfare of the Puerto Ricans in Maplewood. In the process, the confederation had been purified and was being given its distinctive character as an action group. As such, its members had developed the desire to attain external goals and accepted the invitation to fuller participation.

During the meeting Mrs. Estebán had reacted to the attack with great fortitude, at times even lashing back at her accusers. Her inner doubts, anxiety, and uncertain feelings about her capacity for leadership, so evident during the preparations for the visit to the mayor, were replaced by an optimistic self-assurance, perhaps because she thought she had been an exemplary spokesman for the group at city hall. Yet the violence of the attack upset her more than was apparent at the meeting. The following day she had a long talk with Carmen Sylvia García, my research assistant, and confessed:

> At last night's meeting there was a lot of confusion and misunderstanding and it was because of the vice-president's attitude. He and his wife came there to attack me. All of this because when he was the chairman of the last meeting, they decided to do a lot of things, and I disregarded them. They were angry about that. They do not accept me. . . . Even my own brother attacked me. The confederation right now is not backing me. It does not want to help me. I didn't think there was anything out of order last night, but some of the members — especially one — said that I was out of order. Imagine telling the president that she is out of order! . . . Yes, I am sure I'm not the one who is ruling there anymore. I am not the authority

there. Now we have to do what the confederation decides. . . .

I was tense at the meeting. I was laughing, but with tension. Sometimes I laugh because I am healthy, but last night my laughter was not natural. . . . I was about to blow up. If Mr. Amador had continued with his negative attitude I was going to ask him to leave. What he did is not acceptable at our meetings.

But, Mrs. Estebán went on, her suffering was the price to be paid for the resolution of tensions in the group:

I left the meeting a little sad but satisfied because it was I who gave the members the opportunity to bring out a lot of things that had never come out before. Now they feel better toward me. . . . They say nothing has been accomplished, but I think we accomplished a lot because we had an opportunity to discuss and clarify the questions and feelings, and to understand the confusion in which we live.

Since the thrust of the attack seriously challenged Mrs. Estebán's usual way of doing things, she did not know how to proceed. She said, "I must now wait until the members decide what to do." After a moment, she continued:

I think all our confusion is due to the lack of norms and procedures and bylaws. We are just working and working, in a crazy way, without bylaws, without parliamentary rules. We have been working just by trust and friendship. But that is not the way a group should work, and that is why we are going back and back. We need rules! We need laws! At the next meeting we have to consider these things very seriously. . . .

Mrs. Estebán's efforts to understand the meeting were indicative of her talent for insight and objective analysis and statement, even when she was under the stress of violent attack. She saw at that time the need to alter her role—the cathartic effect of the explosive confrontation, the change toward a more impersonal form of organization, and the error of disregarding the group's decision — all with much greater clarity and depth than I did. In retrospect it is clear that, if her understanding was flawed in any way, it was in her failure to see the powerful sense of urgency which had overwhelmed the members. Thus, at the next meeting a week later, she introduced a new and different topic — the critical need for a constitution. She explained that in addition to the basic premises of the organization, the constitution would prescribe the procedures to be followed at meetings so that in the future the disorder, conflict, and unpleasantness of the last meeting could be avoided. No one disagreed, but the central concern of the members was brought up by Alemán:

Mrs. Estebán, in your presence, the mayor designated the director of APA as the person who would take care of this problem [the development of the Hispanic Office]. Carlos Otero reported to us that McCall said we didn't really have a plan, that we did not know what we were doing. We must show these people that we can define points, that we can arrive at a plan. We have to show them that the plan will work, that it is necessary. We have to convince them.

When Mrs. Estebán turned again to her own plan to visit the superintendent of schools, no one would discuss it. Finally, she agreed to make an appointment with McCall the next day.

Before the meeting ended, Mrs. Estebán said her brother had an announcement to make. Alfonso Vilá declared that he wanted to resign as secretary. Mrs. Amador asked him why, and he replied, "Because there are two persons from the Vilá family among the officers of the group, and it should not be that way." Mrs. Estebán interrupted to explain that, in the near future, the group would adopt parliamentary rules, and such rules prohibited relatives from holding office. She had recently discovered that APA would not employ two persons from the same family, and she felt that outlawing nepotism was a sound organizational principle. She recalled her embarrassment at city hall when in the course of introducing the members to the mayor she had identified her father and brother, and the mayor had commented: "There are sure a lot of Vilás in this organization!" No doubt, she had pressured her brother to resign, but no one questioned her, for this was a family matter.

Without delay, Enrique Zamora, a young articulate Colombian, was nominated and elected as secretary. Zamora and his wife had joined the confederation three months before, soon after moving to Maplewood. Zamora's aunt was married to a brother of Mrs. Estebán, and he, himself, had developed a close friendship with David Alemán. Already, by studying English at night, he was piecing together a working knowledge of the language.

When Mrs. Estebán telephoned McCall the next day, he told her the Urban Redevelopment Agency had been assigned the responsibility of providing the group with space for the Hispanic Office. It was his understanding that the group simply wanted office space for meetings. Mrs. Estebán did not correct his misunderstanding, but that afternoon the members would not accept either the recommendation that they turn to the Urban Redevelopment Agency or Mrs. Estebán's plea that she not be forced to telephone him again. She had been instructed to make the appointment, they reminded her and insisted that she telephone him again and not explain the purpose of the appointment so he would have no opportunity for evasion. If he was annoyed at being called, they said, she should tell him that the group had ordered her to do so. Mrs. Amador said, "Tell him that the persistence we displayed in wanting to see the mayor we again display in wanting to see him. Why not? If we insisted with the mayor, why not with the director of APA who is an employee of the mayor?"

David Alemán interrupted, "Yes, one gains their respect by doing it that way."

Mrs. Amador continued, "That's right, but we ought not to get too excited because, as a friend of mine said, 'In the United States if you get too excited about anything, immediately they want you to see a psychiatrist.'"

The reference to psychiatrists was an indirect comment on the American inability to understand the natural excitability of Puerto Ricans, and it evoked laughter. But, again, pressure was brought to bear upon Mrs. Estebán, until finally, very nervous, she telephoned McCall and made an appointment to see him a week later. The battle against the once authoritarian leader had been won!

A planning meeting was held the night before the appointed time. Although Mrs. Estebán was expected at the planning meeting, she did not come, and the group went ahead without her. With the assistance of Carlos Otero they defined the purpose of the Hispanic Office as a bridge between the Puerto Rican *colonia* ("colony") and the service agencies of the city; it was to be staffed with a supervisor, a secretary, a social worker, a vocational counselor, and a male and female interpreter. When a question was raised about the need for two interpreters of different sexes it was answered by Mrs. Amador: "Take, for example, Mrs. Zamora, who is now quite pregnant. If she had to go to a hospital she would need a female interpreter. . . . My husband would not accept it if you [pointing to Alfonso Vilá] were an interpreter for me. He would rather die than have you as my interpreter."

And Zamora agreed: "Yes, we are here to solve problems, not to create them. It would be impossible if she [his wife] had a male interpreter accompany her to a doctor in order to translate what she had to say. It would be very embarrassing."

This topic led Mrs. Amador to confess the difficulty she was experiencing in coming to meetings of the confederation. When she absented herself from home on these evenings, her husband subjected her to a barrage of suspicious questions which, she said, ". . . makes my participation in the group a serious, difficult matter. . . . It is not difficult for you men because you are the head of the household and no one asks you questions when you return home at night."

Among the women, Mrs. Amador's problem was not unique, and this was understood by the participants of both sexes, but Otero would not allow the discussion to stray far from the designated purpose of the meeting — to prepare for the following day's appointment. Playing the role of McCall, he quizzed the members on why they believed the Hispanic Office should be independent of APA. They answered that if the office were independent it could "knock on the door of the welfare department, the employment office, the hospitals, and even APA."

Satisfied with the answers to his questions, Otero then advised Alemán that he ought not to "back away from McCall," that instead he ought to "dish it out to him and fight him back," and "not be afraid to feel angry and show him you are justified in what you want." Then Otero asked a final question: "When should this office be established?"

Alemán replied: "We needed it yesterday. It will be all right if it is set up tomorrow."

The Hispanic Confederation had become an action group, indeed!

8

Cristina Estebán: The Confederation's President Speaks

•

I am a Puerto Rican mother of three children. On St. Joseph's Day I will be 43 years old. I was born in a small village near the Caribbean in the southeastern part of Puerto Rico. In high school my girl friends often criticized me for taking scientific courses instead of commercial courses. With commercial courses you can work as a secretary in a sugarcane refinery, but I told them my father would never let me work as a secretary. They tried to act superior to me and asked where I would ever get the money to go to the university. I simply wanted to study, learn, become independent, and fend for myself. Nothing more.

After high school, I attended the University of Puerto Rico for two years, but my grade point was not sufficient for the Normal Diploma of an accredited teacher. I did qualify, however, as a provisional teacher, and everyone in my hometown wondered how the daughter of a poor man could become a teacher. My girl friends were left with their mouths open in admiration. My father was proud that through hard work and determination I became a professional, the first one in our family ever to be one. To this day, he will not let anyone in Puerto Rico know that I worked in a factory in Maplewood, because they would gossip and say that Cristina, after sacrificing herself for an education, ends up in a factory.

From the moment I arrived in Maplewood, I began to learn about the city. I got to know the majority of the Puerto Ricans living here by teaching English in the adult education program, working in church, making arrangements for weddings and baptisms, finding them jobs, taking them to see doctors and nurses, and interpreting for them. I also became aware of the many programs and services in the city which could benefit the Hispanos. But I kept to my own kind, not wanting to let myself be known to the Americans, at least not until I was more familiar with the city. To this day I have not exposed myself completely. Now, I am beginning to, and it is mostly through the confederation.

Although Americans want to help the Hispanos and try to do many things for us, it is difficult for them because of our cultural differences. Puerto Ricans are being Americanized, but we still retain much of our own way of life. Because the world is changing, we must prepare the Hispanic community and our children to cope with change. Even here in Maplewood, there is an evolution which must be understood. If we don't prepare, if we just sit and wait, then our problems will be overwhelming. I prefer the American way, and for this reason I am teaching my children to be independent. The Hispanic attitude that the husband works and the wife stays home, never going out, must change if we are to live here.

By this I don't mean that American ways are always good and our ways are always bad. Americans are so individualistic that there is little giving of personal help and, consequently, problems are more difficult to solve. Puerto Ricans value friendship and one can have implicit trust in another person in discussing a personal problem. The Puerto Rican may not know psychology or medicine, but he is always willing to be of help.

It is wrong to think Puerto Ricans come here to get help from the government. Public welfare is the last resort we use to solve our problems. When we do seek assistance however, and are required to reveal the most intimate problems of our lives, we expect immediate help. The welfare people do not understand this. When we don't get help and are just given another appointment the following week or month, anger overwhelms us. Some even commit suicide. In the grocery stores, Americans try to cheat us. In the office of the public-housing project where I live, they treat us like criminals. We have problems with American teachers, American doctors, American landlords. When Americans look down on me as a Puerto Rican, I feel bad and wish only that I could put the same coldness in my eyes to return the look. To deal with such people, you have to be strong, act with character, and have confidence in your capacity to conquer difficulties. This is what I do.

As my children grow into maturity, they have come to perceive differences between the Puerto Rican and the American character, and they long for the day they can return to Puerto Rico. While it is true that here they are assimilating American customs, they also are absorbing the wretched problems arising from being Puerto Rican. Because they are young I tell them to be strong, courageous, and never, never to feel weak or fearful.

Some Americans are worse than animals, but others are good-hearted. My priest is among the good ones. He helped us get the apartment in the housing project. Recently, my oldest son fell into a fit of depression and did not want to be the leader of the altar group. He told this to the priest, but the priest would not permit him to quit. The very idea that my son was disobedient to the priest made tears pour out of my eyes. Finally, my son told me that he was too big to belong to a group with only small boys. But my son is responsible and not disobedient. Apparently, the priest and the sisters had been talking to him, because a few days after this he got up early on a Saturday morning and cleaned the entire apartment without being asked. Little by little, he changed for the better.

Americans treat their children differently than we do. They leave their children at home with instructions and the children obey. Puerto Ricans fear that if they leave their children at home alone, they would fight or cry or destroy the furniture. Also, when American children play in the street, they solve their own problems and go to their parents only when it is necessary. Even then, American parents try not to interfere, but Puerto Rican parents become involved in their children's arguments. If someone gives a Puerto Rican child a dirty look he cries, and if someone throws a rock at him he runs to the arms of his parents.

I had trouble with my younger son. His teacher called me in for a special conference and started by asking me his nationality. Then she said he was lazy, did not want to work, and always turned in his written assignments with smudges on them. I admit that my son has an explosive temper, but he is not lazy. I explained to the teacher that when he gets nervous the palms of his hands sweat and dirty the paper on which he writes. Also, he feels that she hates him. She said that could not be so, but I had to explain to her that even a gesture or a glance can convey hatred. As a teacher I know this. Then she turned nasty. She said my oldest son and my daughter take after me, but this son takes after his father. She had never even met the father. What abuse! What a lack of respect!

Then last week, I took this son to a woman doctor for a physical examination. She started off by asking my son's nationality. His records were right in front of her, so she did not have to ask that. He was born in Maplewood; he is an American. But if he were not, what difference would that make to his physical condition? Then she said that my son has cavities. I told her that I always remind him to brush his teeth after each meal, but he doesn't listen. She contradicted me in front of my son and said once a day is enough. When my son complained that I gossip about him, she said I should respect him. Imagine, she was attempting to give my son power over me! I told her I demand obedience from my son, but she said she was only giving me medical advice. That was medical advice? She was so harsh that I never had the opportunity to tell her my educational level.

We live here with problems. We eat with problems. We work with problems. We are surrounded by problems. We live with Italian neighbors who are prejudiced against Puerto Ricans. It is not what people say but that special way they say things that expresses their prejudices. Events, experiences, and most of all problems arrange themselves like a chain linked together in the form of a circle. People are treated badly so they act badly, then they are treated worse, and so on around the chain. To bear the burden of the chain, one must be strong. I am strong. I suffer, but in silence.

My husband is another problem. He has a bad temper. When he gets angry he is oblivious to everything. He forgets he has a wife, children, compadres. He cares little how or to whom he speaks. Whatever comes to his mind, he says it to the person involved. His anger is usually provoked by some problem in the community. He reads about it in the newspaper, gets angry, and erupts. But the anger allows him to undrown himself. Then he feels better.

He resents my going out alone. It is only to be with other women, to go to an organization meeting, to study American customs, but he does not care who or why or where. He does not permit me to accept the invitation. Once after I had accepted an invitation and paid for a ticket to a dinner and was dressed to go out, he suddenly said I could not go. Another time, *he* insisted on going along and I was so ashamed — there was Mrs. Estebán with her husband, the only man among 15 women. How humiliating!

I have had the desire to leave him and travel the world. I have considered every possibility except divorce. No, even that I cannot say. Ideas suddenly come to mind, only to leave me suddenly. I don't repent marrying, but the little problems of marriage can suddenly take a serious turn. I am happier now than I was in Puerto Rico when I was single. There I lived a narrow life because my father confined me to the house and allowed me to go out only to church, school, or to work. The few parties I went to were at school or at work. I never went to the movies, or social dances, or had boyfriends. Even the relatives who came to visit us came only to speak to my father. It was not an environment in which to attain independence, so it was not until after marriage that I began to have more freedom. With freedom I developed confidence in myself.

No, I am not sorry that I married and came to Maplewood. When my husband is upset, however, it is difficult for me. He is upset about the confederation. He knows that no Puerto Rican group has ever made progress. He has every right to get upset, but instead of trying to help, he mortifies me by saying that no one will ever hear us out. Important people *are* going to hear us! But you cannot go to them with an angry voice. My husband thinks that by yelling one gains respect. I think noise never brings respect or for that matter anything of value.

The important thing about the confederation is the struggle we have had to move the group to where it is now. Ever since we first got together we have had problems, all of which are difficult to explain. The group started when Mr. Frank Joyce asked me why Hispanos were not joining neighborhood groups, and I told him to invite them to a meeting and listen to what they have to say. But the Hispanos have a complex involving aggressiveness, and at the meeting this complex was apparent. They complained about bad housing, discrimination, public welfare, and other things that only revealed their psychological problems.

At a later meeting, Rafael Zayas made the motion that I be president and his brother Diego vice-president, but I opposed it, arguing that a man, not a woman, should be president. The truth is that I did not want to be president because, seeing what was going on, I felt the group would not accomplish a thing. Also, I had a personal thing too, a complex. People look upon me as a leader, yet I feel I am not a leader. Were I to become president, I reasoned, people would turn against me because of envy and jealousy. I wanted to be an active member, but to step aside and not be president. Diego was elected president by one vote, and I was vice-president.

The group's purpose was to help Hispanos have better food, housing, employment, education, and to eliminate prejudice against us. Without voting, we decided not to be a religious or political organization, and not to collect dues. The plan was to make the group the nucleus of all Puerto Rican organizations in the city. The persons I invited to join the group were those I felt would respond to their duties. I did not invite persons who would not work, not even friends. Just a moment, let me think about that. Yes, there were some I knew would not be interested in whom I telephoned and visited. I did not want them later to accuse me of not wanting them or of choosing only my own people. Now, when I am asked why the confederation isolated itself, I reply that at the start no one would work with us. It is important to emphasize this point both to the Puerto Ricans and to the Americans.

From the very start, Diego showed his inexperience as president. Because the American advisors insisted upon our working on our own, he once told me, "They are cheating us and treating us as if we were stupid." I told him to be patient and not to speak without facts. He began meetings with, "Well, what shall we discuss today?" When I said he should start with the reading of the minutes, he said that as president it was for him to decide what to do. You see, he was doing worse then than I am now.

One day, quite by chance, Diego met Vicente de Serrano, who was angry over our not inviting him to join the group. Serrano persuaded Diego to convert the confederation into a political organization. Diego kept this plan secret by claiming he had been consulting a lawyer friend, but Rafael [Diego's brother] told me of this plan, so I invited to the meeting persons I knew would be against it. Many members had been complaining about Diego, and we were looking for a way to retire him. Without being president, I had to act to prevent Diego from damaging the group.

When Diego presented his plan at the meeting, I stopped him to insist we review the agenda I had prepared, but he argued so loudly that he drowned out everyone else. Suddenly, he stood up and said, "This group should have only Hispanos, no Americans." I answered that we needed Americans and that we should strive to make them happy by conducting orderly meetings which they were used to. Even Romero Ponce, who had been sent by Serrano to aid Diego in making our group political, agreed with me.

"If we live here," Romero said, "it is because Americans give us homes. If we work, it is because Americans provide us with jobs. The food we eat is American food. We cannot be without the Americans."

The arguments upset everyone. Arturo Prieto stood up and said the arguments were contrary to his religion and if they continued he would leave and never return to the group. I tried to quiet it all down, but Diego threatened to resign if his plan was not accepted. I called upon the members to accept my proposal to disband the executive committee and establish a new one. A majority raised their hands in agreement with me; then I passed around a sheet of paper so they could sign in approval. Persons who would not sign were to be eliminated from the group. Diego, of course, did not sign, but his brother Rafael felt bad about not signing. He said, "Ay, Doña Cristina, I want to continue in the group, but how can I if my brother does not?" Diego then said he eliminated himself from office, and the problem was solved.

At the next meeting, I hardly had to speak. There was complete agreement that we should work to help the community, and each person spoke about the lack of group discipline and how poorly Diego had done as president. They repeated the same thing at the following meeting. Someone then proposed that the vice-president become president. Even though I did not want the position when the group began, this is how I became president.

About that time, I suddenly began to have personal problems. My memory was failing me. As president I had to push the group ahead, but I had to think of writing the newsletter for the neighborhood group, of the Spanish classes I taught, and of the five college courses I was taking. My three children were in school, and I had responsibilities to my husband, my household work, and my church activities. I felt compelled to accept invitations to the Mothers' Club and the Neighborhood Advisory Board of the antipoverty agency. Imagine doing all of this without even counting the help I was giving to my friends.

Then I began to have problems with my classes at college. If I spent four minutes concentrating on an interesting assignment on the history of the medieval period, the next three minutes my mind would wander off to things which had no relationship to what I was reading. Often I thought about the confederation, what to do at the next meeting, and jotted notes on paper. A few minutes of history and again my mind would be smack in the group and again more notes on paper. Afterward I could not find the notes, but I don't think they had much importance. What was important was that I could never finish the history assignment.

I worried, too, about my sister Juana who is not a normal person. I didn't have time to take her to the hospital when she wanted to go. I worried about my brother Lorenzo. Although young and capable, he has a lot of pride, and his imagination tells him that his family does not like him. Once at a psychiatric hospital, one of the psychiatrists said under his breath, "Why do they let such people into the country?" I was offended and told the doctor that my brother's problem involved his nationality and language difficulty. The doctor's reaction registered in his face. Before he had just asked me questions about age, the number of children, and so on. After that, he took an interest in us and asked more relevant questions. Had I told him from the beginning that I was a professional, not a factory worker, he would have treated us better.

Please understand it is not that I don't trust doctors or reject them. I just want them not to be prejudiced against patients because of their nationality. Today, for example, I went to see my doctor and I feel good, good, good. He started off by asking me about myself and said I should tell him whatever is on my mind. I did, and I did very well. My counselor at the antipoverty agency referred me to this doctor, and the agency pays for his services. The counselor did this when he found out about my health problem. When I am under tension or have a problem, sometimes I feel a hot, painful sensation in my stomach, as if the nerves inside had shrunk. I choke up bitter liquid, bile. I take pills to alleviate the pain, but I don't like the sleeping pills the doctor prescribed. When I take them, I sleep as if I were a sleepwalker, but if I don't take them I awaken many times during the night.

My counselor at the agency also helps me make decisions, and he has advised me to cut down on my activities. At a recent meeting of the Neighborhood Advisory Board, I burst out angrily when someone criticized the confederation. I know I was right, but I was ashamed at my outburst. After the meeting I apologized to Roger Davis. He replied, "Poor Mrs. Estebán is tired. She wants to take a rest but will not say no to anyone who needs her." Now, if a person asks me to do something, I refer him to my counselor, who always replies that I am too busy. You see, the agreement between us is for him always to say that I am too busy.

A while back a doctor asked me why I worked so hard and belonged to so many organizations. This question I cannot answer, even to myself. Surely, it is not to have fun, because in an organization you have to use your mind, which is harder than working in a factory. Maybe I am trying to compensate for not being allowed to do other things, the idea being that anything is something. But if one stays home and is not involved in civic or cultural activities, one lives in the dark. By participating one learns what is going on, which is precisely what the Puerto Ricans must do if they want to be integrated. We must study our problems, form groups, and develop solutions. By organizing ourselves to construct a better community, we become a part of it.

Many people think that because I do so much community work I have a special position or appointment in the city, but the truth is that I work voluntarily without pay. I am automatically included in activities and invited to join groups. The more involved I get, the more I learn, and the more I am called upon to help. In turn, I have come to be known as the only reliable Hispana in Maplewood, the only one who can lead our people. Nonetheless, I cannot really explain why I am so active. I am the only one who can understand my own situation.

I have the same trouble explaining how I first got tied up with the antipoverty agency, but let me try. I used to work in a factory sewing ladies' bathing suits. I did this to punish my husband who, by forcing me to come to Maplewood, made me quit my profession as a teacher in Puerto Rico. He did not like my working in a factory, but to me it meant nothing. When my friends asked me why an educated person was doing factory work, I would hold up a dollar bill and say, "It has the same color and value as any other dollar." Yet, it is true that after years of sacrifice for an education, I was doing the work of an uneducated person. Suddenly I decided to quit my job. I told my husband, who said, "Good, good, good. I will work to support you." He was so happy he cut down on his drinking. When I reminded him we would have to live on his salary, he agreed. He never wanted me to do factory work, because I was a professional.

When my friends heard I quit, they became curious about my plans. I thought I would see what I could get from the antipoverty agency, but I kept my friends in suspense over what I was going to do. I also did not tell the agency about my transcripts from the University of Puerto Rico and the fact that I had been a teacher on the island. (Imagine with these qualifications, I had been working in a factory!) The agency did not know that in Maplewood I was in charge of the Hispanic community, not officially, but in fact. The agency was being criticized even by Americans, who said that the agency could not be of any help to Hispanos if the employees knew only two or three words of Spanish. The Hispanos in Maplewood are a people who come from the mountains of Puerto Rico and first put on shoes at the age of 12 or 14. They know little about living in a place like this. With two or three words of Spanish, an American can never understand their customs and problems. Such criticisms were correct, but for some reason the agency asked me to help without offering me a job. Maybe they wanted me to take the initiative, but I would not; that was for them to do.

No, they did not offer me a job, but it is clear that the agency supports the confederation. They have always paid for the paper, envelopes, and postage for the letters we send out. The agency director, Arthur McCall, has instructed one of the neighborhood antipoverty offices to help our group. Because of our visit to the mayor, the agency is pressuring the department of education to get me certification to teach in the state. Before this, the agency devoted itself only to blacks and whites, but now Puerto Ricans are included in the programs. We fought them through the confederation to the point where now we are recognized as the group representing the Hispanos. Serrano wanted his group to be *the* group, but the agency does not recognize his group.

Now the agency has given me the power to recommend Hispanos for employment in their programs. Take my brother Alfonso's case. Although brave, Alfonso is shy and reserved, so the agency was cheating him as they did with other Puerto Ricans. They gave him a job one day and laid him off the next day. I reminded some of the important people in the agency that Alfonso is a good worker and should be given a permanent job. I believe they will take my advice, but I suddenly realized that I had not mentioned that Alfonso is my brother. I feared that they would think I was recommending him for this reason, so around the agency Alfonso never mentions my name. The important fact is that I do have the power to recommend people.

Many Hispanos don't believe this and fail to recognize that now I am a force in the community. Before, I was only a name to the agency; they did not know me personally, nor I them. But through the confederation they have come to know me, and I have come to be involved in the broader affairs of the community. The Puerto Ricans used to live on promises, but because our group has tangible goals, we now have something substantial. The day I do not get what I want is the day I return to my own country.

Another reason I know the agency supports the confederation is the advice my counselor at the agency gives me. Because he is concerned over my health, he wants me to restrict my activites to the confederation, the Neighborhood Advisory Board, and teaching in the adult education program. He has never advised me to leave the confederation. Should he do so, I don't know what I would do. As long as the members accept me, I think I would stay in the group. Away from it, I would miss it very much. Also, were I to quit, who would replace me? There is no one!

The agency pays attention to the confederation because I direct the group. Not that they want to satisfy me personally or cater to me, but under my direction the group has taken the right course, and the agency knows that I am determined. I move ahead without ever giving up. I do not care personally if I come out well or badly, but I care about the group.

It is important, however, to understand that the agency's support of us began only recently, for even a short time ago there was the problem of deciding whether the confederation or the Pan-American Association was to be the valid Puerto Rican organization. When Antonio Tejada was president of the association, he was working for the adult education program, visiting Hispanos to persuade them to take classes, and using his work as a means of recruiting members for the association. The confederation never had this advantage, but everyone knows this about Tejada. Once when he was giving a speech, he said his job was important because he was selling education to Hispanos. Some in the audience, knowing what he really did on his visits, broke out in laughter, but others were offended, thinking that he meant Puerto Ricans are uneducated.

Puerto Ricans are sensitive and must be treated so. Often they are reluctant to ask questions because they think they demean themselves and lose character. They are easily upset. If Tejada wants to be a leader of Puerto Ricans, he should know these things about Puerto Ricans.

The trouble with the Pan-American Association is that it is like the now defunct Puerto Rican Civic Club, which charged membership dues, made a lot of rules, and tried to draft a constitution. Yet I never knew its objectives, because all it did was to have one dance after another. And even though the group officers changed swiftly, Serrano, as usual, was in charge. My husband and I refused to join because the club was against a Catholic organization to which I belonged. Then as now, one group against another, just the way I told my doctor: "We Puerto Ricans are against ourselves."

On the other hand, maybe the Puerto Ricans don't need unity. Maybe what is needed is a small select group which works on behalf of the community without attempting to incorporate the entire community into its ranks. This is how I view the confederation — a respected group, open in membership but seeking more professionals regardless of their nationality — an integrated group, such as we've had by including Americans as counselors, observers, and visitors. When we get jobs, we are not going to be working in Hispanic stores, factories, or businesses. We will be working with and for Americans, so Americans should be welcomed. Then, if we succeed in pressuring the agency into establishing the Hispanic Referral Office, all needy Hispanos will be served, no matter what their religion, race, or political party.

Yet I am fearful that the confederation is going backwards. We can be ruined by one member who imposes wrong ideas on us. Diego Zayas means well. Sometime ago he telephoned me to talk about Vicente de Serrano. He said Serrano told him the confederation's failure to support him [Diego] was aimed at cutting down Serrano's power in Maplewood, and that the confederation still has to be destroyed, because in Maplewood only the Pan-American Association can represent the Puerto Ricans. Diego said he was ashamed at having colluded with him. He even challenged Serrano to a public debate over Puerto Rican affairs. When Serrano refused, Diego wrote a letter to Antonio Tejada, who was president of the Pan-American Association, challenging *him* to a debate. This shows that Diego is repentant over his past mistakes, still is angry at Serrano, and wants very much to work for the confederation again.

We should set aside the errors of the past and accept Diego. Surely, we all commit errors, for none of us is perfect except Jesus Christ. Our duty is to correct our mistakes and never to lose faith in accomplishing something of value.

Serrano is a good person too. When he loves you, he loves you as a good friend. But he has such uncanny skills that he can take a grown man and fool him as if he were a child. Right now he could fool anyone in the confederation except me, but one must be forever alert to what he will do next. I have never understood his effort to destroy the confederation. Maybe he, as well as others, feels that because nothing *has been* accomplished through groups of this type, nothing *should be* accomplished. But they can all rest assured that if *I* lead an organization, something will be accomplished. Definitely! But the others, ay!

Our early failures resulted from Diego Zayas's inexperience. And now David Alemán makes impatient threats to quit unless we respond instantly to what he says. Alemán strives to do excellent work, but he has to develop patience. We must take one step at a time. I think Fidel Amador could be a great leader, but he has been regressing ever since he was elected vice-president. He does not give the group credit for its accomplishments, nor even give us his support. Just recently, for an example, he did not come to a meeting because his daughter was going to have a visitor. Excuses! Both he *and* his wife don't have to stay with the visitor. The trouble now is that he doesn't come to meetings but he won't resign his office. This is a delicate issue. And Mrs. Amador is not like me. She swallows her problems which, by itself, detracts from a person's well-being. If pressured, she might even end up in a psychiatric hospital.

All of this illustrates how difficult it is to be a woman. I feel it myself. While we were planning the visit to the mayor, for example, I was told that a man, not a woman, should represent the group because a man's opinion carries more weight than a woman's. This was true in the past, but now we have as much power as men. The mayor of San Juan is a woman, and she speaks on behalf of the whole city. Had a man represented us at the mayor's office here, we would not have received the attention we did.

Through all of this, one works hard and plans for the future, time goes by, and one gets older, but one feels older only at the moment when someone asks your age. I don't feel old, nor have the years weighed heavily upon me. It is just that when I write my age down . . .

Life turns out badly only when one yearns to do things for which one does not have the ability. I have never been a lover of the impossible. Imagine life as a river. The river was not born by itself. It began from tiny rivulets which united into streams which then grew powerful and wound their way to the sea. In the sea the river loses its name and ceases being a river. If only the flow of life could be understood, from tiny rivulets to the open sea. But in life, one must always be going backward and forward, attempting to collect what has been left behind. We should attempt to understand the details as they appear and capture their significance much as the river captures the streams, and the streams capture the rivulets. Then everything would be okay. To do this, one must have courage and valor. No matter what happens, I maintain my valor.

My problem now is that I cannot understand what is happening to me. My mind feels as if it is being spent and my brain feels as if it is full of water. I do not believe my brain has suffered an attack or somehow been gravely injured, for if this were so I would be unable to recall the past. You see that I can recall everything that has happened, but I feel as if my brain has turned into a substance incapable of understanding.

It is worth repeating again that the important point is not what I have done for the confederation, but how far the group has come. To this day I seek no recognition as a leader. Being president does not mean being a leader, for anyone can preside over an organization. To be a leader, one must be supported by two-thirds of the membership, or at least by a majority. Although I have not tried to determine the extent of my support, I don't believe I qualify. If by some miracle I should become a leader, that will be that. My only wish is to do something good for the Puerto Rican community. This is what counts in the end.

PART IV

The Development of Institutional Ties

9

Entanglement in the Politics of the Antipoverty Agency

•

As our meeting in the main office of APA began, Arthur McCall greeted Mrs. Estebán warmly and effusively, but she quickly explained that Alemán was the spokesman, not she, and that the members, not she, had insisted upon the conference. Before Alemán could speak, McCall said APA could make available a conference room for meetings and provide pencils, paper, and secretarial services, but under no circumstances would APA rent an office for the confederation. He said emphatically: "Were I to give you office space and foot the bill, then 15 other organizations would come pounding on the door to get office space." Mixing specific advice with general instructions, he suggested the group ask the Urban Redevelopment Agency to rent office space for as little as a dollar a year in some building appropriated by the city. He said:

> There are two main points in an organization: that it have money for what it needs to do and that it be sufficiently independent of other organizations. If the confederation wants money, then it should raise it on its own. It should learn to do things in its own way. Do things by your own efforts. We cannot help!

Otero's warning that McCall's reaction would be unfavorable and that the group would have to fight back proved to be accurate, but the suddenness and finality of his refusal without even having heard their arguments caused the members to withdraw into a sullen and confused silence. Alemán's self-assurance crumpled as he tried to make an explanation. McCall, however, interrupted again to explain his position: "Look, we try to help people out and then when we help them they don't help themselves. When we try to get them to help themselves they say we are not helping them."

Despite the thorough preparations for the meeting, no one was able to counter this argument. Beyond the damned-if-you-do-and-damned-if-you-don't contradiction, McCall was implying that poverty programs are all wrong and their success only leads to failure. This criticism of the program aimed at helping the poor concerned McCall, as an administrator, but not the members of the confederation. Finally, Alemán disregarded it and attempted again to plead the Puerto Ricans' need for a referral center to help in solving their problems. Again, McCall interrupted: "We cannot duplicate efforts which are already going on. We need new programs and ideas. We need proposals from which we can begin to work out new ideas. . . . If you bring in a new program, a contribution to the community, then we will consider it."

Although nothing like the referral center was or had ever been in operation in Maplewood, somehow McCall failed to realize that the proposal was for a "new program." Now he was rejecting what he thought the group wanted and inviting what he believed the group was not proposing. McCall was a tough, incisive, and articulate man. The group was put on the defensive immediately by his aggressive stance; they felt an additional disadvantage because the Puerto Rican culture pattern calls for deference to a status superior and because the difficult task of arguing had to be carried on in a language not their own. Unable to fight back under these circumstances, they were angry, anxious, and did not know how to proceed.

At this point, I could no longer remain silent. Abandoning my self-imposed restriction on participation, I told McCall that the group *did have* a proposal to offer but that his repeated interruptions made it impossible for Alemán to present it. My angry outburst opened the way for Alemán who then spoke of the need for the referral center. At first, the proposal was met with skepticism. McCall said much of what was being proposed was already being done by APA. He reviewed the city programs developed both in and out of APA, finishing with a statement on the need for Puerto Ricans to develop channels to avail themselves of such programs. Alemán replied that this was precisely what the confederation aimed to do through the development of the referral center. McCall's assistant, Edgar Gordon, asked, "But why couldn't the Puerto Ricans working in APA do the referring?" Alemán replied that the referral function should be assigned to one office rather than fragmented among the employees scattered throughout APA. A central office would be more efficient and less costly, he continued; it had the additional advantage of letting the Puerto Ricans know they had a place of their own to which they could turn in time of need and with which they could identify.

McCall said: "We don't want to do anything special for the Puerto Rican community because what you are looking for is status and recognition for your own group, the confederation. If you want to do something, do it through your own efforts."

120

By this time Alemán had regained his usual self-confidence. Having rehearsed the arguments with Otero, he was on familiar ground and he concentrated on the confederation's desire for the betterment of the Puerto Rican community, avoiding any intimation that he or the members sought personal gains. He quickly rebutted McCall's argument: APA programs had to be adapted to the needs of minority groups; the confederation's capacity to initiate efforts could be seen at that very meeting; Puerto Ricans were economically impoverished and could not finance the referral center; and the group sought the establishment of the office not for its own benefit but to aid all Puerto Ricans in the community.

After Alemán finished, the members appeared more relaxed and McCall seemed to be satisfied with the argument. Finally, he admitted that it was a good proposal and he said: "That's an excellent idea. We should start working on a proposal right away. We can start modestly and then develop from there."

He explained the details of the procedure to be followed: The confederation and APA would collaborate in drafting a grant application to support the Hispanic Referral Office; the application would be submitted through channels to the Office of Economic Opportunity in Washington; it would take from three to six months to process the application, but McCall said he was confident that it would be accepted and funded because it was a "sound proposal." His parting advice was: "When you want something from a public official, you have to pester him by coming back time and again."

The officials of APA felt Alemán had done very well. They saw him as an exceptionally able spokesman and recognized the fact that another Puerto Rican leader had emerged. Alemán himself, however, was critical and thought he had done poorly as a spokesman. Mrs. Estebán was reluctant to express her evaluation of the meeting, but the others thought it was a success.

When it came to my intervention at the meeting, the members were very surprised. They thanked me gratefully, but my feelings were mixed — happy with McCall's promises to cooperate; concerned at having departed from the norms governing the participant-observer role. By then I had been in the confederation for a year, and Carmen Sylvia García for five months, so the role of participant-observer, having evolved from an effort to cope with an intricate research problem, was firmly implanted in the group. Some time later, I asked David Alemán what he and the group would have done if McCall had refused to cooperate and if I had not intervened. Alemán replied: "We would have gone back to him again and again."

Five days after this meeting with its promise of cooperation, six of us returned to the APA office to start planning with Edgar Gordon, the assistant director, and another official in charge of writing grant applications. According to procedure, the agency would write a preliminary draft of the proposal for the Hispanic Referral Office and the confederation would revise it.

The meeting began with Gordon rejecting Alemán's request for five employees in the referral office. He explained that although APA had been very successful in the past in funding its projects, serious difficulties lay ahead. Now, many cities were bidding for Office of Economic Opportunity money and competing for funds. The APA would no longer enjoy the advantage in funding it once had in its widely recognized and celebrated poverty projects. For this reason, Gordon continued, the confederation would have to settle for a staff of two persons — one to head the office; one to serve as a neighborhood worker — and a secretary to assist them. Alemán was concerned, but the issue seemed to be non-negotiable.

Gordon emphasized, however, that the confederation would have administrative control over the office. He said: "Whatever you want. You decide. We [APA] are the intermediary between the funding agency and the persons and groups who get the money. I prefer you to handle the money yourself. That way *you* would be making the service available to the Spanish-speaking community."

Thus, two conferences five days apart accomplished much for the confederation. To proceed further it was necessary that the confederation be incorporated in the state and then sign a contract with APA; the funds would come from the Office of Economic Opportunity and be disbursed through APA for the confederation to administer the referral office.

Ever since the political assault, when it became known that the Pan-American Association was to be incorporated, Mrs. Esteban had yearned for the incorporation of the confederation. Usually she referred to the Pan-American Association with scorn, but she actually stood in awe of the legal status inherent in its incorporation and had lingering fears that the confederation would be at a disadvantage. She told me: "Their papers of incorporation are their greatest pride. . . . Now they can do things to frighten us because of their lawyer and incorporation."

Mrs. Amador added to Mrs. Esteban's apprehensions by suggesting that, the establishment of the referral office having been arranged by the confederation, it might now be taken over by the Pan-American Association which could legally and rightfully make claims to it since they were an incorporated group. Mrs. Esteban did not take this threat lightly and it added to the urgency with which she called a meeting of the confederation the following day.

As the meeting began, Enrique Zamora, the newly elected secretary, rendered a detailed, accurate, and complete account of the events at the APA office. This evoked murmurs of delight and surprise, for his understanding of English was still rudimentary. What he had not understood at the meetings, others translated into Spanish for him, and all of it was duly recorded in the confederation's official minutes. So competently was this done that no misunderstanding or argument arose as to what had transpired. This was a notable moment in the group's life, because from its inception the confederation had suffered difficulties in keeping written accounts of occurrences and decisions. Along with factual report-ing, Zamora devoted some time to praising Alemán for rebutting McCall's hostile arguments.

Taking the floor from Zamora, Mrs. Estebán began what promised to be a lengthy account of her impressions of the meetings, but she was stopped by Mrs. Amador who insisted that the discussion proceed to the next item of business. Mrs. Estebán did not want to stop. Alejandro Rico, perhaps the group's quietest member, said, "No one ought to act as if our time was unlimited." The members agreed, feeling Zamora's account was sufficient and wanting to move ahead, but Mrs. Estebán argued with them. As voices rose heatedly, Alfonso Vilá suddenly advanced the motion that the confederation seek legal incorporation, and the motion was quickly seconded by Alemán. Somehow, the discussion which fol-lowed the motion enlarged itself to include the problem of who should administer the referral office and the funds for it.

Zamora said, "The group should be reminded that the responsibility of han-dling money is serious, indeed, and delicate. If we have such great difficulties managing ourselves, in making our own plans, how can we confront the responsi-bility of administering anywhere from $20,000 to $50,000? Not knowing how to administer money, then all our work will have been in vain. We are not ready to administer money."

Alemán, his closest friend in the group, argued, "If we let APA take charge of it [the referral office] we will have been defeated. We have been struggling to demonstrate that we Latins are capable of solving problems, of taking the initia-tive, of forging ahead. Now that we have the opportunity, are we going to re-treat?"

Appealing first to ethnic pride, Alemán then turned to the failures of APA: "One reason APA should not run the referral office is that they have many other centers and have spent millions of dollars and have done nothing specific for the Latins. That is precisely what we are fighting to achieve. . . . We have to show these people that we can take the reins in our hands. If we reject the opportunity the first time, the second time will be more difficult. . . . To have such an oppor-tunity and not to take it!"

Others contributed to the debate, but the central and most articulate oppo-nents were Zamora and Alemán. Mrs. Estebán wanted incorporation, yet she did not take sides or attempt to organize the debate. Zamora continued to argue that, if the confederation proved incapable of managing funds, within one year the Hispanic Referral Office would dissolve and the Puerto Ricans would be left with nothing. Incorporation, he insisted, was not to be confused with the group's power or devotion to compatriots: "Without being incorporated we have gone before the mayor and the director of APA and gotten what we wanted. I ask for a vote from those who have always worked for the welfare of Puerto Ricans. I ask that we take advantage of the opportunity the Americans are giving us. I ask for a vote that the referral office be in APA."

In the heat of debate, friends became antagonists, and even those who seldom spoke took their turn. It fell upon Justino Vilá, the president's father and revered elder member, to conclude it:

> After hearing the debate, and the many clarifications, I get the impression you are timid about getting a lawyer to incorporate the confederation. But either now or later you will have to get a lawyer. And about those allegations that no one here is capable of managing money, let me say that APA has professionals, experts in such matters, who will help us administer the money. Their experts know how to write little numbers. They will help us because they are not going to send the money to us in a big cardboard box. . . .

Just as the vote was to be taken, a question arose about a quorum and about Adolfo Valdés's right to vote since he was attending his first meeting. No decision had ever been made about the number of persons comprising a quorum or who was eligible to vote. According to Mrs. Estebán, every meeting had a quorum unless challenged by a specific motion. She went on to explain that Americans could not vote but Valdés being a Latin "automatically belongs in the confederation." This was as close an approximation as had ever been made at defining a quorum and the right to vote. The motion was carried 6 to 3.

Originally the motion presented was in favor of incorporation for the confederation, but during the discussion the meaning of the motion had become confused so that a vote for incorporation also meant a vote for the referral office to be administered by the confederation. Both ideas were voted on at one stroke. Of all the decisions resulting from formal deliberations, this was among the most important ever made. Now the confederation had to attain legal status, enter a contractual agreement with APA, become the recipient of federal funds, and by administering the referral office assume responsibility for referring Puerto Rican clients to the numerous agencies, programs, and services Maplewood provided. At the end of the meeting, Zamora summed it up by concluding: "The confederation now has to confront the monster of responsibility. . . . Even those of us who voted against it must assume the responsibility."

A week later, 18 members attended a meeting of the confederation. Mrs. Estebán opened the meeting by attempting to report her experiences with another group the night before. She did not clearly identify the group, its purpose, why she attended the meeting, and how it was relevant to the confederation. Then she departed from her already confusing report and mentioned that a man, whose name and identity she did not know, had told her that office space would soon be available to the confederation. The members began to express their bewilderment. Alemán said, "I am completely out of it," and Mrs. Amador added, "I am so confused. I understand so little, it seems that I am sleeping, as if I were in a dream."

Concerned about not being understood, Mrs. Estebán repeated the story with new details apparently unintelligible to the others who were becoming more exasperated each moment. At last, her close friend, Matilda Abelando, a quiet, shy woman, spoke: "There is nothing basic in what you have presented here, nothing at all that has justified this discussion. Do you believe, Mrs. Estebán, that this is the way we should eat up our time, on the same topic, on and on? Why continue to waste precious time on something for which we have no basic information, something which is unclear?"

Mrs. Estebán attempted another explanation. Mrs. Amador was completely mystified, befuddled, and incensed at the interminable disorder. One of the most reliable members, she suddenly stood up and said, "I shall have to resign from the confederation effective tonight. So confusing is this that one could lose one's mind. I don't know if I am stupid, or what it is, but gentlemen, even though I don't speak English, I defend myself. With your permission I will excuse myself and go, and I tell you I no longer belong to the confederation. I resign because I cannot belong to a group I cannot understand."

Mrs. Estebán inquired: "Are you doing this because you don't understand what is going on at this meeting?"

Mrs. Amador replied: "I cannot understand any of the meetings for they all confuse me. I cannot continue this way."

Mrs. Abelando tried to explain: "The issues we take up here are like branches on a tree — they grow in all directions and for that reason one gets confused."

But Mrs. Amador was adamant: "What good am I to the group if I continue confused, confused, and more confused. Let my chair be taken by someone who has more brains than I do."

Mrs. Estebán told her firmly: "If you oppose what goes on here, all you have to do is present a motion to halt the discussion. You shouldn't deprecate yourself by saying you surrender your chair to someone who has more brains."

Mrs. Amador retorted: "From coming here my brains have turned to water."

Mrs. Estebán was dumbfounded because the resignation reflected upon her running of the organization, but she soon collected her thoughts and moved to attack Mrs. Amador. No one could expect the special privilege of getting private reports, she said. "We are not going to destroy this organization because of one person. We shall excuse her. We shall pardon her."

Mrs. Amador cried angrily, "Pardon me? For what? I am not asking for pardon. I resign!" And she left the room.

A storm of indignant criticism followed this sudden explosion. Alemán expressed sympathy with Mrs. Amador, then condemned talk which was unnecessary to the group's business. Mrs. Estebán attempted to tell the others how to clear up the confusion: "When there is a long discussion, the members should present a motion to end the discussion. Okay? Mrs. Abelando presented such a motion, not as a motion, but as a clarification. I asked that it be presented as a motion. What do the members say about that?"

Alemán corrected her: "She did not present it as a motion."

Mrs. Estebán retorted: "But I asked that it be presented as a motion."

Mrs. Abelando said, "Here we go again. Some time ago I protested that we talk in vain. . . ."

Zamora interrupted: "Well that was a protest, not a motion."

Mrs. Estebán then repeated: "I ask that the protest be presented as a motion."

Ironically, her effort to invite a motion to stop the confusion she herself had introduced was not successful. The same sequence was repeated amidst noisy and exasperated outbursts. When she was blamed directly for the chaos, Mrs. Estebán took another tack:

> If you feel impatient about these discussions, let me tell you they are not foolish. Any and every detail brought up here is important, and it is good to know about it. We should come here with patience and not rush to a meeting saying, "My kids are over there, my husband is waiting, this, that and the other." This organization has to get reliable, constant members who are willing to sacrifice . . . if we are going to help the Puerto Ricans and have a decent community. Mrs. Amador comes here with one purpose and we with another because she wants to rush. We cannot rush things! To rush is against the discipline of the confederation!

But Mrs. Estebán's appeals were not persuasive. All other sentiments expressed were on behalf of Mrs. Amador, and the members were driving toward some standard of relevancy at meetings. Finally, Alemán asked her: "Every meeting is supposed to have a purpose. What is the purpose of this meeting?" Mrs. Estebán did not answer this question but after another round of debate, she became conciliatory and ended the meeting with an apology: "Pardon the many errors of this meeting. Let us hope that at the next meeting we will not make as many."

The president was a reflective woman and this meeting, perhaps the most unpleasant for her in the group's history, led her to reexamine her role much as she had done after the rebellious aftermath. During the rebirth of the group, the rule proscribing personal talk had an unequal effect upon the members' contributions to meetings. It distinctly favored Mrs. Estebán because she could dominate meetings without referring to personal problems, instead, offering lengthy accounts of her participation in civic affairs, conversations with agency officials, and ancillary activities of a more or less formal type. No one else's life was so saturated, so no one else had as much to talk about and could still observe the rule. But the members' desire to move ahead caused the desire for relevance. In contrast to her idea that any and every detail was important, was the insistence by Zamora, Alemán, and Mrs. Amador that relevancy was contingent upon the purpose of the meeting and the group's broader objectives. The trauma of Mrs. Amador's resignation, the sympathy this act evoked, and the blistering attack upon Mrs. Estebán all accentuated this point. Loquacious she was, but she was by no means insensitive to the members' opinions, and she decided to control her talkativeness.

At the next meeting, mindful of Alemán's comment that every meeting should have a purpose, she omitted the customary resumé of her outside activities. She did not mention her participation at a meeting of the Council of Churches nor of the city's department of education, although both meetings involved the confederation officially. She turned to the business at hand, the selection of a lawyer who would write a constitution and incorporate the group. Very shortly, two motions were passed, one to pick a lawyer from the city's Legal Assistance Office to represent the group without pay and the other to designate a committee to contact the lawyer. Before the meeting ended, Rafael Zayas made a plea that "out of courtesy" a letter be sent to Mrs. Amador inviting her back to the group. This was done, and Mrs. Amador again took her place among the most reliable of members.

A month elapsed before the confederation received the preliminary draft of the proposal for the Hispanic Referral Office from APA. Its revision and approval by the confederation was of the utmost urgency, for the confederation was to meet with APA and the agenda subcommittee of the Neighborhood Advisory Board to review the application before it was submitted officially to the NAB for a formal vote.

The draft included a statement of the purposes of the referral office, the scope and content of the program, a timetable — the office would open in ten weeks, in July, and be fully operative by the middle of August — and the budget. The proposed annual salaries for the staff were: social worker-coordinator, $6,000; neighborhood worker, $4,500; secretary, $3,000; total salaries, $13,500. Additional budgetary items included 10 percent fringe benefits for the staff, travel expenses, office supplies, rent, and so forth, which increased the total annual budget to $19,000. The only unusual feature in an otherwise standard format was a question mark in the statement — "The Hispanic Confederation (?) will have overall responsibility for the program." Edgar Gordon had made it clear that the confederation would have overall responsibility for the referral office, an arrangement he himself preferred, and the confederation had voted for incorporation to assume this responsibility, yet the question mark in the draft statement cast some doubt on the situation.

Because the time was short, Mrs. Estebán immediately convened a meeting to act upon the drafted application. She told the 18 persons present that Alemán would continue as the spokesman for the group because as a member of the Neighborhood Advisory Board she could be accused of a conflict of interest if she presented the application on behalf of the confederation and then voted on it as a member of the Board.

The group was impressed by the application's authoritative format and numerous bureaucratic expressions: "program staff," "liaison," "catalyst," and they felt proud that an organization described in such official-sounding language would be under their control. But Carlos Otero insisted on scrutinizing, discussing, and revising the draft. He said if APA had taken a month to write it, the confederation could not be expected to approve it in two days:

> This is not sufficient time for a real discussion of the proposal. . . .You must decide how many people you need to have on the staff in order to do what you want to do. Do you think two is sufficient. . . .There are organizations in Maplewood getting 40 to 50 thousand dollars a year, and if one wants to get money, one has to fight for it.

Otero went on to explain that the referral office had to build a solid reputation in the Hispanic community and the coordinator had to be paid more than $6,000, for in addition to being bilingual he had to be "capable of supervising the office, [one] who can talk with officials . . . including the mayor . . . [who] will be responsible to you and to the federal government."

Mrs. Estebán had been making a valiant effort not to intrude too much, but she suddenly interjected a completely different topic, a letter she had received from the mayor requesting that the group meet with top officials of the city's school system. The other members practically shouted her down, and the discussion went on. Diego Zayas, who had frequently expressed suspicion of APA, wanted to accept the draft without alteration. He said, "If you try to increase the budget, APA may not give us the office at all."

Most of the members agreed with Zayas, and the discussion turned into a debate, with Otero arguing the need for a thorough revision of the draft. Finally, Alfonso Vilá advanced a motion to accept the draft as it was because "The budget is appropriate to serve a population which is only four percent of the city." Otero's arguments, however, had convinced some members; the motion was defeated 7 to 6; revisions would be made; the meeting with the agenda subcommittee would be postponed.

Otero had long been concerned with APA's neglect of the Puerto Ricans in the community, and he saw the draft as a "bone thrown to the confederation to keep it quiet." He thought it poorly written, hastily conceived, and miserly. (I privately thought he was right, because with only three employees the referral office was a caricature of what was needed.) In addition, Otero was an employee of APA and he knew from daily experience the inner workings of the agency. Relative to its size, Maplewood had led the nation in poverty dollars received. Soon the agency was to submit an application to the Office of Economic Opportunity for $3,318,536 to fund its programs during a 14-month period, and according to OEO guidelines, this was almost six times the amount a city of

Maplewood's size should receive on a per capita basis. Now there were fears of imminent cutbacks, and the agency recognized the need for innovative programs such as the Hispanic Referral Office. Thus, the confederation's proposal had captured the agency's interest. McCall and his aides saw it as something to further enhance APA's reputation of leadership in poverty programs.

Four meetings of the confederation over a period of one month were devoted to the task of revising the draft. Otero presented ideas, stimulated discussion, and solicited criticisms. Then he wrote what turned out to be a new proposal, seven pages long. It included more factual information on Maplewood's Puerto Ricans and their assimilative problems, but the most important change involved the enlargement of the purpose of the referral office. While APA had centered the application on the referral function of linking Puerto Rican clients to ongoing programs and services, the new draft proposed a wide-reaching attack on the Puerto Ricans' problems:

> The development of knowledgeable, effective, and responsible leadership and citizenry within the Spanish community. . . . Remedying substandard housing, health, and living conditions which have debilitating effects in the life of the Spanish resident. . . . To secure and guarantee equal opportunities in the areas of employment and training. . . . To effect a change in all existing social and economic conditions that have detrimental effects on the Spanish family and its organizational life. . . .

Underlying what was, indeed, a new and ambitious program far beyond that of referral, was a basic change in the stance the Hispanic Referral Office was to take in relation to the Puerto Ricans' problems; instead of passively receiving clients, the office was to project itself forcefully into the community in an attempt to eradicate social ills afflicting Puerto Ricans and reshape the social environment creating such ills.

Along with this change, Otero's new proposal included additional staff and some increase in individual salaries: coordinator, $9,000; community-service worker, $7,000; two neighborhood workers, $10,000; secretary-receptionist, $4,000; research-advisor (part-time), $2,500; total salaries, $32,500. Otero realized the budget increase to $45,755 carried the calculated risk of rejection of the whole application, but he thought it more likely that subsequent negotiations would bring about a compromise between the original budget and the new one.

Neither conflict nor confusion marred the four meetings devoted to the new application. Mrs. Estebán ceded the chair to Otero. The discussion was orderly without formality, and a feeling of involvement and mutual affection swept over the membership. Discussion focused almost entirely on the problems and technical issues of writing the application. Otero commanded the group; the members deferred to his judgment while maintaining their sense of participation. It became unmistakably clear that his primary commitment and loyalty were to the group when, in writing the new draft, he put no question mark in the sentence about the confederation retaining control of the referral office.

Yet Otero was apprehensive that his employer, APA, would discover his collusion with the group. He asked that his work be kept confidential. The members, including Mrs. Estebán, complimented Otero on his work and took part in a feeling of general good will at their accomplishment. Otero, however, did not want to dwell on the topic. He began to advise Alemán on what to say at the agenda subcommittee meeting: "You have to sell this proposal. You should know it backwards and forwards. If necessary, memorize it. Fight for its main content. Don't get into details on the exact amount each person should be paid or you will get bogged down."

Armed with this advice, the confederation presented its application for a referral office to the agenda subcommittee of the Neighborhood Advisory Board. The chairman of the subcommittee did not delay in picking out "troublesome points" and "questionable material" in the new proposal which, if not eliminated, would raise difficult problems at the meeting of the full Neighborhood Advisory Board. Should the Hispanic Referral Office involve itself in consumer education, home care programs, family budgeting, cultural exchange programs, etc., other APA projects would be preempted. Employees in such projects would be antagonized and would wonder why the Spanish-speaking community could not use services already provided. He said, "Why don't agency programs already in operation fit into the Spanish neighborhoods? If your reply is because of a lack of communication, then why can't persons who speak Spanish be put into the existing programs?"

Once before Alemán had served the confederation as spokesman and because he believed his performance on that occasion was poor, he had reflected on how he could improve it. Also Otero had again tutored him. This time he was not startled by the criticism nor did he become angry and confused. In a firm voice he described the need to consolidate the referral function and to bring Puerto Ricans into the mainstream of opportunities provided by Maplewood. He concluded by saying, "The simple fact is that APA does not have any programs which attempt to reach the Puerto Ricans."

Unexpectedly, Mrs. Estebán intervened to defend APA: "APA *is* trying to do a lot and I know that. Just today I was at APA and one can see how much they are doing for the Spanish-speaking people. There are Spanish-speaking teachers for students in prekindergarten. . . . The thing is that there aren't enough [Spanish speakers] working in the neighborhoods."

Mrs. Estebán had just begun working part time for APA, interviewing in a manpower project, and her increasing involvement in the agency continued to be evident at meetings and elsewhere. Her attempt to criticize Alemán and thus undermine the presentation of the application did not pass unnoticed among the five confederation members who were present. She had betrayed the group's solidarity and placed herself on the agency's side.

The chairman of the subcommittee then raised an issue of central concern to him — the precedent of supporting an organization which had an ethnic base: "If we send this proposal through and it is approved, then somebody may come along and say, 'We want something for the German-speaking people.' Someone else will say, 'We want something for the Polish-speaking people.' Someone else will want something for the Italians, and so on."

This statement evoked a ripple of laughter from the subcommittee, for it conjured up an image of a conglomerate of nationalities speaking a babble of different tongues, each bidding for its own interest. But Alemán saw no humor in the situation. Indignantly, but with control, he said: "If there is justifiable need for the other centers, then each should be considered. Here we have given reasons which are sufficient. No matter how much money APA spent, or has left to work with, unless there is a link to bring us together, the Puerto Ricans will not benefit. Those present should remember this. . . . If what you say is a joke, it is a joke on a very serious proposal."

Alemán's sobriety disarmed and embarrassed the group, and several persons including the chairman apologized, for they had meant no ridicule. To change the topic, the chairman asked Alemán if the confederation's members had persons in mind to staff the referral office. Alemán replied that they did, but Mrs. Estebán, again asserting herself, denied it.

Toward the end of the meeting, the chairman confided that, as a second-generation Italian still strongly identified with his cultural background, he understood how persons "had an instinct for their own culture going back many years." He was sympathetic to the proposal because he could understand the Puerto Ricans' concern for their compatriots. He told Alemán the questions he had raised would prepare him for the meeting of the Neighborhood Advisory Board. This was a group of 21 persons, three elected from each of the seven inner-city neighborhoods in which APA had developed poverty programs. The chairman of the agenda subcommittee closed the meeting by warning Alemán: "There you will have to face 21 persons. You will walk out of there with your head spinning in circles. . .[I advise that you] change the proposal without really changing the meat of the text. Take out some phrases and reword it so it does not sound as if you're stepping on somebody's toes. Tell them you are willing to work with other groups [APA]."

In a discussion after the meeting, Zamora and Otero said they thought Alemán had been an excellent spokesman, his quick temper having demonstrated devotion to the cause of helping his compatriots. Otero, privy to relevant circles, knew the representatives from APA and the Neighborhood Advisory Board had reacted favorably to Alemán, and he felt the proposal now had an excellent chance of being approved. Zamora and Otero both had noted Mrs. Estebán's tendency to ally herself with APA.

Mrs. Estebán said she was shocked at Alemán's hot-tempered outburst and thought he had damaged the confederation's reputation irreparably. She had convinced herself that Alemán harbored a private wish to be the referral-office coordinator. To combat this possibility she decided that the referral office would be best administered by APA, not the confederation. She explained to me that the spending of federal funds would impose too heavy a burden on the confederation and mistakes in either accounting or management could bring forth legal prosecution.

At a meeting the following week, five days before the group was to present the proposal to the Neighborhood Advisory Board, the bad news came suddenly. Reversing its original promise, APA informed the confederation that they would control the referral office and would relegate the confederation to an advisory role. As Otero spoke of this change, Diego Zayas asked: "Do I understand this right? APA will take over the office as if the confederation does not exist?" Otero said this was so, and Zayas retorted angrily: "I am sure that if Professor Rogler writes a book and I would then ask him to let me put my name on the book, he would say, 'No! No! No!' If he writes a book, he wants credit for himself, not for me. It is the same with us!"

The lawyer from the Legal Assistance Office who had been contacted to work on the incorporation procedure was present at this meeting. He now warned the members of the need to control the referral office without interference from APA. So imbedded was the agency in the city's political system, he explained, that if the group depended upon them and then acted in a politically inadvisable way, serious difficulties would arise. He said, "If you are independent of APA, you would not allow political barriers to stop you from speaking and taking action. You cannot be with APA and take an independent position without endangering your programs. It is better the confederation be independent so that it can do what it wants.

The agency's reversal had caught him by surprise, and he saw the inconsistency of APA's avowed purpose, to encourage with its actions the development and growth of groups, such as the confederation. Otero, however, said he had been doubtful all along of APA fulfilling its promise. He said:

> I was really surprised when Gordon gave you the alternative of controlling the referral office. I knew it would be impossible. They wanted to see what we would do. Then when we turned up with a concrete proposal, they let it run along for a little while. . . . They are afraid that many other groups would want to do the same thing, have their own organizations. . . . APA is saying if you want to play the game with me, play it according to my rules. APA is a big organization and they want control over everything. They want control over this operation.

Diego Zayas found it difficult to accept the whole situation. "I don't understand it. APA was started with funds from the Ford Foundation. Did the Ford Foundation then decide and insist upon controlling APA?"

The discussion swung between the dilemma — to permit APA to have control of the Hispanic Referral Office or to fight for the confederation's control over the office as planned — and the duplicity of the agency. As Alfonso Vilá put it, "The proposal was submitted to APA for *our* benefit. Now they have changed it for *their* benefit." Otero wanted to focus discussion upon the decision now facing the group. So great was APA's enthusiasm over the referral office, he said, that plans were being made to begin service the first of July, in less than six weeks. If the Neighborhood Advisory Board and the governing board of APA approved, the agency would start the office with its own funds even before the Office of Economic Opportunity in Washington had made a decision on endorsing it. Accompanying the opening of the office would be a publicity campaign advertising the agency's innovative thrust and sensitivity to the needs of economically impoverished cultural minorities, such as the Puerto Ricans. On the other hand, said Otero, should the confederation insist upon administering the office, there would be a difficult period of renegotiation with the agency; then if the confederation won, it would confront the usual delays of funding from OEO.

The alternatives were clear, but neither was to the confederation's liking. Finally, Zamora made a statement which gave birth to the group's decision: "It is true that APA would not have established the referral office without the confederation because Puerto Ricans are in the minority, but the important thing is that the office be established and the advice of the confederation be heard and taken."

Amid considerable grumbling but with no organized opposition, a motion was passed to give APA control over the referral office but, strengthening the confederation's role beyond that of advisory, to require the "advice and consent" of the confederation in the hiring of the staff. With the assistance of the lawyer, the relevant part of the proposal was changed so that the confederation would be given the primary advisory function in decisions about the Hispanic Referral Office.

The hiring of staff, particularly the coordinator, was already a lively subject of conversation outside of the group's meetings. Through gossip Zamora had heard that Mrs. Estebán suspected Alemán of wanting the job. Now he proceeded to correct and reprimand her publicly for her actions at the subcommittee's meeting. Alemán had acted wisely, he told her, to say the confederation had persons in mind for the positions available. His statement gave the impression that the confederation had prepared itself so thoroughly that it had thought through to the basic problem of staffing. Anyone who served as spokesman, Zamora went on, deserved the full trust of the group, and Alemán should not be repaid with suspicion but should be given credit for being such an able spokesman.

As the meeting came to an end and the members lingered to talk about staffing, Mrs. Estebán and her brother, Alfonso Vilá, suggested Carlos Otero as coordinator of the referral office. They knew that Otero himself was interested in the job and the agency had already selected him to be the coordinator when they administered the referral office.

10

The Taste of Triumph

•

The night before the meeting of the Neighborhood Advisory Board, Alemán studied the application for the Hispanic Referral Office for six hours. Then, his wife, playing the role of a board member, rehearsed with him by firing questions at him. Thus, Alemán went to the meeting satisfied with his ability to answer the questions and confident that he would represent the group well. The first question, however, caught him unprepared. A board member asked: "Have you computed the fringe benefits on the basis of the standard 15 percent?"

But, quite unexpectedly, the confederation had acquired a powerful and articulate spokesman, the NAB chairman himself. Having studied the application, he was touched by the plight of the Puerto Ricans and concerned at their neglect by the Antipoverty Agency of Maplewood. Although he was black, the chairman felt that the impetus of the black civil-rights movement had overshadowed the problems and interests of the Spanish-speaking persons living in Maplewood.

"I think the Puerto Rican and the Spanish speaker are the forgotten person," he said. "If these persons are forgotten, I don't think we will have won a victory." The chairman thought the application did not even need to be debated, but he did not want it to be given perfunctory approval. He said, "We could say, 'Yes, we approve' and boom, stamp, and continue to the next proposal. I think that now as a committee we can really do something ... I am for going back and expanding this program. I think we should put the full weight of this committee behind the expansion of the program and not wait until later for the possibility of increasing the funding of the program."

After scanning the application's budget, he continued, "This is a paltry sum considering some of the projects we have looked at for which we have had few questions and just said, "Great, go ahead!" The landscape proposal comes to my mind now, and that was a half-million dollars. Everybody has been grabbing and getting, but for the Spanish-speaking community it has been too little and too late. It is time to give strong recognition to this kind of plan."

The chairman's enthusiasm restored Alemán's self-confidence. He then quickly told the board that Puerto Ricans were removed from the city's poverty programs even though they were "the most poverty-stricken people in the city." Unless immediate help was given, he continued, 20 years would pass before Puerto Ricans adapted to the city, and he concluded, "I am sure no one here wants us to suffer for 20 years." But his plea was unnecessary because the members, already convinced by the chairman, were ready to act. One cautious voice was raised by the APA representative who served as a liaison between the agency and the NAB to warn that if the budget was increased too much the agency would not be able to start the Hispanic Referral Office from its own funds and there would be delays while resorting to the Office of Economic Opportunity for funding. The chairman, ignoring this advice, replied, "I do not want to go off on another tangent with my enthusiasm about this program."

Alemán said quickly, "I would like to see the number of neighborhood workers increased."

The chairman asked, "How many more do you want?"

Alemán answered, "Three more."

The chairman said, "If you are making the recommendation that the number of fieldworkers be increased from three to six, then we will add $15,000 to the budget."

Very quickly, a motion was passed unanimously to increase the budget from $32,500 to $47,500. It was unprecedented for the Neighborhood Advisory Board to increase the budget of an application under review, but also unprecedented was the recommendation then made by the chairman: "This proposal needs a cherry on top. I suggest that, as a rider to our acceptance of the proposal, a letter about the needs of this program be sent to the APA governing board which would express the consensus of this board that something needs to be done for the Spanish-speaking population."

The official review over, the Neighborhood Advisory Board members were still enthusiastic. They told Alemán that if, for political reasons, the confederation was in need of further support, each of the 21 members of the NAB would pressure the antipoverty agency. The chairman concluded, "It is a top-priority program, and all resources should be made available to it."

The following day, Alemán reported to the confederation members the NAB's enthusiastic endorsement of the application and how the office's budget was to be increased. He indirectly criticized Mrs. Estebán's leadership by emphasizing the efficiency with which the NAB chairman had conducted the meeting. Stimulated by the good news, the members then turned to three problems facing them: the need to advertise the confederation's success in a newsletter, the legal incorporation of the group, and the advisability of increasing the membership by asking former members to rejoin the group. In this regard, Mrs. Estebán had objected to the renewal of membership by Antonio Tejada after he had been deposed as president of the Pan-American Association. She had not forgiven his betrayal in forming a rival group. Now when the name of a minister from the Christian Damascus church was brought up, Mrs. Estebán strongly opposed inviting him back to the group. She had observed the minister at a meeting of another group, she said, and noticed that he "goes to meetings with his own problems. A person who brings his problems to an organization will destroy the organization."

Mrs. Amador grasped this opening to bring up a complaint. At the confederation meetings, she said, the members had censured her for bringing up personal problems, but this was wrong because often her own personal problems illustrated the common problems afflicting all Puerto Ricans. Since the confederation dealt with common problems, individual problems provided specific cases relevant to the group's formal business. Her reasons for disagreeing with the prohibition of personal discussions were not just pragmatic, but moral as well. She said, "We should behave as if we were brothers, so that if one person has a problem, the others ought to help by giving information to solve the problem."

Reaction to this complaint indicated that the enforcement of the norm during the past year had created discomfort among the members, but only now was such dissatisfaction expressed openly. Obedience to the norm implied the rejection of a Puerto Rican cultural tradition of giving help to other persons within the primary group or circle of acquaintances. The members felt deeply the loss of Puerto Rican communal life — of a *Gemeinschaft* society — and the erosion of the much-treasured help-giving tradition. Participation in the confederation's early life had been a way of restoring the loss, but during the last year the members had been obliged to suppress the inclination to help and to be given help, and even the natural impulse to speak about their need for help.

When we interviewed the confederation members systematically, we asked them to compare life in Maplewood with life in Puerto Rico. Sixty percent replied that life on the island was better because people were "better" than in Maplewood and almost always the reason given was that in Puerto Rico the people tried to "help each other." Even members who did not think persons were "better" in their homeland bemoaned the loss of help-giving patterns among friends and acquaintances. They said: "Here you can be seriously ill, and nobody cares whether you are alive or not." "In Puerto Rico people know how to treat each other. There if you have a problem, somebody gets interested in helping you. Here nobody cares, not even the Puerto Ricans." "I have had problems and nobody helped me. I was sure that some of my Puerto Rican neighbors knew about them."

Mrs. Amador was the first to express the pain of this feeling and the members were sympathetic and understanding, but the group did not discuss the problem at great length at that time. The issue was to remain dormant for several more weeks.

The confederation was never officially informed by the governing board of APA of their decision on the referral office. They read in a report of the meeting in the afternoon newspaper that the NAB had placed top priority on the proposal by the Hispanic Confederation for the Spanish-speaking residents of the city; that the NAB chairman had made a strong pitch for the $47,500 proposal at the meeting, but was advised that the money situation was tight; that he was assured that there would be an effort to find the funds to get the project started.

Through unofficial channels, the confederation found out that the office was scheduled to open on July 1 of that summer. The agency's choice of Otero as coordinator of the office also became known informally. The members were grateful to him for guiding them through the successive revisions of the application and for allying himself with them against APA. They had no objection to his appointment as coordinator, but Otero wanted their approval to be voiced in an official vote, which, he said, was necessary if the confederation was to exercise its power of "advice and consent" in the hiring of the office staff.

For this purpose, Mrs. Estebán convened a meeting in the middle of June, which was attended by 27 well-dressed members. The event was unique in the history of Maplewood's Puerto Rican community: An Hispano organization was going to select an important public official. A feeling of good fellowship and self-importance pervaded the meeting. Members addressed each other in the informal Spanish *tu* ("you") instead of the more commonly used formal *usted* ("thou"), and stood together proudly to have their pictures taken by a professional photographer hired by APA.

After Mrs. Estebán's customary introductions, Enrique Zamora rose to read the minutes, but he was overcome with emotion and began to recount the confederation's arduous struggle against APA to establish the office. In grand style he compared the need for unification among all Spanish speakers to the United States unifying itself during the colonial period and after the Civil War. He went on to speak of the ideal of equality shared by Spanish speakers, regardless of national origins and differences in income, of the need to work hard, obey the law, and never resort to violence. He said:

> Even if Americans do not practice democracy, we should strive to make democracy a reality. . . . Americans emphasize the difference — whether or not a person is a Puerto Rican. I have heard it commented that because he is an Hispano he is stupid. But that is not true. That is a lie! He may be ignorant, but then again that is something else. It is not that he is an idiot or suffers congenital defects from an accident at birth. We are all sufficiently intelligent to be integrated into the American community, so that in the future no one will say, "There comes a Puerto Rican." Let it be said in the future, "There is an American citizen." If we talk about democracy, it is exactly at this point that democracy begins. . . .

Zamora went on to denounce the American press and television for identifying the ethnicity of criminals, credited some Americans with respecting their neighbors, loving their brothers, and helping strangers; then he concluded: "So members of the confederation, let us make our community but one group. . . . Let us cast aside the [inferiority] complex which afflicts the Hispano, and demonstrate our capacity to absorb education and use the opportunities given to us. Make them forget the idea that Hispanos are stupid!"

A burst of applause followed the half-hour speech, along with shouts of approval and comments on how well Zamora had expressed what each Hispano knew and felt. This was another first in the confederation's life, and everyone was deeply moved. The members suddenly felt that to be a member of the confederation was to be involved in a set of universal concerns, a meaning which never before had been given to participation in the group.

Antonio Tejada chose this moment of good feeling to ask some technical questions about the confederation's rules and procedures, the lack of bylaws, and the qualifications for membership. Such questions, touching as they did on divisive and unresolved problems, were always disconcerting to Mrs. Estebán. Now she floundered in an attempt to answer, while the members seemed ready again to plunge into controversy. Quickly, Zamora, still under the influence of his own oratory, said: "By simply being a Latin, you are a member of this group. By feeling pride in your Spanish background dating back 600 years, you are a member. An active member is one who comes to meetings and assists in improving the community, who sacrifices himself on behalf of the community." Tejada was silenced and the ceremonial character of the meeting was not disrupted again.

Zamora then made a motion that the group approve of Otero as the coordinator of the office. The motion was seconded by Mrs. Otero. Unexpectedly and incongruously, Diego Zayas, who favored Otero, opposed the motion. The group should follow democratic procedures, he claimed, by nominating at least two candidates. The members shouted in disagreement that no one else had Otero's qualifications, so the proposal was unrealistic. Zayas then withdrew his motion, and amidst a round of applause Otero was unanimously approved as coordinator of the Hispanic Referral Office. The president was authorized to sign the letter that Otero had already drafted to be sent to APA consenting to the appointment. Then a committee of eight persons was selected to write a newsletter which had been planned for the confederation, and the meeting came to an end. Still uplifted by their feeling of shared satisfaction, success, and importance, the members lingered in the room talking informally, having their pictures taken, and enjoying the refreshments the women had brought.

Thirty persons attended the next meeting of the confederation held on the night before the HRO was to open. Upon being asked to read the minutes, Zamora reported his own impassioned speech which then stimulated him to make another speech. This time he dealt with the motivations of the members or what they ought to be if the group were to succeed. He said:

> It is important to avoid the attitude of a person who comes to the confederation to solve his own problems and who says to himself, "If they do not solve my problem I will not return to the confederation." Rather than this, we should think of the future because of our children, that they not suffer the problems we suffer. We should always remember that we are attempting to construct the future, a future which will be better for our children.

Always before this, Mrs. Estebán had justified the norm of avoiding personal discussion at meetings as a means of avoiding disorganization and confusion, but now the rationale was going beyond the utilitarian to the moral. By appealing to the members' concern for their children, Zamora was using deeply rooted feelings to buttress the norm and to counteract whatever tendency there might be to revert to traditional, primary-group relationships. Now, Mrs. Estebán expressed her agreement with Zamora and repeated the group's modest legacy: "The premises of the confederation are that it is not religious or political, and does not devote itself to the solution of private problems. . . . This organization addresses itself to general problems in the community."

Alemán and Zamora then began to criticize the antipoverty agency for not officially informing the confederation of the governing board's decision regarding the referral office. Here it was the night before the office was to open, they said, and still nothing was known officially about the office staff and budget. Otero then reported that APA would provide only his own and a secretary's salary.

The members were angry and confused, remembering the enthusiasm of the Neighborhood Advisory Board. A two-person staff fell woefully short of the recommendations and promises made to them. They wanted to demand an explanation without delay, but Mrs. Abelando advised caution: "We ought to have patience and wait. Tomorrow the office will open. I would like to take it easy and wait so that when we ask, we ask with all our rights. We ought to wait a week."

The others, however, thought the right was already theirs, and they concurred on a motion to write to APA for an appointment. Also voted through was Otero's recommendation that Mrs. Alemán be appointed secretary of the referral office.

Still infected with a sense of urgency, the members assigned to the newsletter committee the task of designing an emblem for the confederation. No one had thought before of the need for a tangible symbol, but it was a natural result of the commonly felt, openly discussed desire for an external object to represent the personal attachment and love for the confederation everyone was experiencing as a member of the group.

As the meeting was drawing to an end, Otero distributed a slim pamphlet, an abbreviated version of Roberts' *Rules of Order*, and advised the members to read it carefully and bring it to meetings. He invited everyone to come to the opening of the office early the next morning.

On the first of July of the second summer of the confederation's life, the Hispanic Referral Office of Maplewood's Antipoverty Agency opened its doors to serve the Spanish speakers of the city. It was a hot, dry summer day, the culmination of 20 months of struggle, trial, and error in the group's life. The ancient, two-story, red brick building, housing the office, was in the city's largest Puerto Rican neighborhood; reputed to have been a jail at one time, it had been there many years before Maplewood had ever had a Puerto Rican community. The building was in disrepair, and the office in an upstairs room was shabby and badly in need of paint. Yet the room was symbolic of the confederation's success, and it was there that the members got together to relish the occasion.

In one corner, Antonio Tejada was recounting to several men his army experiences while stationed in Spain. About the opening of the office he declared, "Yes, today is as important as the day the Declaration of Independence was signed." Then, reconsidering quickly, he said that the office was just a trivial gesture designed to appease Maplewood's Puerto Ricans, and the high-salaried, well-educated APA officials would continue serving their own selfish interests. Then he returned to his personal experiences and began a lengthy explanation of how to make bootleg rum.

In another part of the office, Mrs. Amador expressed her pleasure, ". . .because we have taken a step forward. True, everything is not as it should be, but still I am very happy." She was happy, too, she said, because soon she and her husband would be using their small store for the production and sale of *mavi*, a fermented tropical drink made from the bark of a tree of the same name, never before available to Maplewood's Puerto Ricans.

Others members spoke happily, but Mrs. Estebán sat by, unusually subdued. To my question of what the day meant to her she replied, "I did not come here to make speeches! At meetings I always have a lot to say, but I did not come here to a meeting. I came to look at the office."

The very first client in the Hispanic Referral Office was a 20-year-old Puerto Rican who had failed the preinduction physical examination for the army. Although his parents had been given no diagnosis or explanation, they thought it was a case of "weak blood." Otero rapidly made arrangements for the client to have a thorough examination at a local hospital. The challenge of the job excited Otero. To his knowledge, the office was the first poverty project explicitly designed to serve an ethnic minority, and he wanted it to succeed. At the same time, he was wary and somewhat anxious that Vicente de Serrano would attempt either to gain control of or interfere with the office by working through the inner political circles of city hall. (Serrano had once accused Otero of meddling in Puerto Rican affairs.) Also, Otero was worried by the confederation. He believed the success or failure of the office was very much dependent upon the confederation's stability. He thought that Mrs. Estebán was an energetic and well-intentioned president, but a disorganizing influence. For this reason, he planned from the very beginning to involve the group in the office's work.

Accordingly, at the next meeting of the confederation, two weeks after the opening of the office, Otero presented a case to the members involving a newly arrived Cuban refugee family in desperate need of clothing and furniture. Mrs. Abelando was the first to speak: "All of us present should help this family even if it is nothing more than a little quarter that we can contribute right at the moment. Even if we can only give a set of [drinking] glasses that cost only $1.00 or a frying pan for $.35, we should give something right away."

Alemán disagreed: "No, this is the kind of problem that will come up today and tomorrow. It will come up repeatedly. There are many agencies available to help in cases of this sort. We would all be glad to help; but if each one of us is going to contribute a dollar, soon all of us would have to go to welfare too."

Mrs. Estebán agreed with Alemán: "Yes, this is an important issue. If this is going to be repeated time and again we have to consider the possibility that other refugees and other poor families will come and want help."

Zamora added, "This family is in need of help immediately. When one has hunger, one is hungry now, not tomorrow. But even if we should help this family, the important thing is that there are agencies established to deal with these problems. The problem that we should address ourselves toward is not one of helping the family directly but trying to see whether the local agencies can develop emergency procedures for dealing with families such as this."

Soon, the discussion turned to the proscription of personal discussions at meetings which effectively ruled out mutual aid between members. The question was raised: Should the confederation help the Cuban family and give them assistance denied to its own members? When stated out loud, this question disturbed the members because it brought out the contradiction between the norm of the confederation and the Puerto Rican tradition of mutual help. Even those members who saw value in conforming to the norm and argued on its behalf could not help identifying with the plight of the Cuban family. The dilemma led to a thorough examination of the norm. To act with the good intentions embodied in the tradition of mutual help would harm the confederation as a group. Thus, undesirable consequences would result from desirable motives.

The conscious emphasis on future decisions — the belief that rules formulated now should be enforced in the future and the view of the Cuban family as an instance of a general problem requiring a standard not an individual solution —

was indicative of the confederation's transformation into an action group.

Zamora finally provided the way out of an apparently insoluble problem: "Local agencies," he said, "should assume responsibility for cases such as the Cuban family." The group decided that when they met with the APA officials to raise questions about the understaffing of the office, their failure to notify the confederation about the decisions of the governing board, and the plans for the office, they would also request contingency funds for the office to meet the emergency needs of families. This solution enabled the members to cope with the problem without setting a precedent difficult to maintain, and yet it permitted them to have the feeling of giving assistance.

Thus, the norm first stated and then enforced by Mrs. Estebán now belonged to the group as a whole, and newcomers to the confederation, not present when it originated, were contributing to its evolution. David Alemán was one such newcomer. The day after this meeting I asked him his opinion of the group decision about the Cuban refugee family. He told me:

> I think they [the members] decided wisely because most of them are barely making it. The money they earn by the week is hardly enough for them to meet their own needs. And when somebody comes up with a problem and needs money, I think very few, if any, of the members of the confederation can spare money with which to help these people. It is okay if it is a group of high-class citizens who have businesses and could spare money to help others, but we cannot. So together we have to try to get help from the right agencies. Maplewood is getting $10 million a year to fight poverty. We just want our fair share of that. That's why we organize you know . . . when a case like this [the Cuban family] comes up, there is no doubt that everybody is moved with compassion and right away you want to give your last dollar. It would be okay if this was the only case but there will be many other such cases in the future. I, myself, right away was eager to make a collection for this. Right! But I don't think it's wise to do that, because if we do it for one, the same case will come up again and they will remind us, "Well, you did it for him, why not for me?" It's not good. You see again, people might hold it against you because you say no. You really have to do it the right way at the beginning.

After the discussion by Otero took place at the meeting, Mrs. Estebán announced a new rule: henceforth information could be brought to meetings only when officially authorized by the group. The rule was consistent with the confederation's efforts to depersonalize decisions, establish precedents, and adopt impersonal procedures for conducting meetings, but Mrs. Estebán presented it as a result of an angry exchange with Alemán over a member who had quit the group. She accused the member of defaulting in his promise of support. Alemán defended the man, a personal friend, on the grounds that other duties kept him from attending meetings. Mrs. Estebán declared Alemán was out of order because his information stemmed from a personal friendship and was unofficial. In the immediate situation, the rule was designed to silence Alemán, but it also expressed a norm that she was trying desperately to follow. Ever since the chaotic meeting when Mrs. Amador had resigned in a storm of protest, Mrs. Esteban had said little about her activities outside the confederation. If the group's president, its most active and best-informed member, was attempting to restrain herself, she reasoned, then others should be expected to do the same.

With the exception of an occasional argument between Mrs. Esteban and Alemán, the confederation had experienced an unprecedented period of peace and tranquility, beginning with those meetings in which Otero led the group through successive revisions of the application and continuing into the first meeting after the opening of the office. Mrs. Esteban's determined effort to control her talkativeness, the secretary's detailed minutes and moving speeches, the decison to design an emblem, the development of an elaborate but satisfying ideology which reconciled the differences between traditional and emergent norms, and, perhaps most important, the triumph in attaining the long-sought goal of establishing the office, all caused rivalries and antagonisms between members to recede into the background. An impression of stability and consensus was created, much stronger than in fact existed. But by the end of July at the second meeting held that month, the euphoria began to evaporate.

Once the secretary read the minutes, 11 separate items, the president announced to the other 24 participants that the meeting had been convened to elect a new vice-president to replace Mr. Amador who had long been absent from meetings. Discussion quickly turned to other topics, one person after another volunteering observations about the many failures of Puerto Rican organizations and the kind of leadership needed. Suddenly and angrily Alemán interrupted:

> Some time ago there was a pamphlet distributed here describing parliamentary rules, which are being disregarded at this meeting. Procedures dictate that when the secretary completes the reading of minutes, the group must turn to decisions which are pending. Now we are discussing new issues without having resolved old ones. . . . This is breaking the rules we have been trying to institute.

Zamora agreed, and Alemán, stimulated by his support, became more pointedly critical:

> I can give you an illustration of why rules are necessary. Two weeks ago we discussed the letter to APA officials, and to this day we have not had an appointment with them. Had we been following rules, the appointment would have been made and not still pending. This is an example of what happens when we don't follow rules.

Though she was not mentioned by name, Mrs. Esteban felt the criticism was aimed at her. She countered with the argument that the group had been so busy with community problems it had never had time to develop procedural rules; moreover, she continued, the vice-president never cooperated and she had been burdened with almost all of the group's work. Then, recounting the group's history, a technique she used often when attacked, she denied the allegation that she was to blame for their difficulties.

But this time Alemán declared that the group's history was irrelevant. "What is relevant," he said, "is that as president you are *the* example, *the* model. It is therefore important for you to run the meetings according to procedure."

Zamora interposed: "This is not the time to find someone to blame. If there is guilt, we are all guilty. This discussion should cease right now!" But Mrs. Esteban, offended by Alemán's criticism, was not about to stop defending herself. To demonstrate how thoroughly she had prepared for the meeting she read the agenda aloud. Listed was practically all of the work which remained undone. When the list was read aloud, however, the effect was just the opposite of what she had intended. Now all the items on the agenda were open for discussion more or less at the same time and in no particular order. Motions were presented, buried in discussion, then brought up again almost transformed. Mrs. Amador, who had resigned from the confederation at one time because of the confusion at meetings, made an attempt at levity: "Look at this [confusion]! And we don't even serve alcoholic beverages. . . . The trouble is that the person who presents a motion and then hears it discussed can no longer remember what motion he has advanced."

When the discussion finally touched upon the need for a constitution, Alemán insisted that the meeting return to its original purpose — the election of a vice-president. Before nominating candidates, several persons attempted to define the traits of an ideal vice-president. Zamora said it must be ". . . a person who can collaborate with the president, is familiar with the work and history of the confederation, has participated in decisions, and has contact with outside agencies." With the exception of the first phrase, Zamora's description fitted Alemán, for it emphasized skill in dealing with the group's official business. But Antonio Tejada, having recently been deposed from the presidency of the Pan-American Association, emphasized traits of leadership binding together the vice-president and the members: "Three things must be present when you elect someone to represent you: sincerity, honor, and trust. If you don't feel the person has these characteristics, don't elect him. A leader needs the trust of his followers."

Neither definition was unusual or unexpected, but what came as a surprise was Eduardo Esteban's motion that the vice-president be a woman. He explained that the Hispanic organizations in Maplewood had always been run by men and had always failed. Therefore a woman should be the leader. But Esteban's motives were suspect to some members who knew that recently, despite his wife's strong objections, he had accepted Vicente de Serrano's offer of the presidency of the Pan-American Association (now renamed the Hispanic Democratic Club). As a result, the president of one of Maplewood's Puerto Rican organizations was the husband of the president of Maplewood's other Puerto Rican organization, its bitter rival.

In the election for the vice-presidency, eight votes were cast for Alemán and eight votes were split among the other four candidates. Estebán left the room in anger, for the one person neither he nor his wife wanted as vice-president had been elected.

Alemán accepted the congratulations of the group. When asked to say a few words, he turned to Mrs. Estebán and said, "My election as vice-president will in no way restrict me from criticizing you whenever I think you are doing things incorrectly. I shall do this exactly the same way I have done in the past. That will help us both as well as the group. Should we fail to call each other's attention to the things we do wrong, we would not be helping the Latin community."

After the meeting, Mrs. Estebán approached Alemán angrily. Criticism was important, she told him, but so were cooperation and patience. As the group's main officers, they had to appreciate the confederation's strength, which was greater than that of any other organizations formed over the years, and, she continued, "If we adhere to strong rules we will lose the membership of the confederation. I say this because I understand the capacity of the people in the Latin community. With them, you have to use rules in a very measured way. Use them, yes, but understand also that these are human beings with whom we are dealing."

Alemán objected: "But the problem we have here is that sometimes we follow rules and other times we do not. The person who comes for the first time gets confused, as we all do. He observes that there is no order and that the meeting is disorganized."

But Mrs. Estebán insisted: "The important thing is to learn how to mold the persons who come here."

On the surface, the disagreement appeared to involve different concerns, by no means mutually exclusive. Yet the issue was suffused with bitter feelings because Mrs. Estebán had heard recently through gossip that Alemán had vowed that he would make her a "good president." When she repeated this gossip to her husband, he, too, was offended, and advised her to resign from the presidency of the confederation because it was time consuming and embroiled her in conflict. The advice turned into outright pressure when both husband and wife interpreted Alemán's election as disapproval of her presidency and alienation of the members from each other. Mrs. Estebán explained to me:

> They do not like me anymore . . . I see myself moving away from the group. . . . When I go to meetings, I do not know what to do. . . . If they do not like me and think I have not done well for them, I shall leave the way open

for them to do things their own way. Then see what happens! Everybody wants rules, but they forget that Puerto Ricans do not like rules. Maybe it is time for me to leave the presidency to see if one of them can do better work. Everybody wants to be president.

But the business of the confederation went on. A week later, Alemán headed a group of members who went to the APA office to talk with Edgar Gordon about the referral office. Gordon denied the agency was remiss when it opened the office with only a coordinator and a secretary. He said that the antipoverty agency had not been consulted about the increase in staff and budget. Alemán ignored this and explained that if the office was limited to a two-person staff, its reputation among Puerto Ricans would be damaged and already the demand for referral services was so great that the secretary (his wife) had to leave her desk to do fieldwork in the Puerto Rican neighborhoods.

At this point, Mrs. Estebán interrupted: "I do not think we have to take the secretary from the office to do that work. The secretary is not supposed to leave the office anyway, unless there is an emergency. She is doing the work of a receptionist and she has to be there."

Disregarding her, Alemán repeated that, as the situation was, the office was hopelessly inadequate. Gordon told him, "But it is better than nothing."

Mrs. Estebán interrupted again: "We had nothing."

Alemán, trying to answer Gordon, said, "It is better than nothing, but. . ."

Gordon retorted, "It is better than what you had before."

Mrs. Estebán, agreeing with Gordon, repeated, "We had nothing before."

Alemán then asked why the agency had reversed its promise of giving the confederation administrative control of the office. Gordon replied that he had assumed the arrangement was agreeable to the confederation because APA had the know-how, the office space, and experience in such programs. Again, Mrs. Estebán agreed with Gordon, and finally the only concession Alemán could wring from him was an agreement to maintain a contingency fund of $150 at the office to help clients such as the Cuban refugee family through emergencies.

The group was no sooner outside of the APA office when Alemán attacked Mrs. Estebán for siding with the agency against the confederation. He told her bitterly, "I do not understand why you had to say that there is an interpreter at the hospital. They did not know that and when one is fighting for something, we have to keep such things to ourselves."

Mrs. Estebán shrugged: "But that is the truth and I cannot keep that information from them."

Alemán retorted, "They are the ones who should give us that information. You are always on the side of the Americans and do not defend our point of view."

"When?" She demanded. "Give me an example of what you are talking about."

"Remember the meeting with the mayor? You went there and the first thing you said was that Puerto Ricans do not have problems. Then, why were we there?"

Mrs. Estebán said in a conciliatory manner: "You cannot force these people."

Alemán raised his voice, "Indeed, we have to force them . . ."

But she interrupted, "No! No!"

He continued, ". . . with words and with the truth."

Mrs. Estebán tried to explain her philosophy: "We have to be humble. We cannot go in there . . . in an aggressive way. We have to go there with modesty and understanding. . . . We have to have patience. . . . We have to be conforming."

Alemán retorted: "When we go to ask for something, we first have to agree among ourselves."

She objected, "But I cannot."

And he argued, "You cannot ignore our problem. When we go there, you ignore our problem to be on their side."

Mrs. Estebán tried again to explain:

I am not ignoring our problem, because when I began all of this [the confederation] it was not out of ignoring our problem. If we do not get things by doing it the right way, we shall not get them by doing it wrong. Do you understand?

I am a person who has lived in poverty in the country and in rural areas. My father had ten children and never asked anyone for milk or for a spoon of salt with which to cook. If we had no salt, we cooked without it. Then why should we present ourselves to the Americans as a hungry people? Do you understand?

Alemán answered: "When we go to present something to them which is our right . . ."

"No! No!" she interrupted:

We have to present ourselves in a peaceful way. Be patient and understanding. . . . We cannot have everything. Right now, I would like to own a house with all kinds of facilities, but I cannot have them. I am not going to steal. I am not going to kill anybody to get what I need and want.

This is the way I feel. If you think otherwise, then we cannot come to an understanding. . . . You will have to look for someone who will fight your way.

But Alemán was insistent:

Every time we have gone there [APA], we have gone to fight for our rights. We have not gone to beg. . . . There are $10 million spent in this city, and we are not receiving the part we deserve. Those people are responsible and they are not doing what they ought to do. What they have given us is just for appearance . . . inconsequential, worthless, and this will bring discredit upon the confederation.

Increasingly heated and far-ranging, the argument returned finally to the old, much-debated issue of how to conduct meetings. Mrs. Estebán wanted relaxed and informal meetings; Alemán was for strict obedience to parliamentary rules. Irreconcilable differences seemed to separate the president and vice-president.

Mrs. Estebán did not attend the next meeting. As she told some of the members, it was not because she was ill, but because her husband was pressuring her to resign. Alemán, conducting the meeting, saw it as an opportunity to test his capacity to enforce orderly procedures. He was assisted by his friend Zamora who, after reading the minutes, warned the members that old business was to be taken up before new business could be introduced.

Alemán immediately reported the results of the visit to APA. It was unfortunate, he said, that the Hispanic Referral Office had not been inaugurated with a staff of eight persons, as the Neighborhood Advisory Board had recommended, or even with five, as the confederation had originally planned. Instead, it would have to remain a two-person organization until the beginning of the calendar year when possibly a new fieldworker would be added. Alemán confessed his disillusionment and then recognized Tejada who wished to speak.

"Their words," Tejada said, "are fictions and fantasies." He went on:

I know that the APA budget is $8 million a year, an amount which I remind you is not as trivial as the act of peeling a banana. Unless the agency has exorbitant salaries, more money should be available. APA is a secret organization. By this I mean that it is ruled by persons who do not come from the Puerto Rican population, the black population, or from other minorities. The agency is a group from the majority, and they treat the organization as a toy out of which they get big salaries. Now they throw a bone at us because we are a minority. . . . We should unite ourselves with the other minorities who have complaints against APA. United with them, we can write a formal petition to the president of the United States and then talk to him about this.

Alemán quickly ruled the proposal out of order because an appointment with the president of the United States represented new business, but much of the old business was entangled in APA's reversals of decisions and the general confusion of their relationship with the confederation. No decision was made about how to proceed, although it was agreed that from that time on Bartola, the tape recorder, would bear witness to APA's promises and commitments and, if necessary, testify to the agency's duplicity. Before the meeting ended, Zamora brought up Mrs. Estebán's name and cautioned the members against her attitude of "patience, patience, and more patience." This attitude, he said, would leave important projects undone.

The agenda having been discussed, Alemán requested and got a motion to end the meeting. If the members wanted, he said, new business could now be discussed, but no one seemed to want to stay on and talk. Although the meeting had been orderly, there had been a feeling of suppressed silence; each person seemed to stop and ponder his thoughts before speaking. Self-conscious and constricted, the usually talkative members gave an impression of regimentation and apathy. The meeting lacked the spontaneity and free-wheeling excitement characteristic of prior meetings.

The APA official newspaper carried a photograph of Carlos Otero, his wife, and Mrs. Estebán on its second page of the July issue of that year, and reported in the caption under the picture that Otero's appointment as "program coordinator" of the Hispanic Referral Office had been unanimously approved by the confederation. In the August issue of the APA newspaper, the referral office was given full publicity with the large black headline on its lead story for the front page: "HRO Serves Spanish-speaking." A smaller headline ran the news "Agencies team up to help new arrivals." And below these headings, the story ran for several paragraphs telling of the assistance given to the Cuban refugee family. All the public agencies mobilized to help the family were described in the article, but reference to the confederation came only in the very last paragraph:

> The program [the Hispanic Referral Office], assisted by the Hispanic Con-federation, a group of Spanish-speaking residents, and a wide variety of wel-fare agencies geared to help in situations of this kind, may eventually reach 5,000 people in Maplewood.

The taste of triumph was sweet but short-lived. By the time the August issue of the APA newsletter was circulated, the confederation was no longer meeting regularly, and the members had no opportunity to get together to enjoy the publicity and recognition they had finally received for "assisting" in the establishment of the referral office.

11

A Family Dynasty

•

Nine weeks passed without a meeting of the confederation, and some members
concluded that the group had collapsed. They had become accustomed to the
death of ethnic organizations. The birth of such organizations also was a part of
customary experience and, during this period, another Puerto Rican organization
was formed — The Latin Cultural Association of Maplewood. Much like the Pan-
American Association, the cultural association was started by confederation
members who felt that the parent group was neglecting important needs in the
migrant community — group activities that would "instill pride in" and "bring
prestige" to the ethnic ingroup by focusing upon Puerto Rican culture as the
"heritage of our ancestors." Whereas the confederation aimed to forge links between the migrant and the city's agencies, the cultural association sought to
revitalize the valued traditions of the ethnic community. As the founders of the
cultural association, Alfonso Vilá became president and Diego Zayas vice-president. Carlos Otero backed the group, and plans were made for banquets, dances,
parades, the annual coronation of a Puerto Rican queen, the development of
artistic talent in the ethnic community, and other such symbolic activities.

The rise of the new organization went unnoticed by the confederation as a
group. Also unnoticed was the departure of Carmen Sylvia García who during
the preceding eleven months had assisted me in the study. She was well liked by
the members, and later on several of them told me how embarrassed they were
that the confederation had failed to thank her for her understanding friendship.
At this time, Mrs. Sona Mahakian Caro became my assistant-in-research, and we
began to have long talks about the participant-observer role. I was not sure
whether or not the group would ever meet again, but if it did I planned to have
Mrs. Caro take Miss García's place.

Early in the second week of August, disturbing rumors spread in the racially
mixed neighborhood where the Hispanic Referral Office was located. Four blacks
were said to have attacked and beaten a Puerto Rican at a bar. A Puerto Rican
gang, then seeking revenge, assaulted an elderly black vagrant so savagely that he
was hospitalized in critical condition. The rumors flew; the blacks were expected

to retaliate; both camps were arming themselves for a fight. Even Alfonso Vilá, a timid and mild-mannered man, reacted to the feeling of an impending clash; he told me, "If they [the blacks] come looking for us, they will find us right here!"

The city authorities, agency workers, and neighborhood leaders were fearful of a riot. They organized separate meetings for the Puerto Rican and black residents of the neighborhood, then brought both groups together to discuss their grievances in the presence of representatives of the police, the department of education, and APA. Agency employees and local leaders walked the streets of the agitated inner-city neighborhood, listening to complaints, countering rumors, and attempting to alleviate fears. The effort was helped immeasurably by several days of heavy rainfall which cleared the streets, and finally peace, at least the usual form of peace, returned to the neighborhood.

Because he was the HRO coordinator, Carlos Otero was involved fully in the effort to still the hostility between the two neighborhood groups, and he was helped by Enrique Zamora and David Alemán, but the confederation as an organization did not play a role in averting the riot. Although Mrs. Esteban was aware of the group's potential value in mediating conflicts between Puerto Ricans and blacks and she still believed in the confederation's accomplishments, she was torn by cross-pressures which made her either unable or unwilling to activate the group again. The lapse of nine weeks without a meeting was an unprecedented gap in the group's life and an abrupt change from the preceding two months when there had been a meeting once a week. Mrs. Esteban was pushed one way, then another, and as a result she did not convene a meeting.

Alemán's election to the vice-presidency had upset her, not only because she often disagreed with him, but also because she took it as a personal rejection of her leadership. It seemed that the more power he gained, the less she possessed. If she resigned, Alemán would now step into the presidency, and this was the very thing she did not want. Once, in discussing this possibility, she told me: "Absolutely not! Alemán is impatient, much like my husband. If anyone should be president, it should be Alejandro Rico. He is humble and patient."

To my knowledge, no one had ever proposed Rico as president; very likely no one except Mrs. Esteban had ever thought of it, including Rico himself. A year before when he had been nominated for the vice-presidency, he had hastened to withdraw himself from candidacy pleading that he did not have the education for such a high office. Rico was quiet and very shy; he hardly ever spoke at meetings. Unlike Alemán and Zamora, he was not a rising leader in the group, yet his was the only name Mrs. Esteban could advance for the presidency.

Although Mrs. Esteban's husband had attended only a few meetings, the group made him angry. He could not understand why his wife was the target of such pointed criticism when her sacrifices for the confederation were obvious. Also, at times he felt that her attachment to the group conflicted with her

152

loyalty as a wife, so immediately after Alemán's election as vice-president, Mr. Esteban stormed out of the room, fully expecting his dutiful wife to follow him. When she did not, his anger at the group turned against her. He insisted that she resign as president, but she countered by asking Otero and me to explain to her husband how the group conducted its meetings. There was no need for me, however, either to deny or avoid this request because Mr. Esteban would not discuss his inalienable right of authority over his wife's activities.

Mrs. Esteban's devotion to the group was central to her problem of whether or not to resign from the presidency. As often as the members might reject her, her emotional identification with the confederation went beyond the membership itself. She thought the confederation belonged to her more than to anyone else. *She* had been the key member when the group originated and she had rescued it from the first crisis of disorganization. *She* had delivered it from Diego Zayas's untutored hands, protected it from Vicente de Serrano's political assault, led it into the mayor's office, and remained constant through the ups-and-downs of entanglements in APA politics. She was devoutly Catholic; often it seemed to me that her civic activities formed a part of her religious life and her support of the confederation was derived from a sacred oath.

Finally, Mrs. Esteban's commitment to the group won out over her desire to please her husband, and she resolved to continue as president at least for the time being. Then, in an apparent effort to mitigate her husband's anger, she urged him to participate in the group. Thus, Eduardo Esteban began to attend meetings regularly.

At last, Mrs. Esteban was ready to call another meeting. Fourteen persons came. After reading the minutes, the secretary, Zamora, rebuked the president: "Forty years have passed since our last meeting." He then went on to speak of the need for a constitution and legal incorporation. "Otherwise," he said, ". . .we shall remain a phantasm, a group of persons with no legal status. A constitution is the spirit of an organization." He presented the motion that all members participate in the writing of the constitution, but this was defeated five votes to two and the task was assigned to the group officers only. Zamora exclaimed in anger: "We are always avoiding the obligations of this organization. We cannot work this way! If only the officers are going to work, then why invite the other members? We need the cooperation of all. Our president has a lot of work and a lot of problems. She belongs to many organizations which prevents her from responding fully and with force to her duties as president. A constitution takes a lot of work. Why don't you cooperate?" But the members remained indifferent.

Since the last meeting of the group, Mrs. Alemán had quit her job as the secretary of the Hispanic Referral Office. Otero had replaced her without securing the consent of the confederation for the new secretary. Alemán expressed concern that the group was being left out, and he scolded Otero: "You had a lot to do with the writing of the HRO application which clearly states that appointments to the office are made only with the advice and consent of the confederation. In appointing a new secretary you did not consult the confederation."

Alemán also did not approve of Otero's choice. He complained:

> I did not see sincerity in her desire to help Puerto Ricans. . . . She told me she was there to help the good ones [Puerto Ricans], not the bad ones. I asked her how she distinguished between those who were good and bad and I told her, "My dear lady, you are not here to act as judge. You are here to listen to problems and to try to solve them through channels." That was my first conversation with the lady. Afterwards, she gossiped, telling me bad things about persons working in the office.

Zamora then recounted other unpleasant incidents involving the new secretary. Otero was taken by surprise by their criticisms, but a number of Puerto Rican clients who had turned to the office for help had voiced the same reactions to her, vowing never to go back to the office as long as she was there. Otero quickly defended himself. He had not sought the confederation's advice, he said, because there had been no meetings; if the president did not call meetings, then the vice-president should have done so. It was the group's fault, Otero explained, not his, that meetings had not been held, and the office could not function if it had to wait for the group to meet. If the members wanted to apply the advice-and-consent rule, he charged, then they should question the fact that Alfonso Vilá was working at the office. (Vilá had been transferred to HRO from another APA unit.)

Alemán countered that the office was working inefficiently. Otero replied that such an accusation had to be documented, but Zamora went on, charging that the new secretary did not have the interests of Puerto Ricans "in her heart." Mrs. Otero hastened to defend her husband: "No one can tell what is in a person's heart," she said.

Mrs. Estebán, who until then had kept out of the argument, commented sarcastically, "Perhaps they [Alemán and Zamora] are psychologists."

Thus, the first meeting after a nine-week lapse ended with a new source of conflict, this time involving the HRO coordinator. Still proud of the group and unaware of the effect the bickering among members might have on outsiders, Mrs. Estebán asked a priest she had invited to the meeting, "How did you like it?" He murmured that it had been interesting.

Five persons came to the next meeting a week later to begin work on the constitution. The first five articles, taken, with minor modifications, from a copy of the constitution of the Neighborhood Advisory Board brought along by Mrs. Estebán, specified the officers and their responsibilities: that elections would be held every two years by secret ballot; that meetings had to be held once a month on Thursdays with a quorum comprised of 50 percent of the active members; and that Roberts's *Rules of Order* would be followed at meetings.

Unlike the first five articles, the next two were distinctive to the group. Article 6 stated: "The Hispanic Confederation is not a religious or political organization. The confederation does not solve personal problems."

Article 7 defined membership and qualifications for voting: "(1) Any person who can speak or understand Spanish can become a member of the confederation. The spouse of a member can be a member even if he or she does not speak Spanish. (2) Before a member can vote on any issue, he must attend two meetings to acquaint himself with the discussion on the floor."

No one except Diego Zayas had ever insisted upon excluding Americans as members, but since he was not an officer and not present at the meeting, no one opposed the liberal qualifications for membership. The requirement of attendance at two meetings before voting was reached by a compromise between Mrs. Estebán and Alemán. He thought a newcomer's vote, based upon ignorance of the issue being discussed, would serve to nullify the informed vote of a long-standing member. She wanted persons to vote as soon as they came to a meeting so that they would immediately develop a sense of participation. The disagreement, however, lacked the usual sting of their debates. The work on the constituion was done with great lassitude, as if it were cumbersome and uninteresting, and the repeated plea that a constitution was needed did little to stimulate the members.

Two weeks later at the next meeting, Mrs. Estebán and Alemán disagreed again, this time on a proposal to limit each member to ten minutes of talk at a meeting. She said, "We must remember that we cannot restrict the members too much, because if we try to include something [in the constitution] which is specific and rigid, the members would not be able to discuss the issues the way they want to. They would quit."

The argument that an unlimited amount of talk by members disorganized the meetings did not sway her, and no such rule was written into the constitution.

The writing of the constitution was a half-hearted attempt. It produced only a few pages, which were soon relegated to the group's files, never to be brought out again. Those articles which were distinctive to the group did reflect important problems and decisions made during the confederation's history, but as a document the constitution had practically no effect upon the group.

Zamora and Alemán then submitted their resignations as officers. Zamora wanted to devote his evenings to studying English; he said if he did not master the language soon, he would return to Colombia, his home country. He also was dissatisfied with the members' passivity, as if they were not a part of the community, and he brought up another point: "As far as objectives or plans, I don't know what they are. I have been coming to meetings for a year and I have never known what the group's plans were. Things are done according to whoever speaks at the table, not according to a master plan, which never has been formed in the two-year history of the group."

Alemán explained, "I resign because the meetings last too long and too little is accomplished." He said another serious problem was the assumption that group action could proceed only with the full approval of all members. He believed that two or three persons should take the responsibility of pushing ahead, even if it meant disregarding some opinions. He concluded his explanation by asking: "How can one accomplish anything if the concern is whether you, you, or you like this or that?"

Thus, an ironic reversal revealed itself: the opponents of a strong leader now wanted a strong leader, and the president, once having been a strong leader, now wanted democratic procedures to widen the base of participation. Since the time the members had expressed dissatisfaction over the president's singular control of the group, Mrs. Estebán had displayed great sensitivity to their opinions. Sometimes after a motion was passed, she would still question if this was what the members wanted or if it was agreeable to them. She was reluctant to act without their unanimous support. When she explained that the group dictated to the president, not the president to the group, Zamora, who had been a key member in the revolt against her authority, replied: "Yes, that is the case ideally, but what happens here is that people come to interrupt and fight even though they do not know what decisions were made beforehand."

The group was at a low ebb. With the resignations from office of Alemán and Zamora, solidarity and momentum had been lost. I expected the confederation to collapse, but Mrs. Estebán acted as if she were insulated from the depressive mood of the group. A third resignation, this time from a newcomer who wanted to devote evenings to studying, provoked her to scold him: "Yours is a selfish plan. . . . You should devote yourself to working for the community. My problem is that I work all day, then go home and take care of the children, then go out and work for the church. After church, I work for the people [Puerto Ricans], helping them, and then I go home to study. I have to do all that and I do it. No one can do what I do."

Mr. Estebán added, "Yes, she works all day, comes home to cook, then goes out to work, sometimes until midnight." Despite her husband's pride in her busy schedule, Mrs. Estebán was well aware of the conflict in their home. She went on to admit that the burden was heavy: "Now, if a woman is single, she has more freedom. And if she is married but with no children, she has more time. But if she is a mother and a wife, she has many problems. The man rules the woman, and that is why a man walks with his head bare and a woman with hers covered."

The president still considered the confederation a going concern. She announced that at the next meeting there would be an election for new officers,

and 30 notices were mailed to the members announcing the meeting and election
on the first of December of that year. When only 14 persons came to the meeting,
Mrs. Estebán made reference to the article of the constitution which specified
that 50 percent of the active membership comprised a quorum. Although the
constitution had not been completed or adopted officially by the group, she
cancelled the election because of the lack of a quorum. Some members thought
the attendance was poor because the group was still relatively unknown in the
community and in need of publicity. They thought this meant advertising on the
radio and in newspapers; others suggested a raffle; still others were in favor of
serving free drinks at meetings. When Mrs. Estebán wondered if a party would be
effective, the members reacted with enthusiasm. Very quickly, they decided to
organize a Three Kings party the following month, on January 7, actually the day
after Epiphany. Eduardo Estebán then spoke up.

> I have organized five dances since I came here [to Maplewood]. The first
> dance we made tickets and gave each person five to sell, and we made $158.
> One man controlled the bar and he made $400. The second dance we made
> $100. We even raffled a gallon of rum. The third dance we made $60, the
> fourth $20, and the last one $1. We were going backwards, but they were good
> dances because there were no fights.

The trend of decreasing profits did not instill confidence in Mr. Estebán's
organizational skills, but he assured everyone that now he knew the trick of a
profitable dance: "To make money, you mix a quart of whiskey with a quart of
water before you sell it." His wife rebuked him sharply: the objective was to
attract new members, not to make a profit.

All of the confederation's work which remained undone was forgotten, as
were their many unresolved problems. The recruitment of new members was
certainly a part of the group's official business, but the talk among the members
made it clear that the main reason for the dance was to have fun. One man put
it this way: "Everything cannot be ... formalities ... and always calling upon
people to work and work. Some time must be spent in having a good time, and
we Puerto Ricans are enchanted by the idea of having a good time. Our blood is
tropical. We like entertainment and there is nothing that stimulates us more than
a dance."

Participation in the confederation had involved formalities and work. In fact,
compared to other Puerto Rican organizations, the group had become a sober,
almost austere, undertaking. The dance would satisfy the wish to relate to each
other in the group as convivial friends, not just as collaborators in a common
cause, but under the pretense that an official purpose — to attract new members
— was being served. The group's character required this form of mild self-decep-
tion.

At Mrs. Estebán's request, Enrique Zamora withdrew his resignation until after the new endeavor and took on the responsibility of organizing the dance. All the work had to be done during December and the first week of January. There was an immediate need for money to reserve a dance hall, to pay for the dance license and liquor permit, and to print the admission and raffle tickets. Several members voluntarily contributed money out of their own pockets and cooperated in the sale of raffle tickets. Five thousand raffle tickets were printed, with the prize a round-trip airplane ticket between New York and San Juan. Supplies were purchased including cases of whiskey. Arrangements were made for the dance hall, for advertising, for an out-of-town Puerto Rican band, for hiring two policemen to maintain order, and for invitations to the dance to be sent to eight local notables, including the mayor and the new director of APA.

The evening of the dance was cold and windy, and there was an accumulation of slush. Less than a hundred persons came to the dance. They sat in groups scattered about the cavernous hall which would have accommodated many times that number. Alfonso Vilá said his worst apprehensions were fulfilled. He had warned the members to sell tickets in advance. He knew from experience that once a person purchases a ticket, he will go regardless of the weather, but, Vilá said, his advice had been disregarded because, "When a person such as me brings up a point at a meeting and the point is rejected by a person such as Carlos Otero [his boss at HRO], I cannot continue to argue."

Even after the dance started Vilá attempted to attract more people. He went to Vicente de Serrano's Democratic Club, where a well-attended dance was in progress, and persuaded five persons there to come to the confederation's dance. Despite such last-minute efforts, however, when Zamora balanced the books there was a loss of $30. Of the eight notables invited, only one came.

At the next meeting, two weeks later, one member said the dance was a resounding success and all agreed. Never before had they had such an evening together, dancing, drinking, and having a good time. As they exchanged anecdotes about the dance, they laughed uproariously, relishing every incident in that brief interlude of fun. One member said the dance was successful because: "Even though we lost money, we gained in the favorable opinion of the police, the manager of the dance hall, and other persons who came. This view of the confederation will spread so that soon the view will be unlike the way other Puerto Ricans are viewed."

Indeed, several Americans had said, seemingly in surprise, how well the group had conducted itself. Mrs. Estebán was elated by the compliments, and she congratulated the members on their "high class" behavior. What kept many from the dance, she explained, was not so much inclement weather, but a fear that Hispano dances turn into brawls.

The treatment we [Puerto Ricans] receive is, to a large extent, our own fault.

You ought to see how some of us behave when we go to bars and drink and how the evenings end up. Fights break out in which chairs and bottles are used to attack bartenders, even the owners of the bars. It is for this reason that some bars will not serve Puerto Ricans, out of fear or hate toward us. How many do you think end up in jail on Sunday morning, persons with their ears mangled by the clubs of the police?

Zamora submitted a detailed typewritten report of the party's finances to the members, then reprimanded them for not cooperating with him until the last moment before the dance. He said they had to learn to accept the sharing of responsibilities. The objective of bringing new members into the group had not been attained (not one person joined the confederation because of the dance), but one member still in the mood created by the party suggested that preparations begin at once for another dance in order to get back the $30 lost.

Zamora became very angry:

The confederation has done nothing during the last seven months, in fact since we elected a vice-president. Since the Hispanic Referral Office opened, we have neither cooperated nor collaborated with it, and the office has not reported to the confederation. This is because of a lack of communication and because the group is not doing its work. We are in no position to have another party. We did not have a meeting for two months and then when we did meet we did not talk about anything relevant to the group. The group has been inactive and losing its value. . . . Our problem is not that someone from the outside is tearing down the group. We are tearing it down ourselves. We are regressing.

Indeed, four meetings had been devoted to planning the dance and one to discussing it afterwards, and the group still had the problem of finding the winner of the raffle ticket. He was not at the dance and his name and address on the raffle ticket were barely legible. After much discussion and some actual effort, he was identified and given the ticket to San Juan.

Zamora's stern words ended the group's six-week involvement in an activity viewed as fun, but the feeling of companionship awakened by the dance did not revitalize the group, for Mrs. Estebán was still pondering the troublesome cross-pressures arising from her role as president. She did not call a meeting for another five weeks. Finally, after making careful plans, she resolved to hold elections.

As the meeting began, she recounted the group's history to the other 26 participants before calling upon Otero to report on the Hispanic Referral Office. Otero spoke about the number of families seen, their problems, and what the office had done to help. But Antonio Tejada was not satisfied. He rose to attack Otero and called the office a fantasy. Mrs. Estebán cut him short. "We are in need of constructive questions," she said, "not destructive comments."

Then, another problem was brought up. An official of APA, who directed the poverty programs in the neighborhood where the office was located, had been bothered by what he called the suspicious attitude of the Puerto Ricans. He proposed that the confederation collaborate with other neighborhood groups. Zayas jumped up to argue: "We are Spanish! So, the very first thing the police commissioner and the mayor would say is, 'How come the Spanish people who have their own problems have to mix with other nationalities in order to fight?' . . . Are our problems the same as those of other nationalities? No, they are not! We must try it our way before joining other forces. Until then, we shall fight our own way."

Zayas then suddenly turned to Otero and asked in a hostile tone: "Is it not true that you told me the Hispanic Referral Office came into existence of its own accord?" A tense silence followed this attack. Otero at one time had been central to the emotions which bound the group together, and he was still a status superior. The members felt it was improper to put him on the spot in public as Zayas had done. Before anyone else could speak, Mrs. Estebán hurriedly said the topic had been discussed long enough and they would proceed with the election of new officers. Without further delay, she presented the candidates for presidency and vice-presidency: Fernando Vilá, one of her younger brothers, and Eduardo Estebán, her husband. She asked them to stand to be identified and then spoke of their qualifications:

> Fernando Vilá is my brother, but I did not select him because of this. Rather, I selected him because when I spoke with him, he demonstrated to me that he is a person of character, that he has drive, that he would assume the responsibilities of the organization. He demonstrated to me an interest and a desire to join the group, to work, to attain the goals of the organization. In church groups he is active and responsible. I have observed how responsible he is in his work.

Then she turned to Estebán:

> Here is Eduardo Estebán, my husband, with whom I have spoken about this. He was one of the very first to come to Maplewood and has worked for many years for the Hispanic community. He has served them as an interpreter even though he does not know much English. But he helps whoever asks for help and he has worked in the church and organized athletic clubs. He thinks of himself as responsible and wants to do good work so that we can continue.

Exactly a year and two days had passed since Mrs. Estebán had invoked a rule against nepotism to dismiss another brother, Alfonso Vilá, from the position of secretary of the confederation, but the rule was never discussed again, not even when the members self-consciously reviewed the group's legacy of norms for inclusion in the constitution. Now, after citing the candidates' qualifications, Mrs. Estebán suggested that with one election the group choose both of its top officers — the one with most votes would be president, the other would be vice-president.

There was a trace of discomfort among the members, as if they sensed an irregularity in the procedure. (Without further nominations, Mrs. Estebán's husband *and* her brother would have been elected.) Perhaps Mr. Estebán sensed the discomfort, for he suddenly withdrew his name, although he had known beforehand that his wife was going to nominate him. A motion was made and voted on to have separate elections for the two top offices and to nominate additional candidates. Fernando Vilá said he was in accord: "Let me defend my own skin. If you have other candidates, then present them. Whoever is elected, there ought not to be any doubts afterwards."

Diego Zayas then turned to an unknown woman sitting by him, asked her name, and nominated her for the presidency, but his attempt to devalue the procedure backfired as the woman turned out to be the wife of still another of Mrs. Estebán's brothers. Mrs. Estebán ruled her out as a candidate, not on the grounds of kinship but because the well-prepared president had planned to nominate her as secretary. Had the plan succeeded, the president, vice-president and secretary would all have been Mrs. Estebán's relatives.

During the election Fernando Vilá became president with 11 of the 13 votes; Irma Amador, vice-president with 10 of the 17 votes; and Mrs. Estebán's sister-in-law became the secretary with 14 of the 18 votes cast. Because the Three Kings dance had involved the management of money and other dances might be held in the future, the office of treasurer was added to the slate, and a newcomer was elected to it.

Mrs. Amador expressed her surprise at the ubiquity of the members of the Estebán-Vilá family. Mrs. Estebán asked her not to blame the family, and Mrs. Amador replied that she meant no criticism, rather just the opposite; she was struck with the vast experience of the family in directing organizations such as the confederation.

Mrs. Estebán's tenure of office came to an end after ten months as vice-president and 18 as president. As she looked back upon this experience, she confided to me, "I don't think the confederation could have accomplished more than it did." It was necessary to emphasize this point because she had been criticized, particularly by Alemán. She believed Alemán had always coveted leadership of the group, but if this meant a desire to be president, his actions were inconsistent with the motives she imputed to him. He had resigned as vice-president and did not even come to the meeting called to hold elections. Zamora likewise did not appear at the meeting. In addition, Alemán had confided to me what he thought was one of his basic flaws — an inability or unwillingness to persevere. He believed that perseverance was necessary for leadership, but when things went wrong he was quickly disillusioned and wanted to quit the group. His one driving interest in life was to write poetry and music.

Mrs. Estebán's election plan fell short of complete success, but she did begin a family dynasty within the confederation. It was soon clear, however, that even then she was not ready to relinquish the power she had wielded for so long. As the former president, she declared herself an ex officio member of all committees and proceeded to convene a meeting on her own one week after elections. The purpose was "to orient" the new officers. She said, "The fact that I retired as president does not mean that I will be out of the group. I intend to continue as a member and I shall come to meetings. I will always cooperate with the group. You people must continue to work according to the principles and objectives of the confederation."

She instructed the new officers to invite representatives from the police, the local hospital, and the welfare department to speak to the group, thus reverting to a plan the group had once made but not carried out. Although she had often been critical of Otero in private, now for the first time in public she expressed her growing dissatisfaction with the Hispanic Referral Office. "If the coordinator does not think he has enough staff to do the job, then he is supposed to communicate this difficulty to us as well as the needs which exist in the community. If he does not do this, the confederation cannot do a thing. If we are aware that something is lacking, then we will try to do something right away."

Otero was not at the meeting, but he heard through gossip that Mrs. Estebán was about to demand from him an accounting of the office's work beyond what he had already reported at the election meeting. He felt the office could not improve its service as long as it remained understaffed. Since its opening, he had been overwhelmed with clients seeking help on problems of abortion, crime, mental illness, unemployment, housing, and even marital disagreements. When the clients did not get the help they expected, their complaints reverberated throughout the migrant community. Otero felt he was losing the support of both the Hispanic community and the confederation for reasons that were beyond his control.

The problem was likely to become even worse as a result of the reorganization of APA planned by its new director, which involved the placement of all subunits into the main hierarchy of command. This meant that HRO was to be put under the control of the neighborhood unit where it was housed, separating it from APA's central office by an intervening administrative level. Otero thought such an arrangement would reduce the office's power in the agency's inner circle because, in effect, it demoted the office and the coordinator himself, and would restrict the office to serving the immediate neighborhood only.

Since the opening of the office, Otero's involvement in the confederation had been casual and his attendance irregular, but now, feeling pressured from all sides, he sought the group's support and attempted to use it as leverage against APA. At a meeting five weeks after the election, he rallied the members with the following: "The idea is being proposed that the office serve only this neighborhood. You should think this over very seriously. With such a change the office would not be for all the Hispanos in the city, and this is what the APA director wants. I am not in agreement with this plan, and I think it is something which should be discussed in the confederation."

Turning from a new problem to an old problem, he continued, "Additional people [staff] are needed. I think it is time for the confederation again to present its ideas and plans to the directors of APA. Three persons [in the office] are not sufficient to provide all the services required in this city. . . ." He recommended that ". . . a letter be sent to the director and also to his assistant. Tell him that you are not happy with the arrangements being made and that you want to discuss the issue with him personally. Send copies of the letter to others. Do this as soon as possible. . . ."

Otero ended with a nostalgic reference to what the group had once accomplished: "Then, there were people who really worked in order to establish this office, people who went to APA not just to say hello and good morning, but to argue strongly for their points. They achieved success. Now the critical question is: Are you going to continue as you are doing, or are you going to revert to the old ways of accomplishing things?"

Otero's speech was successful in arousing the members' emotions, but at the start of the next meeting a week later, the new president, Fernando Vilá, expressed deep concern over APA's attempt t ⸝ limit the confederation to the immediate neighborhood. Both Zamora and Alemán, who had returned to the group, corrected Fernando: It was the office, not the confederation, that would be affected by APA's reorganization, they said. Fernando admitted that he did not know the difference between the two, and it became evident that he had not understood Otero's passionate speech. The situation was explained to him.

Because she was a member of long standing, the new vice-president *did* understand the problem, and now Mrs. Amador attempted to re-create the sense of urgency Otero had evoked: "Is the confederation going to remain silent until APA has decided to restrict the services of the office to this neighborhood? Are we going to come around only after they have done this?"

Moved by her words but not sure how to justify the complaints they wanted to take to APA, the others turned to the HRO application, and there they found legitimate reasons for complaint: "In all other areas," the application stated, "the identification of programs, advice, and in day-to-day operations of the office, the evaluation of programs, the confederation is to be consulted." The confederation had never been consulted on how the office would be affected by the agency's reorganization.

In planning what they would say during the meeting with APA, the members thought of asking for two additional employees for the office, but a motion was passed later to ask for four. Their strategy was that if they asked for two they would get one, and if they asked for four they might get two. This was a new feeling which had its roots in the belief that APA had not dealt honorably with the confederation.

Otero was asked to draw up a list of names of Puerto Ricans who could be employed in the office or elsewhere in APA. Pressures would be put upon the agency to recruit from that list. In addition, there would be a demand that *all* Puerto Rican employees of APA, regardless of where they worked, be put under the office's control. The members looked upon the agency's recent employment of Puerto Ricans in other poverty programs as a calculated effort to subvert the Hispanic Referral Office; since these Puerto Ricans served both Puerto Rican and American clients, the fact that they were Puerto Rican established an appearance of more services being offered the Hispanic community than was actually so. If all Puerto Rican employees of APA, however, worked for the office, there would be a real increase in the services offered the Hispanic community.

Decisions were made on each and every request to be presented to APA. A letter was written to the new director asking for an appointment, a committee was designated for the visit, and three meetings were held in preparation for the visit. But once again confusion returned to the confederation; the meetings were chaotic and the participants were bewildered.

In endeavoring to "orient" the new president, Mrs. Estebán prompted his every action. She was the dominant member of her large extended family, and Fernando was her younger brother by eleven years. As the former president, older sister, and the person who put him into office, she insisted on being heard. Fernando was uncertain in his new role as president. Knowing he had much to learn, he was, at first, overwhelmed by his sister's efforts to orient him, but not so the other members. Otero urged her not to be so critical of her brother. Alemán insisted that it was the new president's responsibility to conduct an orderly meeting. Soon Fernando began to react to her in the same way. At first he tried a feeble plea: "Cristina, with your permission, please." But later he became stronger, even caustic: "Excuse me, I let you get it out of your system and I hope you are through because you have taken all the time we have for this meeting."

When she became aware of the group's reaction, Mrs. Estebán remembered the determined efforts she had made as president to suppress her own talkativeness, and she was moved to complain: "Now that I am no longer president, I am speaking, but now they don't want to let me speak." She nonetheless still attempted to influence specific decisions. When the group was deciding on the spokesman for the visit to APA, she argued, "We have to give a chance to a new person. These people [at APA] are tired of seeing the same persons, and soon they will lose respect for us. If they see a new person who can gain their respect, they will conclude that among us there are not just one or two leaders, but three or four."

I had the feeling that Mrs. Estebán's advice was designed to eliminate Alemán from his customary role as spokesman at conferences with APA, but Alemán himself presented a motion that the new president speak for the confederation. Turning to Fernando, Alemán advised him to impress upon APA the unmistakable fact that everything done for Maplewood's Puerto Ricans had resulted from the group's initiative, not from the agency's.

The night before the appointment with the assistant director of APA, Edgar Gordon, a crisis arose: Fernando lost his voice, and there was no substitute for him. The vice-president, Mrs. Amador, was going to be out of town. Zamora was not fluent in English. Mrs. Estebán worked full time for APA and could not speak for the group without presenting a conflict of interest. Otero, as HRO coordinator, thought he should not even be at the meeting. Alemán was available, but his name was not brought up as a possibility.

Mrs. Estebán finally changed her mind and decided she would be the spokesman. Then, the group reverted once again to the practice of role-playing to rehearse the meeting, with Otero, as usual, pretending to be the top official – this time Edgar Gordon. His questions were tough: "What do you want, a hundred persons working at the office?" As Mrs. Estebán and the others, too, attempted to answer, the resultant clamor plunged the meeting into chaos. So confused was the interaction that at one time Mrs. Estebán assumed a reversal of roles and taking Gordon's part, she criticized Otero, as the group spokesman, for not submitting reports to APA's central office and for "working in a crazy fashion." This method of criticism enabled Mrs. Estebán to attack Otero without becoming personal. Soon, it became impossible to tell whether the arguments were role-playing or not. Noticing this, Fernando turned to his sister and whispered: "For a minute I thought you would be the best person to serve as spokesman."

She replied: "Why, because I have so much information at hand?"

"Well," he whispered back, "I figured that the way you talk you would confuse Gordon, but now I see that Gordon [Otero] has confused you. . . . Cristina is lost. She does not know what we are trying to do."

But all was not lost! Mrs. Estebán apologized for the confusion. Fernando's voice improved overnight, and he was able to act as spokesman the next day.

Edgar Gordon began the meeting with the reminder that the Hispanic Referral Office had been started with APA's surplus funds, but since then APA's funding had been cut back drastically by the Office of Economic Opportunity. For this reason, the new director and Gordon, as assistant director, were intent upon reorganizing the agency and "cutting and slashing wherever we can." Unless a number of congressional amendments were passed in Washington, he said, there was no possibility of increasing the office's budget. He concluded with an apology for not having officially apprised the confederation of APA's financial crisis.

Zamora understood Gordon, but his spoken English was not fluent and he asked me to translate his remarks into English. He said that everyone knew about the funding cutbacks, but why had APA recently employed some Puerto Ricans ". . . [who] were hired by APA but not assigned to HRO. You present the case of a very austere financial program, but the hiring of these persons is not consistent with an austerity program. They very well could have been assigned to the office which is in dire need of help. The inevitable conclusion is that APA has either forgotten or ignored HRO."

Gordon replied that the persons named were employed in old, not new, vacancies, and their being Puerto Rican attested to the agency's concern for this population. Contractual agreements with the funding agencies prohibited the assignment of the new employees to the office, he said. They had to work in the jobs designated. Then he admitted to having always opposed an office such as HRO with a specialized ethnic function because, he said, "We see our neighborhoods, not as racial entities or nationality groups, but as total communities with problems. There *are* problems of people who do not speak English well . . . but the idea is that everyone in the neighborhood can come to [an APA unit] to be served."

Although Otero had not come to the meeting, Mrs. Otero was present, and she disagreed with Gordon: "The reason for the creation of HRO was the realization that the Spanish-speaking people of Maplewood have special problems, that basically they are immigrants. . . . Why have the office if there is the view that other neighborhood offices can take care of their own Spanish-speaking residents? Why have an office? It was created to serve the Spanish-speaking people of the whole city."

She added that all Puerto Ricans in the agency should be made available to the coordinator of the office. Gordon reacted to this suggestion quickly.

> They are! Let me say one thing too. This may come as a criticism of your good husband, but if Carlos would use our services better, and I mean this sincerely, if he would stop being a one-man gang, or a two-man gang, because he and his secretary are running around like chickens without their heads doing 500 jobs, what he has to do is use our neighborhood offices more, and this is where he is falling down, by not using the resources available to him . . . and not try to do everything himself.

Gordon went on to explain that he could not deal with "ethereal hocus-pocus" allegations of persons not cooperating with Otero. If true, he said, the charges should be documented with specific details. The agency's reorganization would put HRO under the control of the local neighborhood unit, but the office itself could continue to give citywide service. He brought the meeting to an end by saying that he had always enjoyed meeting with the confederation.

Fernando Vilá had met his first test as the group's leader successfully. Even though he had said little, the members felt he had represented the confederation very well. Perhaps he knew this, for he began the next meeting with notable self-assurance: "Let me begin the meeting. If all of you who are sitting away from the table would like to come up a little closer, please do. . . ."

In the discussion of the meeting with Gordon that followed, the members realized that, although well-intended, Otero's attempts to deal with the specific needs of every client had led to a diffusion of effort with few cumulative gains for the migrant community. Alemán thought the office needed to identify the common problems and interests of Maplewood's Puerto Ricans, then embark on organizational efforts to make the community a self-sustaining force independent of services of local agencies. Many differences of opinion separated Alemán from Mrs. Estebán, but on this they agreed, as did Fernando.

Thirty-two months before, Frank Joyce had been concerned with the need for Puerto Ricans to join community organizations, but the Puerto Ricans preferred to have their own organizations. Now the confederation had come full circle and returned to the idea that had given it birth.

PART V

Research Methods, Interpretation, and Conclusions

12

The Methods
of Research

•

Before the study of the confederation began, field experiences with Puerto Rican informants had indicated the need to study in depth and detail the organizational problems of urban migrants. The accounts of Puerto Rican informants demonstrated a recent history of group failures and provided information on the organization, composition, and goals of some groups. They also alluded to problems that the groups experienced, from disruptive effects of partisan politics to inadequacies of leadership, but the accounts provided little understanding of how such problems penetrated the groups over time as the members sought to carry on the group's affairs. No informant was able to give the life history of a group from birth to death in sufficient detail to enable the accurate identification of sequences of events, interpersonal cleavages, and group processes. Memories of experiences of failures tended to fade quickly. Although the informants' accounts were adequate for the specification of the study's original observation — the brittleness of Puerto Rican organizations — and valuable as an adjunct to observational data, alone, they were inadequate as data to explain why and in what way Puerto Rican organizations had such a fragile character. Thus, to study the organizational life of the Puerto Ricans, it was necessary to use the participant-observer method. Fortunately, the Hispanic Confederation of Maplewood had been formed only five months before I learned of its existence, and I was able to join it.

The narrative of the Hispanic Confederation of Maplewood — including the epilogue — covers a 44-month period, from November 1964 to July 1968. The group's origins and activities during the first five months of its life were studied by interviews with key informants. During the next ten months we attended 20 of the group's 22 meetings and took detailed field notes. (Those who took part in the two meetings I missed were interviewed about them.) During the following 16 months we attended and tape-recorded all of the confederation's 46 meetings. During the last 13 months we kept in touch with the group by going to occasional meetings, talking with the members, and examining the minutes of the meetings. We kept attendance records and seating charts of each meeting we attended.

To complement the data on meetings, we conducted systematic interviews with group members and intensive interviews with the group's leaders, leaders of other Puerto Rican organizations, city officials, and other persons who came into contact with the confederation. Every telephone conversation, casual contact with a person, formal or informal activity of relevance to the group was written up as a field report. Leaflets, membership lists, letters, documents — almost all of the group's written products — became part of the data, as did local newspaper accounts concerning Maplewood's Puerto Rican community.

Since the confederation was an action group seeking to develop links between the Puerto Rican minority and the dominant North American majority, a day-by-day involvement in both cultures was necessary. Fieldwork had to be coordinated with the group's progress through a network of persons and organizations enmeshing both cultures. It covered a wide range of persons from the city's top politician and executive, the mayor at city hall, to the most humble Puerto Rican living in a deteriorated inner-city neighborhood, speaking few if any words of English and scarcely literate in his own tongue. Between the top and the bottom, there were lawyers working on behalf of the poor, coordinators of neighborhood school programs, agency directors, antipoverty workers and officials, a Puerto Rican political boss and his aides, and other persons in the city's bureaucratic and social structure.

Although I became an advisor to the confederation at the invitation of the group's first president, my main purpose was to observe, collect data, and study the Puerto Ricans' experiences in forming and maintaining an organization, and I was troubled by the possible disparity between the roles of advisor and researcher. The members' identification of me as a Puerto Rican provided me with an inside view of their activities, as well as the meanings they attributed to events and their feelings about them. The role of advisor — member of the ethnic ingroup — seemed to require strong obligations to the group. The members knew that I was a university professor and presumably had skills, knowledge, and social contacts of value to them, but the potential to influence group decisions struck me as being in conflict with the anomic social process I wanted to study. Had I urged the members to attend meetings, attempted to teach them how to conduct meetings and define goals, or had I represented the group in contacts with the city's agencies, my participation in the group could have obscured sources of instability; or, for that matter, it could have created a new, unusual pattern of disruption. In either case my participation would have affected the internal life of the group and its future trajectory, and I wanted to avoid both possibilities.

From the beginning I decided not to conceal from the group my role as a researcher. As such, I would be observing the members of the group, writing about them in field notes, and eventually reporting their activities in publications that would result from the study. Consequently, they had a right to know what I was doing. I felt also that the role of a concealed researcher would have imposed upon me the stress of guilt feelings about hiding my true motives from persons with whom I would be spending many hours, days, and months. As the study eventually unfolded through successive stages of the group's life, it would, in fact, have been impossible to conceal the research. To eliminate ambiguity on this point, however, I adopted the policy of telling the group members and those persons with whom the group came into contact that I was doing a study. At the same time, I gave assurances that the names of the persons involved would not be reported in the research publications.

At first, the idea of sociological research was not well understood by the group members. One suggested that what I was really doing was a history of the confederation, an accurate observation which made the study understandable to them. Subsequently, I made it standard practice to explain the research as a history of the confederation, and it was understood in these terms. On several occasions, the group members called my attention to some event they considered important to the history of the group and urged that it be included in the notes I took. I always followed their suggestions, seeking by means of casual conversations to determine why they thought the event was important. The tasks of historian, thus, were often shared with the members of the group.

Because Puerto Rican groups tended to be anomic, my foremost concern when I joined the confederation was to do nothing that would either obscure or counteract the group's instability. This meant that at meetings I had to be very passive and noncommittal. I had to check any inclination to act out or to react with spontaneity and interest. This was an unnatural and difficult stance both for me and for the group. When I should have been listening to and observing the members, I was preoccupied with the requirement of self-discipline, and note-taking was difficult, indeed. Overly concerned with self-control, I often overlooked what was transpiring in the group.

The confederation, too, suffered from the effects of my highly constricted participation. Socially, I was marginal to their activities and an enigma because they knew relatively little about me. They glanced at me inquisitively, even at times suspiciously, feeling perhaps that my silence meant disapproval of what they did.

Strangers sometimes came to meetings as new members, but soon they would be known and accepted as they participated in the give-and-take. The role of stranger, therefore, was transitional, involving a short phase of participation which lasted only until the outsider became a member of the ingroup. This process, of course, was operative only among those who were identified as Puerto Rican, for American consultants and visitors always tended to remain outside the group's inner life. But to be a member of the ethnic group and to remain a stranger, as I did, departed from what was customary; it made my participation incongruous. Thus, by striving to avoid one error of participation, I was committing another error — the creation of tensions stemming from my continuing role as a stranger in a primary-group context.

Finally, Mrs. Estebán, then vice-president, told me that she and the others wanted to know more about me and that she wanted me to contribute more to the group. Her comments alerted me to the problem I was creating. The wish to observe yet not influence was an unattainable ideal, but it conditioned me to play the role of advisor as passively as I could. Soon I realized that extreme passivity was not the same as not interfering. I was not studying the group to observe the effects of my own anomalous intrusion into it, but without knowing it I was attempting to study the group as if my presence could be subtracted from the situation. Not only was this not possible, but also it tended to frame the problem of participation in the wrong terms. The choice was not between affecting or not affecting the group: observation was necessarily linked to participation, and participation invariably would affect the group. The actual problem was to achieve a form of participation which would minimize those effects strongly conducive to group stability or instability, yet allow me to remain in the group. There was no immediate solution to this problem. Decisions had to be considered as experimental and tentative, subject to revision. Whatever form of participation was adopted, I could never be sure that it was the best response to the problem.

As a result of Mrs. Estebán's comments, whenever I met the group members at meetings and elsewhere I began to talk about myself, my wife and children, relatives in Puerto Rico, and the incidental occurrences of the day. Social distance was reduced. Very soon I was no longer a stranger to them and we became close and enduring friends. Group meetings became more enjoyable and less tiring, and the field notes taken were more thorough and detailed.

On the other hand, the requests that I contribute to the group were more troublesome. Each request had to be considered carefully because there was no turning back. To refuse to do something I had done before would violate an ethical norm and create tensions associated with my participation, again leading to the type of error involved in my initial passivity. But to have responded fully to all of the requests would certainly have escalated my participation into some form of leadership, with the members depending on me. This was exactly what I had planned to avoid when I joined the group. Thus, my role had to undergo continuous examination.

After the confederation experienced an internal crisis and the political assault, group changes enlarged the scope of the study and accentuated the dilemmas of the participant-observer role. Along with the introduction of vigorous leadership, there were incipient signs that the group's original character was changing. This was apparent at the surface of group meetings, and it fascinated me. I was delighted to be in a position to observe such change directly and in detail. What appeared at first to be an unexpected research bonus turned into one of the study's main objectives — the delineation of social change in a small group — but the changes themselves reinforced the need for caution in the participant-observer role. I did not want my contributions to be an intrinsic part of the group's evolution.

The problem, then, was to minimize two types of error: doing too much for the group, thus stabilizing it and influencing its changing character; or doing too little, which would inject a unique but persistent source of tension and possibly threaten my participation. The effort to cope with such errors and develop a suitable form of participation depended, however, upon my status as a Puerto Rican university professor gathering data for a history of the confederation.

Following the practice of many, if not most, first-generation Puerto Rican migrants who preserve the tradition of maternal surnames in their names, I introduced myself as Lloyd Rogler Canino. From then on I was called Rogler or Canino or both. I told them also that I was born and raised in Puerto Rico and that most of my relatives were still on the island. Because of my maternal surname, background, and fluency in Spanish, they accepted me as Puerto Rican. The fact of having a Puerto Rican mother weighed heavily in my inclusion in the ethnic ingroup. David Alemán affirmed this point when I asked him if I was identified as an American in the Hispano community: "No! Just the fact that your mother is Puerto Rican is good enough for them [the Hispanos], good enough for anybody." Thus, in the ritual introductions of members at the start of meetings, Mrs. Esteban identified me as follows: "When he speaks English, he is an American. When he speaks Spanish, he is Puerto Rican. But he is really Puerto Rican. Although when people hear his name, Rogler, it is hard for them to believe he is Puerto Rican."

From their viewpoint, my profession made me an unusual Puerto Rican, and some members were surprised that in Maplewood a Puerto Rican could be a professor. At political rallies Vicente de Serrano always introduced me along with the local notables and candidates for office in an effort to prove that not all Puerto Ricans were uneducated. Although directed primarily at the Americans in the audience, the introduction always evoked the loudest round of applause of the evening from the Puerto Ricans. My profession tended to place me in the American world, yet the ambiguity between my ethnic identity and my profession was resolved quickly by the confederation's members in favor of the ethnic ingroup. To them I was an "educated" or "successful" Puerto Rican.

An advantage of this status was that it made possible my moving back and forth between the two cultural worlds to collect data. To the confederation's members it was natural that I could, if I wanted, be a part of both worlds, but it could well have obligated me to become a pervasive help-giver in the confederation and among the members. Although attenuated, the traditional *patrón* system is still present on the island and is brought to the mainland by the first-generation migrants. The word *patrón* itself is not common in the migrant vernacular, but the patterned interpersonal relationship it stands for easily reappears in the new setting when the social situation is appropriate — when a higher-status person acts as the social, moral, and economic guardian of a less fortunate compatriot in return for a debt of loyalty. In Maplewood, the pattern functioned most clearly in providing cultural support for Serrano's role as political boss, but in my case it accentuated the error I might have committed by doing too much for the group.

From the beginning of my participation in the confederation, I made it a rule that any form of surreptitiousness was forbidden. At meetings, notes were taken in full view of the members and expanded afterwards. The schedule we worked from was in plain sight during interviews, as was the tape recorder when it was used at meetings, conferences between the group and public officials, and interviews. The tape recorder was introduced to the members as an aid to data collection in the study, with the understanding that it would be turned off immediately at the request of any member. To my knowledge, no such request was ever made. The only member who expressed discomfort over the tape recorder was Fernando Vilá, who thought he had a poor speaking voice. Otherwise, the taping was accepted with ease, and it appeared to create little or no discomfort among the members. The tape recorder was given the name of Bartola by my first assistant-in-research (Miss Carmen Sylvia García), and Bartola came to be known as one of the most reliable participants, for she was always at meetings and had, by all odds, the most accurate memory in the group. Late in the study, Bartola made a significant contribution to the group by serving as an official witness to the promises the antipoverty agency made to the confederation (see the epilogue).

At one time Mrs. Estebán suggested that her telephone conversations be taped because she believed (and I agreed) that the information she was providing was valuable to the group's history. But, had her suggestion been accepted, word would have soon gotten out that her telephone calls were being recorded. Then other persons who telephoned me might have thought their comments, too, were being taped. The study might have become suspect, not only by members of the confederation but in the migrant community as well. I thanked her for her interest in the accuracy and completeness of the information upon which the history would be based, but I rejected her offer.

Being known as the group historian and as an "educated" Puerto Rican added flexibility to the participant-observer role. It made understandable cross-cultural contacts and my desire to talk to as many different persons as possible who came into contact with the group. Mrs. Estebán once pointedly reminded me that a valid history of the confederation had to include the viewpoint of the political boss who was her opponent. Along with her concern that it be a complete history, several times she hinted at how interesting it would be for her to know what other persons were telling us, but the information each person provided us was kept in strict confidence and never passed on.

By distributing contacts with members more or less evenly, I established social relationships with many, if not most, of the participants. A norm of inclusion — not exclusion — was practiced in order to maintain communication with as many persons as possible. Data collection made this necessary, but important also was that I not create the impression of alliance to, or collusion with, any single member or subgroup in the confederation. Thus, the pattern of interpersonal relations linked to the participant-observer role differed from what was customary in the group because other members tended to sort themselves into friendship cliques, opposing factions, and subgroups of acquaintances.

Briefly put, in the early days of the study the participant-observer role was partly planned, but it was crescive too, evolving out of unexpected contingencies. By the time the confederation had weathered the political assault, the role had become sufficiently stable and predictable to permit it to be defined verbally. Then it became possible to state explicitly and quite fully the underlying problems and experiences out of which it grew, the prescriptions and proscriptions governing the conduct of the person in the role, and the tone of relationships one should have with other persons. In sum, the role could be taught to another person. Thus, the confederation acquired a second observer, Miss Carmen Sylvia García, who joined the group as my assistant in the study. A trained psychiatric social worker by profession, with a master's degree, Miss García had had many years of experience interviewing in Puerto Rico. Because of her experience, training, and temperament, she was ideally suited to help gather data for the study. She was quiet, intelligent, and competent, but perhaps equally important was her highly developed capacity for relating herself to her compatriots with sensitivity and warmth; without seeming to intrude, she became a friend and confidant.

Before I introduced Miss García to the group as my research assistant, I had long talks with her about the background and purpose of the study, the confederation and its members, and the role of the participant-observer. Unlike the other newcomers, she knew a great deal about the group before ever meeting its members. Also unlike them, she was to guide her participation according to the role of the participant-observer.

At Mrs. Esteban's request, the meetings were held at the university. While I had to be present to make the necessary arrangements, I did not want the members to feel obligated to schedule group meetings or other activities according to my availability. At the same time, the longitudinal character of the study made it imperative to collect information on each and every group activity, preferably through observation. In fact, I was unable to be present at the meeting at which the group deposed its first president, Diego Zayas. Immediately afterwards, I had

177

the difficult task of piecing together the occurrences at the meeting by interviewing the key participants. I wanted never again to lose an opportunity to observe directly a critical turning point in the group's life. Miss García's assistance assured continuity, added flexibility to the study, and alleviated my anxieties that a professional or personal obligation might make it difficult for me to be present. She was always there when I had to be away. Usually, however, we both attended meetings, sitting apart and hardly speaking to each other. Afterwards, we pooled our notes and observations to draft a report of the evening's activities. To supplement our data outside of the meetings we usually worked separately, but in coordination, to develop solid friendships with members, visiting them in their homes, at work, and in their neighborhoods, accompanying them to local agencies, and conducting long interviews with them. Thus, Miss García's participation in the study permitted increased data collection of events both during meetings and outside of these activities.

After Miss García left Maplewood, the role of participant-observer was taught to another assistant-in-research, Mrs. Sona Mahakian Caro. Although born and raised in the United States, Mrs. Caro had lived for many years in one of the Spanish-speaking republics of the Caribbean, was married to a Latin American, and was completely fluent in Spanish. She had a deep appreciation for Latin American culture, which was matched by her understanding of it. In conversation, her gestures, the intonation and rhythm of her spoken Spanish, and the quickness with which she responded to the nuances of interaction and meaning made her an authentic Latin. At the time I taught Mrs. Caro the role of participant-observer, the confederation was not meeting, and it was not certain that it would ever meet again. But it did, and when the members met Mrs. Caro, they liked and accepted her.

Officially, I served the group as translator and letter writer, and from the summer of 1965 to the winter of 1966-67 by making available a meeting place at the university. I translated only at those meetings at which Americans spoke to the group and only when there were Puerto Ricans who did not understand English. At Mrs. Estebán's request, I wrote most of the group's letters with the agreement that a designated member of the group would tell me what was to be included at the time the letter was dictated. I did this to make sure the content was the group's responsibility, not mine. Such letters always carried the president's signature.

We began to meet at the university after the elementary school where the group had been meeting was found to be locked. Mrs. Estebán immediately urged that I continue to make the room available because, in her words, "It is motivating for Puerto Ricans to come to the university; it is something prestigious for them. Also it helps to improve the image of Puerto Ricans." The very reasons she advanced worried me, because I did not want their meeting at the university to serve as a stimulus to participation. To my surprise, however, the opinions of the other members on this subject were by no means as favorable as the president supposed. If it was an inducement to some members, it was not for all of them. One said, "Some persons do not like to go there because the big name [of the university] scares them. We should have an informal place in which to meet." Another one considered it an inconvenience because "persons feel they should dress up to go there." I believe that as time went by, the initial reaction — whether favorable or unfavorable — became less salient and more neutral.

Another problem was the possibility that the meeting place would identify me and the university as the confederation's sponsor, in particular to persons outside the group who did not understand my role. Vicente de Serrano, for one, assumed that I was in control and attempted to pressure me to his views. It took persuasive talk to dispel this idea, but in the very act of explaining my role to show that I posed no threat to his position as *the* political boss and by inviting his cooperation with the study, I probably reduced the thrust of his assault upon the confederation. Unknowingly, I protected the group, for had I not been involved the political assault might have continued for an even longer period of time.

Before I joined the group and during my early participation in it, other advisors had served as translators and letter writers, and one had provided a meeting room. Therefore, such services were not uniquely tied to my participation or contingent upon it, but their importance should not be minimized. They were helpful and indicative of my commitment to the group. I was willing to cooperate within the limits of an established framework of participation.

The limits I imposed on myself and my assistants as participant-observers at meetings, and in all social contacts with members as well as with nonmembers, prohibited us from doing any of the following: persuading members to come to meetings or to stay away; setting the date or time of meetings or their duration; inviting persons, members or not, to meetings; introducing new or old ideas, proposals, or plans for programs; writing procedural rules, applications for programs, or constitutions; taking a turn arguing for or against proposals or motions, or voting upon motions; indicating beforehand what course the group should take or what decision it should make; opposing a decision already made or implying that the decision made was preferred; evaluating the outcome of meetings, conferences with officials, or the way in which any member behaved; acting as if we represented the group; conveying information between persons, groups, or agencies; intervening on behalf of a member of the group at official functions. (Nonetheless, at one meeting with the director of the antipoverty agency I violated the last rule; see Chapter 9.) These proscriptions, designed to make the participant-observer role marginal to the group's official or semiofficial business, were conceived as binding, permanent, and always to be obeyed.

Although the participant-observer role in the research project had been thoroughly discussed by Carmen Sylvia García and myself, she found it difficult at first, as a psychiatric social worker professionally trained to help people, to suppress her inclination to advise the group. She had a deep intellectual fascination with training-group techniques, which are designed to enhance a person's insights into himself and others, creating social sensitivity as a result of experiences in relatively unstructured group situations. She found the confederation to be much like a training group because it lacked orderly procedures at meetings and the members' talk tended to be expressive rather than goal-oriented. Yet, this was during the rebirth phase of the group when Mrs. Estebán was exhorting the members to pursue the goals for the betterment of Puerto Ricans and, in comparison to what it had been before, the confederation was more oriented toward action.

Miss García believed the group was unable to develop formal procedures for meetings and sustain a drive toward external goals because there was, among the members, a set of interpersonal emotional problems, mutual misunderstandings, flaws in communication, and a lack of insight. She believed each member had a "hidden agenda" or a plan to use the group as a means for attaining his own private wishes. However right or wrong the theory may have been, she assumed it was correct and occasionally suggested to the members the need to reveal their own private motives and feelings so as to understand the immediate group process in which they were enmeshed. The members listened to her politely, but they did little to follow her suggestions because incipient changes had caught hold in the group and the members' attention was riveted elsewhere. Beyond this, discontinuity from meeting to meeting made it difficult for the members either to initiate or sustain a process of scrutinizing their own interpersonal relations. Although her suggestions fell outside the participant-observer role, as we held mutually critical talks about the way to participate, Miss García began to hold in abeyance her inclination to apply training-group theory to the confederation. I had the difficult task of developing the role, but she had the equally difficult task of learning it and following it during the 11-month period of her participation. Her success was acknowledged by Mrs. Estebán in a private talk with her sometime later. She said, "I am always the one who does all the talking, and you don't say a thing about your own ideas and plans."

Some of the persons who became reliable members were at first confused, even unhappy, with the way we participated, but as they talked to other members and to us, they understood and, with only the notable exception of Mrs. Estebán, accepted the role. Their reactions depended upon their expectations about an advisor's role, upon their learning of roles in the group, and upon their willingness to accept the terms of our participation. One such reaction was David Alemán's. He told me: "Well, at the beginning I asked Mrs. Estebán why you didn't participate more at meetings. She said you were an advisor. I replied, 'But surely he can give us advice on how to conduct meetings in a proper manner and raise his voice whenever something improper is going on.' Not until that time when I asked you and you explained to me the role you had did I realize why you stayed out of the arguments that were going on."

Unlike Alemán, Carlos Otero was among those persons who were convinced from the start that our way of participating coincided with and even enhanced our role as advisors to the group. He told someone: "I think Lloyd Rogler is a perfect advisor. He says nothing. He does nothing. He just sits there and waits for it to come out."

But those who were in the group for only a short time tended to remain disgruntled with our failure to do more at meetings. One attended just a few meetings and told Miss García in an interview: "If the confederation has advisors, what are they doing? Nothing! The advisors should instruct the members as to how to do things correctly. Rogler Canino is no advisor because I do not see him advising the group and helping the others to understand the importance of the organization."

Mrs. Estebán was the only member who pointedly questioned our form of participation. When under attack by the members or involved in an argument, she sometimes turned to us to arbitrate the dispute or to support what she thought was right. Once in the full heat of a bitter argument with David Alemán over how the confederation should negotiate with the antipoverty agency, she lashed out at Carmen Sylvia García's neutral stance:

> Well, Miss García, say something! You are a consultant! A consultant is like a school principal, like the mayor of a city. She has to talk, give advice, express her point of view in regard to what the others are doing — if it is good or if it is bad. In this case the consultant shall not remain silent. . . . Why do you keep silent, hearing and that is all? We have to come to an agreement. The advisors do not serve only as observers. If there is something wrong, they will have to say so, not keep silent. If he [David Alemán] is not right, then your duty is to . . .

Having chastized Miss García, she turned back to David Alemán.

But attacks were rare exceptions in Mrs. Estebán's treatment of us. Her usual attitude was strongly favorable and she was deeply appreciative of the many months we spent working with her, in particular, quietly listening to her. Several months before I left Maplewood, she again repeated what she had told me many times before: "You are very understanding. You are better than a psychiatrist."

Yet her resentment over our failure to do what she wanted lingered to the very end of my contacts with her and the group. This became evident at the testimonial banquet the confederation gave in my honor two weeks before I left Maplewood. After dinner, each person took his turn standing up to offer a toast as an *homenaje* ("homage") to me for my devotion to the group and the Hispanic community. (Some wanted to know the name of the Puerto Rican professor who would replace me and if he would be as devoted to them as I had been; they assumed incorrectly that the position I occupied in the university belonged to a Puerto Rican.) The speeches were long and the compliments rich. As the last person to speak, it remained for Mrs. Estebán to inject into the occasion a more balanced and accurate perspective. She reprimanded the others in jest for speaking too long, thereby providing even more data for the study and delaying the publication of the book on the history of the confederation. She said she agreed with the favorable comments on what I meant to the group and the Hispanic community, but then, apparently strongly concerned about the need to set the historical record straight, she emphasized that the outpouring of sentiment should not becloud the fact that I had often failed the group. Why had I not spoken out when the group confronted serious difficulties? Had I done so I could have rightfully affirmed my identity as a Puerto Rican truly devoted to the group's cause. The banquet ended with this rebuke.

Mrs. Estebán's pressure upon us at meetings tended to come when either she or the group faced a problem. When the members reminded her that the request fell outside our role as advisors, she retorted, "Why? The advisors have the same eyes and ears we all have." She believed strongly that everyone should put forth maximum effort, and no one was beyond reach of her plea to contribute more. Often when she questioned an advisor, another member would interrupt to reply, thus deflecting the question and relieving us from the responsibility of answering it. At the meetings, questions to advisors or to anyone else were likely to elicit unsolicited comments from those who were not being asked, and soon the point of the question would be buried in the welter of voices. Had the group followed organized procedures at meetings, attention would have centered on our response to questions, but it was not common practice for the president to grant members the floor, either officially or informally. The person heard on any subject was the one who spoke first, monopolized the discussion, could break in to interrupt, or could outshout the rest. For this reason, the advisors' failure to reply to questions usually passed unnoticed.

Sometimes we, as advisors, unwittingly reacted in an evasive way. Our replies would then consist of a nonanswer to the question or an answer to a question not asked. Although our replies were often irrelevant, they were much like those of the other members. Since the usual course of group discussion involved a sequence of loose connections between questions asked and answers given, unconsciously we were following the group's pattern.

When it was necessary for an advisor to reply to a question, the key principle was to make it as nondirective as possible. Often this involved a counterquestion such as "What do you think ought to be done? . . . is the case? . . . is correct?" Loquacious as Mrs. Estebán was, this was an invitation to her to give a speech,

182

and she usually accepted. If we used this technique deliberately, she also deliberately used us. At times I felt she was expecting the question to be returned to her, and then she would preface her well-prepared answer by saying, "Yes, that is an important question." She appeared to be using us as a vehicle for the ideas and plans she wanted to impress upon the group. When she did not make a speech, some other member usually did, and again the group would be stimulated into discussion. Other times, the advisor would reply by alluding to what had just been said, a technique which almost always stirred the group to further discussion. It was hardly ever necessary for an advisor to plead ignorance or to refuse to answer.

Toward the end of a meeting sometimes we would be asked questions that appeared to require no answer whatsoever. Whether the president or another person asked it, the question's intent was merely to evoke a response from one of us, particularly after we had remained silent for a long period of time. Simply put, we were being invited to speak to show that we were part of the group's conversational life and not outside the common social situation. Because we had been silent, we were being told — tacitly but clearly — to identify ourselves socially with the group and the members. Then, it was important to speak, and there was no need to focus directly upon the question originally asked.

The tape recordings are proof of what we said and did not say at meetings. The usual procedure was to place Bartola, the tape recorder, on a chair and extend the microphone to the middle of the conference table. Bartola began to record at about 7:00 P.M., half an hour before the meeting was scheduled to start, and would continue until everyone except the participant-observer(s) left after the meeting, sometimes as late as 10:30 P.M. Bartola recorded our participation in the informal, casual talk before and after the meeting, as we exchanged light and sometimes humorous impressions about the inclement weather, relatives still living on the island, memories of Puerto Rico, and incidental topics of the day. Bartola proves that during meetings we spoke infrequently. Often the tapes carry no indication of our presence while the meeting was in session, although our presence was undoubtedly being taken into account. But the fundamental point is that, having little to do with the usual flow of conversation, we were *not* directing the group, at least verbally.

Quite often the members visited our offices at the university for a cup of coffee or telephoned us, and we, in turn, visited their homes and accompanied them to dances, baptismal parties, anniversary celebrations, and church affairs. But if our relationship to the group can be conceived as one in which we gave and took from each other, then the confederation allowed us to join its ranks to participate according to the role we thought appropriate, and we repaid the group by translating at meetings, writing letters, and providing a place in which to meet. While these services could have been provided by other advisors, I believe our own distinctive contributions were more important in that we related ourselves to the group and its members as compatriots, friends, and confidants.

The members of the confederation were at the bottom of Maplewood's stratification heap and were isolated socially by their ethnicity, residence in inner-city neighborhoods, and as a result of discrimination. They had few opportunities for friendship with persons such as us — concerned professionals who understood their language, culture, and *su manera de ser* ("their way of life"). We provided this opportunity and enhanced the gratifications it brought by devotion, attention, and understanding as listeners. Thus, at first, the members would sometimes ask that we set aside time for them, ostensibly because they had observations "important to the confederation's history," but they soon discovered that they needed no official-sounding reason to visit us. We listened to whatever they said, whenever convenient for them, and for however long they wanted. Our recognizing the member as a friend seemed to afford him some relief from the customary perfunctory treatment he received in contacts with the world outside his own ethnic group and from the sting and indignity of discrimination.

We attempted to cope with the errors of participation apparent at the start of the study by combining efforts to be marginal to the confederation's official business with the establishment of strong informal ties with the members. The informal ties, I believe, by motivating the members to come to meetings and some of them, perhaps, even to remain in the group, somewhat more than compensated for our standing aside from the group's official business. Mrs. Estebán believed this was the case, and so did David Alemán, who once told me: "I think the fact that a man that has as much work as you do and is faithful to the meetings of the confederation sort of inspires other members to come. They see that it is important to come."

Yet, however important we may have been as an inducement to participation, it would be patently incorrect to conclude that our presence was what sustained the group through its arduous course, for the confederation was organized five months before we joined it and continued after we left. While the study was in progress, it attained incredibly high peaks of solidarity — almost as if the members were bound together into a mystical union, but at other times it plunged into disunity, while the members seemed unable to extricate themselves from the confusion, hostility, and mutual recriminations. Late in the study, rumors in the Hispanic community pronounced the confederation dead, but it came to life again. The group did achieve modest victories, extracted concessions from local agencies, established a contractual relationship with the city's powerful anti-poverty agency, and gave birth to a referral office for Puerto Ricans, but, at the same time, it experienced disruptive internal crises, power struggles culminating in revolts against the group leaders, a political assault, and perplexing actions by city agencies and officials. If our participation was a minor influence in drawing the members together, which I believe it was, it did not affect the group's longevity, nor, for that matter, did it appear to have a marked impact upon such striking ups-and-downs.

While the confederation was in the nineteenth month of its life, we began systematic interviews with all of the members who had come to at least one meeting since the group's inception. The main purpose was to gather information on the members' backgrounds, skills, attitudes, values, and experiences that conditioned their participation in the group. Not included as members were the advisors, observers, speakers from agencies and organizations in the city, or those who came under Vicente de Serrano's orders to politicize the confederation. The members totalled 46, but we were unable to interview 4 of them: One had returned to Puerto Rico. Another had moved to a different city in the state. A third was in a psychiatric hospital, and the fourth, his wife, declined to cooperate out of fear of punishment from her husband, whose episodic fits of violence and paranoid delusions had led to his confinement. Thus, 42 persons were interviewed systematically, 28 men and 14 women. All of them were first-generation migrants — 1 from Mexico, 2 from Colombia, and 39 from Puerto Rico.

To gain the members' cooperation, I took the time after one meeting to explain why the interviews were necessary. I said that a valid history of the confederation required information from each of them, individually. I told them their cooperation was of the utmost importance, and Miss García would arrange the interviews at whatever time or place was convenient to them. By this time, I had been in the group 14 months, and Miss García eight.

Our friends cooperated willingly, often wanting the interview to continue even after it had been completed. Only Mrs. Cantero was reluctant to be interviewed. She was employed as the secretary of a small office devoted to helping Puerto Ricans that was part of a local Catholic church and under the supervision of the parish priest. Mrs. Cantero feared the interview would violate the confidential nature of her work, for many Puerto Ricans turned to her with their personal problems. I went to the office frequently to take bundles of clothing for needy Puerto Rican families, to help in adult education classes for Puerto Ricans that were given on the church premises, and to have long talks with Mrs. Cantero and the priest. On one such visit, I explained to Mrs. Cantero that the information we sought would not breach the confidentiality of her work, but she still felt that the priest would prohibit her from cooperating. With her permission, I spoke to him: he said that he would neither order nor deny her cooperation. When Mrs. Cantero saw that the decision was her own to make, she immediately cooperated.

It was difficult indeed, however, to interview those who did not form a part of the informal relationships we had established in the group. These people had had fleeting contacts with us and, being marginal to the confederation, did not know us very well, if at all. The social and cultural barriers which separated the

Puerto Rican migrants from the outside world were the main obstacles to interviewing. Forced by residential segregation to live in the inner-city neighborhoods, the migrants found that they were also isolated by language and culture. We had difficulty locating their addresses, making appointments, and overcoming their initial resistance to being interviewed. The desire to keep prying eyes out of untidy apartments was one obstacle we had to face: the women were ashamed of their housekeeping, and the men at the lack of authority over neglectful wives. Some informants told us that a change of address was a way of keeping one step ahead of bill collectors. Thus, the persons we sought were often reluctant to open their doors.

One time, for example, Miss García knocked on the apartment door of a woman with whom she had an appointment. She heard a commotion inside of furniture being moved and bare feet hurrying about. Then suddenly there was a silence. According to a neighbor, the woman was an abandoned wife living on public welfare payments and she was entertaining her lover. Difficult to contact, she was reluctant to be interviewed until she understood that Miss García was a compatriot, not an investigator. Another person who finally cooperated after repeated visits was a man who had a legal suit pending against an insurance company for injuries allegedly incurred at work. He was afraid of divulging information that would damage his claim against the company.

Nevertheless, once Miss García was able to see the person, identify herself ethnically and professionally, chat informally, and explain the purpose of the visit, she received full cooperation and was treated with the hospitality customary in Puerto Rican culture, including refreshments or invitations to stay for lunch or dinner.

The tendency of the migrants to keep the apartments relatively dark, with the window shades drawn, is symbolic of social isolation. During interviews, the person often pushed the shades aside, and, stimulated by what he saw, expressed his views on the host society. The migrants saw the society as dominant, disciplined, and regimented, even to the point of prohibiting convivial sidewalk get-togethers or the playing of the radio at its usual loud pitch. They see it as a society suffused with laws, rules, and regulations, investigating incessantly what persons are doing. Unsure of what terms the society demands of them, the migrants react to outsiders with suspicion, always uncertain of which acts might be punished. This barrier affected our initial participation in the confederation and the field interviews with marginal members. To overcome it, we placed ourselves solidly in the ethnic ingroup.

The systematic interviews with the 42 members were in Spanish, took from three to eight hours for each person, and from one to 11 visits to each person's home. The interview schedule was developed during the year preceding its use and it had, altogether, ten sections, each containing a large number of items. The specific items in each section were either of the fixed-choice or open-ended variety. Fixed choices were specified for items only when our experience in pretesting indicated that the choices meaningfully and comprehensively covered the replies the members were likely to make. The open-ended items required further probing by the interviewer, as did some of the fixed-choice items. The schedule is described in detail below.

Sociobiographical Characteristics

The section on sociobiographical characteristics included information on the member's age, sex, marital status, education, employment, income, religion, the composition of the family of procreation, marital history, and type and quality of housing. When applicable, the same information was collected about other persons living in the same household.

Personal and Migratory History

The history section focused upon the member's past, including place of birth and upbringing; the decision to migrate; employment before migration and immediately afterwards; the reasons for moving; and the degree to which the person felt the move had enabled him to achieve his aspirations. Also, it asked the person to evaluate Maplewood according to employment opportunities, education, food, friendships, climate, neighbors, entertainment, health facilities, opportunities for the children, and life in general.

Improvements Since Migrating

Information was sought in this section on how the person had improved in education, work skills, and in learning to speak, read, and write English since his arrival in Maplewood. He was questioned about his evaluation of such improvements and with whom he speaks English, if at all.

Perceptions of Maplewood's Social-Class System

The interviewer probed the member's ideas on Maplewood's class system; the number and characteristics of the social classes; his location and that of his friends in the class system; to what level he aspired to rise, to what level he hoped his children would rise; and the importance and influence he believed he had in the broader society; also probed, were his ideas about the Puerto Rican ethnic ingroup and how the person felt he was related to it.

Social Mobility

The section on social mobility included information collected on the family of orientation as a baseline to determine intergenerational social mobility according to education, employment, and income; barriers to mobility as well as opportunities for self and the children; and, the evaluation of life experiences in terms of mobility aspirations.

Views on Groups in Maplewood

The member's views on the treatment of groups in Maplewood were probed, with particular reference to Puerto Ricans; also investigated were his views on patterns of entertainment among Puerto Ricans, visits between the member and his family, and his involvement in marriage.

Health Opinion Survey Items

Used in the health-opinion-survey section of the schedule were the items in Allister M. Macmillan's Health Opinion Survey,[1] which we found to discriminate between schizophrenics and nonschizophrenics in a previous study.[2]

Achievement Values

The section on achievement values contained a large number of items focusing upon the member's belief in such values as the view that man can improve himself through his own efforts; the willingness to trust other persons; and the emphasis on economic opportunities over contacts with relatives.[3]

Social Participation

The section on social participation assessed the member's pattern of participation in formal organizations; the frequency with which he attended meetings; his status in the organizations; with whom he attended meetings; the length of time of membership; and the reasons for belonging to the organization.

Involvement in the Hispanic Confederation

Information collected on involvement in the confederation included the member's views regarding the unification of Puerto Ricans in Maplewood; how he was introduced to the confederation; with whom and how frequently he attended meetings; friends and the persons he disliked in the group; evaluation of the group's objectives, activities, and degree of success; and, the importance of the group in the member's life.

The procedures used to analyze the systematic interviews were simple, straightforward, and uniformly applied: First, items from the schedule were used to define operationally 44 variables of potential importance to participation. Second, the 42 members were rank-ordered on each of the 44 variables according to their replies to the item(s) defining the variables. Third, correlations between the variables were computed.[4]

In addition to the systematic interviews, we tape-recorded intensive interviews with persons whom we felt were exceptionally important to the group, either as members or because of their involvement in the organizational life of Maplewood's Puerto Ricans. Unlike the systematic interviews, which were administered uniformly to a pre-established list of members, the selection of the person for the intensive interview and the interview itself, depended upon and was adapted to the person's experiences in or with the confederation, other organizations relevant to the Puerto Rican community, and the situation of the interview itself. Prior to the interview, the information in the field notes referring to the interviewee was studied carefully in order to develop a set of guiding, open-ended questions.

Although variable from person to person, the intensive interviews shared the common objective of identifying the confederation's experiences with, or relationship to, other groups, organizations, or institutions. For example, during the first summer of the group's life, Maplewood's Puerto Rican political boss organized an effort to take over the confederation by having it join the Pan-American Association, another Puerto Rican organization, which he already controlled behind the scenes. The assault was not successful, but it still had a marked impact upon the confederation. Maplewood's partisan political structure then became immediately relevant to an understanding of the confederation. Data collection focused upon the city's political system as it enmeshed the leaders of the confederation and the Pan-American Association, the political boss and his aides, and the mayor of the city. The information revealed the connection between the main actors, as instigators or recipients of the assault, and those who were at the source of the assault, men in the political system.

We interviewed intensively the following persons: Diego Zayas, the group's first president; Cristina Estebán, the first vice-president and second president, indeed, the most important person in the study; Alfonso Vilá, the first secretary and long-standing member; Enrique Zamora, the second secretary and an emerging leader; David Alemán, the third vice-president, the official spokesman in the group's negotiations with the Antipoverty Agency of Maplewood, and a leader in his own right; Virgilio Blanco, who although he came into the group late in the study, insisted upon being interviewed so he could contribute to the confederation's history; Frank Joyce, whose initial efforts to help the Puerto Ricans led unexpectedly to the formation of the group; Carlos Otero, an antipoverty agency employee who was the group's main advisor; Vicente de Serrano, the city's powerful Puerto Rican political boss and instigator of the political assault; Romero Ponce, the political boss's aide who carried out the assault; Antonio Tejada, the first president of the opposing group, the Pan-American Association; James Finn, one of the founders and the main advisor of the Pan-American Association; Maplewood's mayor, who influenced the group at critical moments. The relevance of these persons to the confederation can be seen in the narrative.

María Porrata appears briefly in the narrative although she was never a member of the confederation and had no identifiable effect upon the group. She was selected for a series of long, intensive interviews because the breadth of her knowledge of the Puerto Rican community was, I believe, as wide and detailed as that of Vicente de Serrano and Cristina Estebán. (Taken together, the three of them knew the entire social organization of the migrant community.) Mrs. Porrata did not know English, was barely literate in Spanish, and, because she lived on meager public welfare payments, was at the bottom of the economic heap in the Puerto Rican community. However, she was centrally located in a large system of interpersonal relations that extended beyond her blood and affinal relatives, friends, and acquaintances into the ritual coparent system. Because her life was rooted deeply in the traditions of this system, Mrs. Porrata's children and grandchildren had godparents of baptism, confirmation, the road (the person who carries the child to the baptismal godparent at church), and water (the person who blesses the child's home in case of illness or misfortune). It seemed to me as if almost all of the rumors circulating in the Puerto Rican community inevitably passed through her interpersonal network to keep her well informed about the ethnic ingroup. Mrs. Porrata's accounts were valuable background information on the ethnic group's reactions to the organizational efforts of Puerto Ricans.

Because of their deep and pervasive influence on the confederation and because they represent the two main types of leadership connecting the migrant to the city's governing circles, Vicente de Serrano and Mrs. Estebán are given a distinct status in the narrative — they speak on their own. Parts of the interviews with them were edited and reorganized and are presented in Chapters 5 and 8. As *the* Puerto Rican political boss, Serrano's role had institutional support in the city's political party system. Mrs. Estebán, on the other hand, was a nonpolitical civic leader; her role was strikingly innovative, yet uncertain, for it had no solid precedent in the Puerto Rican community.

The intensive interviews were tape-recorded, then fully transcribed. If conducted in Spanish, which most were, the interviews were first translated into English. The transcriptions form a file of 2,149 double-spaced typewritten pages.

From the very beginning of the analysis of the qualitative data, I did not want to impose upon the 46 tape-recorded meetings analytical schemes developed elsewhere in sociology for studies in which the objectives were not necessarily those of this research. Moreover, the sociocultural background of the confederation's members differed sharply from the usual subjects of other sociological studies, and the ends the group sought to attain were tied uniquely to the minority status of the Puerto Ricans in Maplewood. I wanted the procedure for analyzing meetings to respond sensitively to the confederation's own character and social situation. The procedure had to account for the members' actions in the group as well as the content and sequence of topics taken up at meetings. It had to identify recurring features of the group and changes in these features over time. To attain these objectives, we developed the assessment schedule.

The assessment schedule was composed of 21 general categories, each designating a recurring feature of the group, with specific questions subsumed under each category, so we had 155 questions in the schedule. The categories and their questions were developed from the translations and transcriptions of three meetings, then pretested and refined by listening to a sample of other meetings. Because they were developed empirically and not in an a priori fashion, the categories reflect much of what was distinctive to the confederation.

For example, the confederation often acted as if it were starting anew at each meeting, as if its history had not culminated in a legacy of decisions. Decisions made at one meeting were often forgotten at the next meeting, or hardly considered, even though discussion focused upon the same issue. In the very same way, topics taken up at one meeting would be dropped suddenly, perhaps never to be brought up again. Yet, there was a time when some members became exceedingly conscious of the decisions they had made and the precedents established. These observations suggested the category of *Continuity-Discontinuity*, which, in turn, subsumes a series of questions. Some of the questions were as follows:

1. To what extent, if any, does the meeting take as its point of departure decisions and proposals made at prior meetings?
2. Are minutes read at the meeting and, if they are, do they accurately convey the group's prior decisions?
3. Does anyone view discontinuity as a problem, or make a consistent effort to keep conversations in line with the topic under discussion? Who? How?
4. Are alien or unrelated topics introduced at some times and not at other times as the group attempts to make a decision? What are the topics and who introduces them? How?
5. Does any member serve a "memory function" by referring to prior decisions, or insisting that the group focus upon unresolved issues? Who? How?

6. In comparison to prior meetings, are there notable changes in continuity or discontinuity? Describe.

And so on through 12 questions under this category.

The categories and a brief summary of the subject matter of the questions that they contained are listed in the following:

1. Attacks, anger, threats: patterns of attack and defense in the discussion, including indirect insults, ridiculing, and mocking; such reactions as transitional, limited in focus and in the number of members who use them; or as broad in focus, sweeping the membership and growing in strength.
2. Attitudes toward each other: negation, hostility, indifference, disdain, or scorn; favorable, support-seeking, or as invitations to collude.
3. Commitment: active or passive commitment to the group; silent commitment, but persistent involvement; views of commitment as a problem.
4. Comportment and presentation of self: as forceful, knowledgeable, shy, confused, ingratiating, hostile, somber, jocular, etc.
5. Confusion: origins in interaction; resulting from too much or too little information; disjunctive descriptions or explanations; attempts to resolve confusion; the feeling of being victimized by confusion; or the projection of idiosyncratic ideas and feelings onto the group.
6. Consensus-Disagreement: topics involving either consensus or disagreement, their origins and forms of expression; efforts to remedy disagreement or create consensus.
7. Continuity-Discontinuity: transitions from one meeting to the next and within meetings; sources of discontinuity; accuracy of the information conveyed; acts designed to remedy discontinuity; persistence of such acts; disjunctive topics.
8. Decision making: as an unfolding or disjunctive process; topics introduced and how viewed; the final outcome as inconclusive or firm; legitimacy of specific decisions in relation to the established procedures; the issue of a quorum.
9. Frustrations and suspicions: stemming from or directed towards members or outside persons and agencies; degree or extent of sharing.
10. Gratifications: deriving from inside or outside the group; forms of expression; relevance to participation.
11. Informal aspects: topics unrelated to the group's official business; familial or other relationships as they affect meetings; traditional or emergent norms in group activities.
12. Information: presentation of information; source in or out of the group; accuracy of information about persons or agencies; relevance to decisions.
13. Objectives: views on short-run or ultimate objectives; objectives of the meeting; how defined, respecified, and related to group actions; origins in interaction; beliefs or feelings about the attainment of objectives;

14. processes that impede their attainment; how viewed in relation to delayed gratifications.

14. Outside contacts: views toward and contacts with agencies, persons, and social groups on the outside; presentation of confederation as representing the Puerto Ricans; tactics of negotiating with persons and organizations outside the group; quality and tone of contacts in negotiating with persons and agencies; gratifications or frustrations resulting from outside contacts.

15. Power: patterns of reciprocal influence among members, and in relation to outside contacts; sources of power and its perceived legitimacy; strategies for acquiring and maintaining power.

16. Procedures: formal sequence of meetings; references to, or the use of, parliamentary procedures; pressures towards acceptance of such procedures; the absence of procedures viewed as a problem and how to cope with the problem; obedience to "strict" parliamentary procedures as it relates to the satisfaction of members.

17. Responsibilities: how defined, distributed, and assigned; avoidance or acceptance of them; attitudes towards them.

18. Roles: definition, interrelationship, and performance of roles; consistency or conflict between roles in and out of the group; pressures for change; validation of role performance; satisfaction with roles of leaders, followers, advisors, and participant-observers.

19. Strategies: interpersonal among the members, or toward outside groups and agencies; their effectiveness; types, diversionary or direct strategies.

20. Structure: general organization of roles; polarization between members; fit between group's organization and the objectives.

21. Tensions: explicit or latent; their source and focal points; how expressed and how to cope with them; enduring or temporary.

As a heuristic device, flexible in application and adapted to the group, the assessment schedule was not intended to measure quantitative variables. Neither the categories nor the questions within each category were mutually exclusive. Nor were the questions designed to define exhaustively the meaning of the category to which they belonged: any sequence at a meeting which resembled the questions in a category was fitted into that category. To repeat, its purpose was to facilitate the narration of the group's experience, identify group features, and detect group changes over time.

Nonetheless, the use of the assessment schedule involved a series of intricate operations. The situation in which it was used was as follows: Bound in a loose-leaf, hard-covered notebook, the schedule was in front of me as I played the tape recording of a meeting. Then, a narrative of the meeting was dictated into a dictaphone, interspersed with information and quotes relevant to the schedule's categories and questions. To dictate, the tape recorder had to be stopped frequently after a brief interval of listening. Often, a particular sequence of the

193

meeting had to be played over and over because of the members' tendency to speak at the same time and to divide themselves into conversational groups or because confusion in the meeting would confuse me. (One category in the schedule was "Confusion.") Excepting those moments when the members were speaking to Americans at the meeting, almost all the conversations were in rapid Spanish. The end result of processing a meeting was a lengthy report in English. To develop and apply the schedule to the 46 meetings required six months of full-time work.

No matter how carefully the work was done, however, this procedure was not free from errors of commission or omission in the facts of the narrative, in the translation of sequences from Spanish to English, or in the fitting of information into the appropriate categories. For this reason, once I finished applying the schedule to the 46 meetings, Mrs. Caro devoted five months of full-time work to replicating the procedures I had used. A third person then spot-checked those sequences of meetings in which neither one of us felt confident of our work. The checking and rechecking did not guarantee the elimination of all errors, but certainly it did minimize their effect. I believe that errors are of negligible importance in the text of the 1,958 double-spaced typewritten pages that resulted from the use of the assessment schedule.

The assessment schedule was developed out of the most intensive, detailed data on the confederation, the tape recordings of meetings. For this reason, it was used to process the 817 pages of observational reports on the meetings which were not tape recorded and were, therefore, considerably less complete in factual detail than the recordings of meetings. Also, because the ideas reflected in the categories were broadly conceived, the schedule itself provided a way of incorporating into the narrative the 368 pages of field observations away from meetings, the 2,149 pages of intensive interviews, and the replies to open-ended questions in the systematic interviews. In brief, the assessment schedule was the main instrument used to bridge the large amount of qualitative data to the reports from which the confederation's history was written.

NOTES

1. Allister M. Macmillan, "The Health Opinion Survey: Technique for Estimating Prevalence of Psychoneurotic and Related Types of Disorder in Communities," *Psychological Reports*, 1957, no. 3, pp. 325-339.

2. Lloyd H. Rogler and August B. Hollingshead, *Trapped: Families and Schizophrenia* (New York: John Wiley & Sons, 1965), pp. 24-27.

3. The subdimensions of achievement values — activism, trust, and integration with relatives — and many of the items in this part of the schedule were taken from Joseph A. Kahl, "Some Measurements of Achievement Orientation," *The American Journal of Sociology* 70, no. 6 (May, 1965): 669-681.

4. The results of this analysis are presented in Chapter 14.

13

From Puerto Rico to Maplewood

•

This chapter will focus on the lives of the members of the confederation: Who were they? What were their social origins? Why did they come to Maplewood? What social standing did they have in the city? How did they compare Maplewood to their island home?[1] What brought them into the confederation? These questions are interrelated, and as a consequence, when we examine the data that bear upon them, it becomes easier to understand the group.

At the time the systematic interviews were conducted, the median number of years the migrants had lived in the United States was 11, ranging from less than 1 to 24 years. Eighty percent had arrived during the 1950s, the decade producing the largest influx of Puerto Ricans to the United States mainland. In the systematic interviews of the 42 members, each was asked where he was born and raised and where he had lived immediately before coming to the United States: the name of the place and whether it was "the country," "a town," or "a city." The locales named are concentrated primarily in the coastal strip circling the island, on the ocean-side plains, or the foothills at the base of the central mountain chain that divides Puerto Rico longitudinally. The comparative absence of persons from the mountainous interior is a reflection of the greater concentration of population in coastal Puerto Rico. There was no tendency for the locales named to be concentrated in any one area. (The members shared ethnicity as Puerto Ricans but not the bonds of compatriotism of region, town, or city.) The metropolitan area of San Juan, a primate urban center, however, was underrepresented. Thus, the forging of the confederation into an action group must be viewed in relation to a membership of first-generation migrants who knew little about the ways of city life.

Table 13-1 shows the geographical mobility of the members during three separate time periods in their lives. The changes in percentage from place of birth, to place of rearing, to place of residence prior to migration to the United States indicate an incipient trend towards urban living. At the end of the sequence, however, only a minority of the members (29 percent) were living in "cities." Moreover, the cities and towns in which they were living had the character of rural villages: small centers of business and trade populated largely by individual entrepreneurs, merchants, and craftsmen. Puerto Rico's industrialization program was barely under way at the time these migrants lived there, and it was concentrated primarily in metropolitan San Juan. Only two persons lived in this area before moving to the United States. Thus, the prevailing experiences of the confederation members were not urban. They had little familiarity with the intricate patterns of city life and the highly differentiated functions and specialties of an industrialized social setting such as Maplewood.

Table 13-1

Confederation Members by Place of Birth, Rearing, and Residence Immediately Prior to Migration to the United States*

Type of Place	Confederation Members		
	Place of Birth	Place of Rearing	Place of Residence Prior to Migration
	%	%	%
Rural	62	60	40
Town	29	26	31
City	10	14	29
N = 42			

*Percentages do not total 100 because of rounding errors.

Eighty-four percent of the members moved from Puerto Rico directly to the eastern seaboard where Maplewood is located, there to join the largest concentration of Puerto Ricans in the continental United States. Forty-five percent moved directly to Maplewood. Some of those who did not come directly to Maplewood lived elsewhere with relatives or friends. Such visits tended to be short in duration and, apparently, were looked upon as temporary by the members. Some came to work as itinerant farm laborers as far south as Florida. Mrs. Zaragoza, for example, traveled a long way with her family before arriving in Maplewood. She told the following story:

> In Puerto Rico my husband earned very little as a farm worker. He had no education and there was no future for him there. Then he heard that farm work in the United States paid much more than in Puerto Rico. We came to Florida to a farm and while he worked in the fields, I had a job cooking for the farmhands. Once when I did not have dinner ready, one of the laborers stabbed me and almost killed me. I spent a month in the hospital. When I returned to the farm I found my children almost starving and my husband still working like a slave. I threatened to commit suicide if we did not leave.

We left and worked our way from one farm to the next, always going north. We heard that Maplewood was an industrial city with lots of work available. We met one of my brothers who knew about Maplewood and knew English too. He said, "Follow me, for we are going to Maplewood." We did, and here we are.

Mrs. Zaragoza is typical of the confederation members with little urban experience either in Puerto Rico or in the United States before their arrival in Maplewood. Almost all the confederation members had relatives, compadres, or friends in the city before their arrival and these persons were their first source of help and information about the city and in establishing a household in an urbanized, industrialized setting.

In order to discover the context in which the decision to migrate was made, we investigated the occupational history of the members and of their fathers. Because the members' origins were primarily rural or semirural, their families' livelihood often depended upon the planting, cultivation, cutting, and refining of sugarcane. For example, Cristina Estebán's father, Justino Vilá, began his working career as a *listero*, the person in charge of keeping a list of names of the men in the canefields; he was eventually promoted to working in the refinery, itself, in charge of throwing the switch of a grinding machine. In the next generation, Cristina's husband, Eduardo, had his first job as a *pinche*, carrying water to the caneworkers in the field.

Table 13-2 presents the occupations of the members' fathers and the occupational history of the members at three periods of their lives — first occupation, occupation before moving to the United States, and occupation in Maplewood — the last column presents the occupations the members *expect* their children to have.

Three-fourths of the fathers were unskilled workers, predominantly in rural employment. Upon first employment, the majority of confederation members had occupations at the same level as their fathers. When we compare the members' employment before moving to the United States to their occupations in Maplewood, there is no change during this time span — a median of 11 years. When the fathers' occupations are taken as the baseline and compared to the members' occupations in Maplewood, a majority of the members still remain in unskilled work although there is some decrease in the ranks of unskilled workers.

These comparatively small percentage changes, however, do not reflect more striking changes in the qualitative nature of the work itself. For example, Hector Salgado started as a cane-cutter, worked in a candy factory just before moving to the United States, and now in Maplewood works in a meat-packing plant. Although all his jobs have been unskilled, he has changed during his lifetime from agricultural work to an urban job, from working outdoors to working indoors. To Salgado, as to other members of the confederation, this is an important change.

Table 13-2

*Confederation Members and Occupational History (Fathers' Jobs,
Members' First Jobs, Jobs before Migration, and Present Jobs),
and Occupational Expectations for Children**

Type of Occupation†	Occupation of Fathers	First Job	Job Before Migration	Present Job	Expectations for Children
	%	%	%	%	%
Higher executives, proprietors of large concerns, major professionals					70
Business managers, proprietors of medium-sized businesses, and lesser professionals		3	3		22
Administrative personnel, small independent businesses, and minor professionals					4
Clerical and sales workers, technicians, and owners of little businesses	10	10	13	7	
Skilled manual workers				5	
Machine operators and semiskilled workers	15	17	26	31	
Unskilled workers	75	69	58	57	4
N = 42					

*Percentages do not total 100 because of rounding errors.
†Scored in accordance with the occupational groupings of August B. Hollingshead, *Two Factor Index of Social Position* (Copyrighted 1957; Yale Station, New Haven, Conn.: Privately Printed, 1965).

Looking back upon their early life in Puerto Rico, they have no romantic illusions about agricultural work; no nostalgia binds them to the soil. They recall agricultural work as poorly paid and brutally hard and they consider their indoor work in Maplewood, far removed from the scorching sun of the island, an improvement.

The symbolic gratifications of urban work are important, but important, too, are the members' beliefs that employment in Maplewood has brought them tangible gains. During the three time periods being considered, the members' mean monthly income increased from $80 earned in the first job, to $141 in their jobs before moving to the United States, to $347 in Maplewood. When all the sources of income of each family represented by a member of the confederation are combined, the mean monthly family income in Maplewood is $512. Inflationary trends account for part of this increase, but the confederation members believe they have made notable gains in their incomes.

Closely linked to the members' feelings of having prospered are their expectations concerning the occupations of their children. The last column of Table 13-2 presents what they expect. It is understood, of course, that an expectation is a prediction of a future state of events which may or may not come about; in this presentation it is not the accuracy of the prediction which is important, but the prediction itself as indicative of the members' views of the future. Seventy percent of the members expect their children to become higher executives, proprietors of large concerns, and major professionals. The expected mobility is greater than that which the members themselves have experienced in their lifetimes, greater even than their mobility when their fathers' occupations are taken as the baseline. Whereas 88 percent of the members are below the skilled-worker category, 96 percent of them expect their children to rise to the top three job strata. According to expectations, the children would bypass not just the skilled worker stratum, but also the stratum of clerical and sales workers, technicians, and small businessmen.

Having been born and reared in a rural setting and presently employed as janitors, dishwashers, packers, and so forth — jobs that keep them outside the framework of skilled work in the factory system — the migrants have little knowledge of or appreciation for skilled manual work. To them, skilled work is but a minor variant of the unskilled or semiskilled work they now do, at best a slim improvement over their own occupational status. The Hispanic traditions of the island strongly devalue manual work, almost to the point of stigmatization. Hence, the income advantages of skilled work are hardly recognized and the work itself is not appreciated. No member of the confederation ever enrolled in a vocational course and, among the 42 members, only one served an apprenticeship after coming to the United States. The motivation for coming to the mainland was first and foremost economic. Then, spurred on by what they considered to be their own tangible and symbolic attainments, the members aspired for their children to soar upwards into the higher ranks of the occupational ladder and to leave behind the need to do manual work.

Along with occupation, education is central to social mobility. Table 13-3 shows the years of schooling completed by the members and their fathers, as well as how much schooling the children are expected to attain. One-half of the fathers received no schooling at all, and an additional 14 percent only had from one to four years. (The fathers' mean years of schooling is three, the mothers' less than two.) This reflects the underdeveloped character of the island's educational system early in the century when the parents were growing up. At that time educational opportunities were very limited, in particular, for the rural or semirural lower-class person. A minority of the members' parents were literate.

Table 13-3 demonstrates that the members received more education than their fathers; in fact, they exceeded their fathers' education by a mean of five years. A solid majority had at least five years of schooling. (Mrs. Estebán with two years of college had the most education among the members.) In the line of succession from one generation of families to the next, the members were probably the first to break out of the constricted world of the illiterate: all of them could read and write Spanish. Exposure to the countless symbolic messages of modernizing Puerto Rico expanded the scope of their experiences and awakened new desires and aspirations.

Table 13-3

Confederation Members and Education (Years of Schooling Completed by Fathers and Members and Their Educational Expectations for Their Children)*

| Years of Schooling | Confederation Members | | |
	Education of Fathers	Education of Members	Expectations for Children
	%	%	%
0	50	2	0
1-4	14	21	0
5-8	22	26	0
9-12	12	41	14
13-16	3	9	84
17+	0	0	3
N = 42			

*Percentages do not total 100 because of rounding errors.

Eight years of schooling was the mean completed by the members, but they *wish* they could continue through four more years. While expressing the wish to reach college-level education, however, they did not take into account their actual life conditions. Consequently, in a follow-up question, they were asked how many years of schooling they could *realistically* expect. Tempered by the question, the mean dropped to slightly less than nine years of schooling, just a fraction of a year beyond what they have now; in fact, 77 percent did not really expect to get any more schooling. While the wish lingered, sober reflection led them to the conclusion that their educational attainments were at an end and future gains in social mobility would have to be made through avenues other than the educational, or would have to be projected on to their children.

Again, in an effort to suppress wishful fancies, we asked each member for a sober prediction: "If you continue in your present situation, how many years of schooling do you expect your children to attain?" The last column of Table 13-3 presents the results of this question. Practically all members expect their children to receive some college education. What they only fancy for themselves, they really expect for their children.

Yet the members do recognize ascriptive impediments to social mobility. When asked directly whether or not all persons in Maplewood have equal opportunities either in access to jobs or in job promotions, 79 percent of the members said they did not. Each member was then invited to identify which group, if any, received preferential treatment, and which did not. At this point in the sequence of questioning, the importance of ethnicity and race was almost always brought up, particularly skin color, and patterns of preferential or discriminatory treatment were recognized. The members thought that the favored groups are "white Americans," "the Irish," "the Italians," "the blond, blue-eyed," and "those with connections," and the groups discriminated against are the Puerto Ricans and blacks. When asked to compare the treatment given to Puerto Ricans and blacks, 71 percent said that the Puerto Ricans were treated "the same" or "worse," and 29 percent said "better." Those choosing the alternative of "better," however, often added that they did not mean to imply that this was good or favorable treatment or treatment equal to that of other groups.

In appearance the confederation members ranged the spectrum of racial characteristics, as do Puerto Ricans in general. The intensive interviews with selected members suggest strongly that they learned, upon arrival in the United States, the breadth and depth of the American pattern of racial discrimination. Quickly, they became aware of the evaluations the new setting attached to racial differences. Practically all of them had suffered the personal indignity of discrimination, often as a result of being classified as black. It is a common topic of talk among Puerto Ricans. Mrs. Pomales said, for example: "I suppose that with my skin color, Americans think of me as a black, but I do not consider myself a black. I am an Hispana, a Puerto Rican, and I do not concern myself with skin color."

Her comment suggests that the prevailing emphasis placed upon the label Hispano among Puerto Ricans is a means of conveying the identity of the ethnic group and an attempt at separation from the classification of black. The stimulus which unexpectedly gave rise to the confederation was, after all, Frank Joyce's concern that Puerto Ricans were not joining the predominantly black groups in the neighborhood. He labored unsuccessfully to bring them into such groups, but the members wanted their own ethnic organization. Afterwards, on various occasions, representatives from black organizations attempted to get the confederation's cooperation, but again without success. Not infrequently, the members expressed racial prejudices and did not want their own fate to be tied to that of the other disadvantaged group in Maplewood, the blacks.

In the vernacular of the city's Puerto Ricans, the term social class is common.

They came from a socially stratified society in which talk about social classes is open, public, and uninhibited. This habit continues in Maplewood. When asked in the systematic interviews how many social classes there are in Maplewood, the members did not resist answering. Seven percent thought there are no social classes in Maplewood; 5 percent thought there are two classes; 45 percent, 3 classes; 26 percent, 4 classes; and 17 percent, 5 or more classes. About seven out of ten members thought Maplewood has either three or four classes. This is a surprisingly small number if we consider that, in comparison to Maplewood, their hometowns in Puerto Rico had little social or ethnic diversity and that the question which was asked, simple though it appears, did impose upon them the difficult intellectual task of taking into account Maplewood's varied groups. But the number of social classes itself was not arrived at through individual calculations; it very likely reflected the ethnic ingroup's prevailing views of the city's class structure. Because the topic of social classes in the new setting was widely discussed among the migrants, each person learned the collective views of the group. Consequently, the effect was to simplify what otherwise might have been a baffling social experience — the diversity of groupings in the new social setting.

After telling us the number of social classes he thought existed in Maplewood, each person was asked to discuss in detail the characteristics of the social classes to see how he delineated class distinctions. Jacinto Badillo felt the class system in Maplewood is organized primarily according to ethnicity and race. He said, "The social classes are the Jews, Italians, blacks, and Puerto Ricans. The Jews are the richest and smartest of all. The Italians are in the middle, but they hate the Puerto Ricans. The poorest and, along with us, the worst off, are the blacks, but they also hate us. Some Puerto Ricans make more money than others, but we are all the same because the Americans see us as the same."

Mrs. Laura Cantero explained her views: "Here we have the rich, the middle, and the poor class. The rich are better educated, polite, and gentle, and having more money they live comfortably. The middle class express themselves correctly, dress nicely, and visit good places. The poor have less education and do not know how to behave correctly. They live badly and are not allowed in the good places. All classes have representatives of different nationalities."

These two views, however, were in the minority, for money or income was the most often cited attribute of social classes. It was mentioned more than twice as often as race, the second most frequently mentioned characteristic. The different characteristics mentioned by members as attributes of social class were as follows: money, 64 percent; race, 29 percent; occupation, 24 percent; education, 24 percent; national origin, 17 percent; and religion and the orderly life, 10 percent.

The intent of the interview question must be kept in mind. We did not want to put words into the member's mouth by asking him whether or not a particular characteristic was important to the class system. We did want the member voluntarily to tell us the characteristics he thought were important. Hence, the percentage distributions above undoubtedly underrepresent the percentages which would have resulted had the members been asked whether or not a particular characteristic is important to the class structure.

The discussion above suggests but does not demonstrate the importance of money in the members' thoughts about the class system. Rafael Zayas, for example, said that in the city's three social classes, the upper class has more income than it needed, the middle class has money sufficient for its needs, and the lower class has less than sufficient. Mrs. Ana Vargas stated pointedly: "The basic fact in the three social classes is the money you have; no matter what your nationality, no matter what your schooling. That is it!"

The members portrayed a class system with a mixture of ascriptive characteristics, such as race and national origin, and achieved characteristics, such as money, occupation, education, religion, and the orderly life. The prevailing view, however, was that it is an open and flexible system with no hard external constraints to prevent a person from attaining class-related goals. Impediments such as ethnicity and race impressed themselves upon the members' consciousness, but they were secondary in importance to the possession of money. With money as the most common denominator, the city's diverse groupings were brought under the rubric of a simplified class system. The members' conceptions of the city's class system coincide with the economic motivations which brought them from their homeland to Maplewood.

We then asked each member where he placed himself in the class system and this, of course, depended upon his views of the class structure. Forty-six percent considered themselves to be in the "middle class," a term which they used; 20 percent considered themselves in the bottom class. The remainder located themselves variously in the "working class," the "nonprofessional group," or the "high class" — groupings which, in their judgments, are not at the bottom of the class hierarchy. But when Puerto Ricans as a group are discussed, they were generally placed on the bottom rung of the ladder; thus, the members thought of themselves as above their own ethnic group. The data hint at a tendency on the part of the members to dissociate themselves mentally from Puerto Ricans in the process of classification.

Nonetheless, the members *are* Puerto Ricans and no matter what objective standards of class placement are used, they were at the bottom of the stratification heap. According to Hollingshead's *Two Factor Index of Social Position*, 74 percent of the members were in class V, the bottom group; 21 percent were in class IV, and 5 percent in class III.[2] Residentially, they were located in the inner-city neighborhoods commonly referred to as ghettos, living either in deteriorated buildings or in public housing developments. Educationally, they had

moved only a step beyond illiteracy. Occupationally, a majority were still unskilled workers. Yet, in the face of these realities, only 20 percent placed themselves in the bottom group of their perceived class system.

Table 13-4 presents data relevant to this interesting point. It demonstrates
that when the base of comparison is changed from the members' social position
in Puerto Rico to that of "most people in Maplewood," *all* members viewed
themselves as at least on a par with most people in Maplewood: 14 percent perceived themselves as "higher"; no one viewed his social position as "lower" than
most people in Maplewood.

Table 13-4

Confederation Members' Perception of Their
Social Position in Maplewood

Social Position in Maplewood	Members' Perception of	
	Social Position in Puerto Rico	Social Position Compared to Others
	%	%
Higher	55	14
Same	26	86
Lower	19	0
N = 42		

In a large-scale survey conducted in Puerto Rico, Tumin demonstrated that
the values of self-worth, dignity, and pride are imbedded in Puerto Rican culture
independent of rank in the usual objective criteria of social stratification.[3] For
a confederation member to have admitted having a "lower" social position than
"most" would have been incongruous with his self-conception as worthy. Moreover, the value of self-worth converged with the belief that, in coming to Maplewood, he had made upward strides. The assimilative process in the new cultural
setting was relevant too, because it led to the acceptance of the American
democratic creed's proposition about the equality of all men. The conclusion
that all persons *are* equal is drawn from the value premise that all men *ought* to
be equal. Nonetheless, the fallacy of the syllogism is as irrelevant as the contra-
dicting facts of the social structure: although the members of the confederation
did recognize discrimination against Puerto Ricans as a group, they did not view
themselves, personally or individually, as having a marginally low status in Maplewood.

This being true, the members should have enjoyed a feeling of equity when
they compared themselves to "most people in Maplewood," and Table 13-5 indi-

cates that this was so. Regardless of the subject they were queried on — importance, influence, achievement of ambitions, opportunities for attaining the "good things in life," the justness of life — a solid majority believed that they were at least on a par with "most people in Maplewood." Their own statements, too, showed the connection between the feelings of parity, of satisfaction, and their progress in Maplewood. Jesús Vargas said, "Ever since I came to Maplewood I have been working. I have a car, an apartment, and all the things I need to live comfortably. I am happy. I have everything I need. When it comes time to die, I will return to my native land, Puerto Rico, but meanwhile ..."

Jorge Rullán commented, "When I arrived here I looked around, then said to myself: "This is the place for me." The job opportunities are good; the salaries are fabulous; and I have everything I need. In Puerto Rico I never made more than $25 a month, but here I have a high salary. I am happy." Such comments were expressed so often by the individual members as to appear repetitive.

Table 13-5

Confederation Members' Perception of Their Lives (Their Own Importance, Influence, Achievements, Opportunities, and the Justness of Life), Compared to Others' in Maplewood

	Comparison to Others		
Members' Perception	More	Same	Less
	%	%	%
Of importance	17	71	12
Of influence	21	69	10
Of achievement of ambitions	34	49	17
Of opportunities	36	43	21
Of justness of life	29	57	14
N = 42			

Also viewed optimistically was the future: 69 percent of the members said the future would be better than the present; 14 percent said it would be the same; 7 percent thought worse; and the remaining 10 percent would not hazard a prediction. When asked what their chances were of attaining what they wanted most in life within the next three or four years, 52 percent chose the alternatives of either "excellent" or "good"; 21 percent chose the "so-so" alternative; 17 percent the "little" or "none" alternatives; and the remaining 10 percent did not know. Finally, 77 percent affirmed that, at present, they were taking action so as to attain what they wanted "most in life."

The perceived open character of the class system as they understood it supports this optimistic outlook, but relevant, too, were the members' specific evaluations of life in Maplewood. All of them had shared the experience of moving to Maplewood, so they found this an interesting and important topic. In the casual, informal talk at the confederation meetings, they often made comparisons between Maplewood and Puerto Rico.

Table 13-6 presents data on how the members evaluated ten aspects of life in Maplewood in comparison to Puerto Rico, from working conditions to friendships.

Table 13-6

*Confederation Members' Perception of Selected Aspects of
Life in Máplewood Compared to Life in Puerto Rico*

Selected Aspects of Life	Members' Perception		
	Better	Same	Worse
	%	%	%
Working conditions	88	10	2
Opportunities for children	77	21	2
Health care	66	12	22
Schooling	57	29	14
Food	43	40	17
Entertainment	26	17	57
Way of Life*	20	37	44
Weather	12	7	81
Neighborhood relations*	10	36	55
Friendship	7	43	50

N = 42

*The total does not equal 100 percent because of rounding errors.

The percentages in the first column of Table 13-6, the "better" column, are arranged in descending order. The column indicates that a majority of members evaluated Maplewood as "better" in working conditions, opportunities for children, health care, and schooling. These represent the tangible elements of the good life that improve man's well-being and the most salient objectives associated with the move to the United States. Although food was not evaluated by a majority as "better," more persons found it "better" in Maplewood than "worse." The consumption of food was closely related to the enjoyment of material rewards in the new setting.

The percentages take a turn away from an evaluation of "better," however, when the members were asked about entertainment, people's way of life, neighborhood relations, and friendships. These evaluations refer to the quality of social contacts. Even the weather, which a majority viewed as "worse" in Maplewood, is related to this point: aside from the physical discomfort of the long winters, inclement weather was seen as inhibiting the development of sidewalk cliques, neighborhood groups, and friendships.

In response to another question, 90 percent of the members said they missed Puerto Rico. When asked what they missed most, 60 percent replied "relatives," and 18 percent "friends." They longed for supportive social relationships, the bonds of primary group contacts, the sense of communal living. Nowhere ever did the members mention missing the quality of working conditions, schooling, health care, and so forth, in Puerto Rico — elements of life in which Maplewood was seen to enjoy a distinct advantage.

We wondered if Maplewood did not have such advantages, where the members would then choose to live. To find this out we questioned each member about where he would live if he had all the money he needed for his wants and desires. The assumption was that if the person had "sufficient money" he could enjoy the same material advantages in Puerto Rico. Seventy-one percent said they would choose to return to their homeland. Therefore, the confederation members experienced both gains and losses by coming to Maplewood. To avail themselves of the opportunities and level of living of a modern, industrialized society, they felt they had to sacrifice the rich psychological experience of a more traditional society.

It is difficult to explain such a feeling of loss. The migrants lived in the inner-city neighborhoods with other Puerto Ricans, many of whom are their relatives, compadres, and friends. It would seem that contacts with such persons should mitigate the loss of primary-group relationships. Moreover, the members did recognize Puerto Ricans as a distinct group in Maplewood. In answer to the question of whether or not Puerto Ricans could be distinguished from other groups in the city because of "their way of life," 79 percent said yes. That nine members (21 percent) should reply negatively was unexpected, considering the migrants' social context; their ecological, linguistic, and cultural separation; the prevailing use of Hispano as a label for the ethnic ingroup; and the frequent references to la raza, a term which translates into commonality of culture, not race. Successive probes clarified the meaning of the negative answer. The question was ambiguous: to these persons, a positive answer implied the acceptance of American prejudice against Puerto Ricans. Bolívar Zegarra at first denied the distinctness of Puerto Ricans as a group, but soon began to illustrate differences between Puerto Ricans and other groups in Maplewood, while insisting that such did not justify the Americans' discriminatory treatment. Not wanting to endorse discrimination, he was reluctant to admit the distinctness of the ethnic group.

If the members considered Puerto Ricans a distinct group, then, from their viewpoint, how unified were the Puerto Ricans? When asked this question, 62 percent of the members chose the alternative of "not unified at all"; 36 percent said "a little unified," and 2 percent (one member) chose "very unified." Practically all members saw little or no unification among Puerto Ricans. Thus, the distinctness of the group seemed to rest upon the perceived common origin, culture, and language of Puerto Ricans.

The members did not see the absence of solidarity in the ethnic ingroup as an abstract notion removed from their immediate lives. On the contrary, it was something which they observed repeatedly and felt deeply in everyday life. It was a salient topic of conversation at confederation meetings and elsewhere in other social situations. To Antonio Tejada, who not only was president of the Pan-American Association but also devoted long hours to organizing Puerto Ricans, the lack of Puerto Rican unity was a matter of deep concern. Tejada said, "Puerto Ricans are self-centered. They really do not like each other. The ones who improve feel superior to those who do not improve; then, those who do not improve resent those who are trying to become professional, even to the point of attempting to harm them. They cannot unite to work for the benefit of the whole group."

And others, even those who had had little to do with organizational efforts, shared Tejada's view. Mrs. Quevedo remarked, "Most Puerto Ricans are noisy and nasty. They are unwilling to cooperate. What is worst of all is that they do not attempt to make themselves a respected group. They pull in different directions and react to each other as if they were enemies."

Neither of these views was idiosyncratic. There was a pronounced tendency to derogate the ethnic group in language that was stinging, pungent, and pejorative. They described in many different ways a stereotype of the Puerto Rican that was unflattering but quite commonly accepted and expressed.

Rafael Zayas said, "Puerto Ricans here care little about improving themselves and that is because they are not intelligent. They abound in perversions such as gambling and prostitution. This is tied to their pessimism and to their indifference as to whether they do right or wrong."

Pablo Vivo said, "Puerto Ricans do not cooperate with each other. I myself feel ashamed at the Puerto Ricans' reaction to Americans whom they insult and defy. For that reason I do not like to associate with Puerto Ricans."

Alfredo Cabán said, "Puerto Ricans do not try to adapt themselves to this culture. They have low moral principles and I am ashamed of them. Around here it is better to identify yourself as a Russian than as a Puerto Rican."

Jorge Rullán said, "I am an orderly person. I like to work and I like Americans. But there are Puerto Ricans who live off the lies they tell, and others who gossip, gamble, and defy American authorities. Almost all of them are hypocrites. Today friends, tomorrow enemies."

And finally, Alejandro Rico summed up the feeling as follows: "The women copy American fashions and then want to go out and be free without the man's permission. They exaggerate in their dress and think they are superior to others.

Both men and women buy furniture without paying for it. They are hostile toward Americans and insult them by speaking Spanish in front of them. Why do Americans think badly of Puerto Ricans? Because they are noisy, gamble, buy without paying, and many of the women turn into whores."

Nevertheless, the prevailing view was that selective migration was at fault, and bad behavior got worse in the new social setting. Héctor Salgado explained, "The ones who come here are from the lower class, from the mud and muck. They had problems there; they have problems here. When they earn more money here, they get even worse."

Alfonso Vilá had a similar thought: "Morally, the Puerto Ricans get worse [in Maplewood] because they attempt to change culturally and adopt new habits, the American habits. But since they don't understand them fully, they misinterpret them, do things wrongly, and act contrary to the usual ways of correct behavior."

Laura Tejada concluded: "Puerto Ricans make no attempt to adapt and they become nasty and negative to the point of mocking Americans. They gamble, disobey the law, and think they can adapt by turning hostile."

Rafael Zayas claimed: "Not knowing the English language, they do not understand Americans, so they become hostile and negative." But Antonio Tejada, Laura's husband, thought learning English was itself a cause of bad behavior. He said, "They learn English and earn a lot of money. Then they buy a car. Because of this they think they have a right to violate the law by carrying arms, getting drunk, and gambling. Eventually, they try to challenge the police."

Arsenio Pomales went further with the point that earning "a lot of money" stimulated bad behavior:

> In Puerto Rico the people are humble, shy, and slow, but as soon as they get here they act as if they had been given an electric shock. They puff up, lose their humility, and develop a sting like a wasp. Dizzy over the money they earn, they forget their good manners and begin to defy others. They forget their old friends, no longer visit each other. . . . I think everything they do is wrong.
>
> Go to the airport and see how our *jibaritos* [country folk] arrive, then see them again a few months later. They become noisy, disrespectful, impertinent — everything undesirable.

Fernando Vilá, however, thought the problem was one of "contamination" by Americans. "They get spoiled as if they had been contaminated. There is no friendship, and one neighbor does not care for the other, each one living his own life. For this reason, they become suspicious of each other and, like the Americans, turn cold and indifferent. Recently, when the newspapers called Puerto Ricans troublemakers, I felt ashamed."

Arturo Prieto, as a lay minister, had devoted much of his life to the "saving of lost souls" among Puerto Rican migrants. Although his views were much like those of the others we interviewed, his expression of them was the strongest.

> Puerto Ricans affect each other like a cancer. They gossip dirty lies about each other. In front of you, they behave one way; behind your back they would like to kill you. Hypocrites! That's what they are. Something makes them selfish, each one looking out for his own welfare. . . . Even the women become worse. So much do they want to imitate American women that the first thing they do is forget the sacredness of their chastity and hook up with a lover. Both sexes are confused and disoriented, crazily trying to copy, but messing themselves up with their excesses.

Whatever the alleged causes of the unpleasant behavior, the end result in the members' minds was an ugly stereotype of the city's Puerto Ricans, quite different from the way they recalled people in Puerto Rico: virtuous, generous, and supportive. "In Puerto Rico," Víctor Queró said, "people act as if they were in one big family." Therefore, associating with their compatriots in Maplewood did not compensate for the migrants' sense of loss of communal life. Perhaps it even exacerbated the loss. The conclusion reached by Mrs. Laura Cantero was her own, but it was not at all uncommon among members. "In Puerto Rico, I felt secure for I was surrounded by friends there. Here I feel insecure and afraid because the Puerto Ricans behave as if they are the enemy of each other and one cannot trust them."

Some of the members drew a direct connection between the stereotype of Maplewood's Puerto Ricans and the history of organizational problems in the city. Arsenio Pomales commented: "We each hold to what we want as individuals, caring little about what others want. Instead of loving each other, we act like enemies. For example, when we go to a confederation meeting and see Mrs. Estebán as president, we ask ourselves why she should be president and not ourselves. We are envious of her because she is what we want to be. But envy makes us work against her. That is the way it is here. Each to his own."

These then were the experiences, feelings, and views of members of the city's most deprived ethnic minority. Rural in origin, few had had urban experiences before arriving in Maplewood. During their lives, they increased their income as they moved into more valued urban-based jobs. They had more education than their parents and, in turn, they expected their children to make even greater educational and occupational gains. They recognized discrimination against Puerto Ricans but were proud of their own individual accomplishments and optimistic about the future. Though aware of racial and ethnic impediments to upward social mobility, they still conceived of the city's class system as relatively open, the difference between classes based primarily upon cash or income. Objectively, they were concentrated at the bottom of the class system; subjectively, in looking at themselves individually, they did not feel marginal or inconsequential. Maplewood had provided them with what they came for.

Yet they missed the warmth of social relations they associated with life in Puerto Rico, and they saw little unity among the city's Puerto Ricans whom they stereotyped in unfavorable terms. From all appearances, they dissociated their own inner lives from the life of the ethnic group whom they derogated — as if one did not affect the other, as if there were no common base of experience between the two. But these same persons were members of the confederation, an action group whose avowed purpose was to correct the inequities afflicting Maplewood's Puerto Rican community. Why, then, were they members of a group advocating the cause of those they devalued — the Puerto Ricans in Maplewood? The answer to this question is to be found in the character and meaning of the members' participation in the confederation, the topic of the next chapter.

NOTES

1. Among the 42 members systematically interviewed, there were two Colombians and one Mexican. Where necessary, the items in the schedule used in the systematic interviews were adapted to their nationality. Because they are such a small minority in the membership, we will not deal with them as a separate group.

2. August B. Hollingshead, *Two Factor Index of Social Position* (copyrighted 1957; Yale Station, New Haven, Conn.: privately printed, 1965).

3. Melvin M. Tumin with Arnold Feldman, *Social Class and Social Change in Puerto Rico* (Princeton, N.J.: Princeton University Press, 1961), pp. 172-173.

14

Participation
in the
Confederation

•

Participation in the confederation ranged from the hardcore, committed members who appear in the narrative time and again to others who quit after only one meeting. Had all the Puerto Rican migrants withdrawn quickly, the effort would have died in infancy, another group failure in the history of the city's Hispanos. To have accomplished what it did, to have endured so long, the confederation had to have reliable members as a base of support. From Frank Joyce's first concern with bringing Puerto Ricans into neighborhood organizations, to Mrs. Esteban's establishment of a family dynasty in the group, the question at the core of the life and evolution of the confederation is: Why did some members remain faithful and constant throughout the vicissitudes of the confederation's life while others did not?

To answer this question, we analyzed the attendance records we kept in relation to the data from the systematic interviews with the members. The attendance records cover 26 months and were used to determine how often the members participated in the 68 meetings or official activities of the confederation. While the group was in its nineteenth month, we began systematic interviews with 42 persons who had attended at least one meeting. They are the persons included in this analysis; not included are those who joined the group after the systematic interviews began. Nonetheless, the time period being considered covers the group's major evolutionary changes and includes the main actors in the confederation's life. We found a pattern of correlations[1] among the following variables: (1) participation in the confederation; (2) social position of the members; (3) use and understanding of English; and (4) social values of the members.

The date of entry into the group established an absolute limit to the number of meetings a member could have attended. If he joined the confederation at the beginning of the 26 months, he could have attended all 68 meetings. If he joined the group immediately before we began the systematic interviews, mathematically he could have attended only 28 meetings. For this reason, the measurement of a person's reliability as a member was based upon the number of meetings he actually attended divided by the number of meetings he could have attended. The resulting decimal figure was used to rank-order the members. Those at the top of the rank order were the most reliable; those at the bottom, the least. It should be emphasized that this measure was not based upon hearsay or upon the members' self-reported attendance; it was derived from direct observation and recording of attendance at meetings. Therefore the variables correlated with membership reliability are relevant to actual behavior in the confederation itself.

When the social position of the members and their fathers were rank-ordered individually by Hollingshead's *Two Factor Index of Social Position*,[2] we discovered a direct correlation between the fathers' social position and that of the members ($t_b = .314$), and between the members' social position and the reliability of their attendance at the confederation's meetings ($t_b = .358$). The higher the rank position on one measure, the higher the rank position on the other measure, and vice versa. The findings are:

social position of members' fathers	$t_b = .314$ $\longrightarrow$	social position of members	$t_b = .358$ $\longrightarrow$	reliability of attendance

The two-step historical sequence indicates a connection between the members' familial origins in Puerto Rico, their social standing in Maplewood, and their support of the confederation. To "flesh-out" the sequence, we introduced into the analysis the members' understanding and use of English and selected social values in their lives.

The ability to understand and use English is the best single indicator of the extent to which the member, as an Hispano, incorporated himself into the American setting. If he understood English, it meant that he was exposing himself to the American world outside the ethnic group, to new and diverse stimuli of social contacts and the mass media of communication, even to the printed advertisements pasted on the front windows of grocery stores in inner-city Maplewood. If he spoke English, it meant that he was interacting with Americans, for Hispanos do not speak English to each other.

Each member was asked a series of questions regarding his understanding and use of English.[3] He was then rank-ordered according to his replies to those questions. We found the higher the rank order in the use of English, the higher the social position in Maplewood ($t_b = .432$).

The social values held by the members should be viewed in relation to the changes in their life history from a traditional rural or semirural social system to one that is modern and industrialized. Though barely into middle age, the members of the confederation had traveled a long road — geographically, culturally, and socially — and, like all migrants, they transplanted their social values in the new soil.

Among the most emphasized values of the Puerto Rican culture is obligation to the broader family. We found, however, that the members vary in the degree to which they accept the value of integration with their relatives. (This is more likely true among Maplewood's Puerto Ricans, since migration, itself, may result from or cause the loosening of family bonds.)

The members were rank-ordered according to their replies to five statements so that the higher the rank the more detached the member from the value of integration with relatives.[4] For example, members were asked to react to a statement such as: "If one has the opportunity to help a person get a job, it is always better to choose a relative instead of a friend." Strong agreement with such a statement implied belief in the traditional value of integration with relatives, while disagreement implied detachment from the value and a step away from the once almost sacred obligation to kin members.

The members whose fathers had a higher rank order in social position tended to be more detached from the value of integration with relatives (t_b = .316). This correlation is consistent with the finding that the more detached the person from the values integrating him with relatives, the higher his rank order in the understanding and use of English (t_b = .375) and in the reliability of participation in the confederation (t_b = .332). In addition, those who tended to have a comparatively higher social position in Maplewood were those who were detached from the value of integration with relatives (t_b = .456).

Another value we tested in the migrants' culture system is trust, or lack of suspicion in others. Suspicion was endemic in the Puerto Rican community of Maplewood, arising from a variety of conditions: the experience of cultural uprooting, relegation to a subordinate minority position, the need to contend with a dominant establishment, and the lack of satisfying social relations.

The members were rank-ordered according to their choice of alternative reactions to statements involving the idea of trust.[5] A typical statement was: "One can only trust in a person one knows well." We found the value of trust directly related to the members' participation in the confederation (t_b = .346), to their social position (t_b = .358), and to their understanding and use of English (t_b = .443).

Directly linked to the value of trust is the value of activism. Activism entails the philosophical view that man's future is not preordained or inevitably fixed and the quality of the future is contingent upon what man does in the present to improve himself by his own efforts.[6] We found the value of activism directly related to the reliability of attendance at confederation meetings (t_b = .415), the members' social position (t_b = .391), to their detachment from the value of integration with relatives (t_b = .335), and to the value of trust (t_b = .403).

Throughout the change from island home to life in Maplewood there was a measure of continuity. The correlations form a pattern in the two-step historical sequence beginning with the social position of the members' fathers and concluding with the members' reliability of participation in the confederation.

Although no member inherited wealth or property from his parents, his present social position in Maplewood was linked to the family background on the island. The relationship between past and present social positions represents a transition from the families of orientation of the members to the members' growth into adult roles — most to the point of forming their own families of procreation: 93 percent had, at some time, entered into marriage, although 7 percent were not living with their spouses because of separation or divorce. Marriage expanded their circle of blood and affinal relatives and joined together earlier obligations to the family of orientation with new obligations to the family of procreation.

Nevertheless, the fathers of members who had a higher rank order in social position represent a minority who were functionally literate and a step above the bottommost occupations. From their comparatively higher, but still modest, social position, they may have imparted to their offspring the view that obligations to nonrelatives were important in their own right. Thus, the monolithic dominance of the family and its monopoly of control over social relationships may well have been weakened or attenuated. When released from superordinate obligations to the broader family, the migrant was freed to search in the outside world for opportunities for self-improvement and to participate in other social settings.

The persons who were most willing to forgo the value enmeshing them with relatives, who saw persons other than relatives as possible sources of assistance, who would separate themselves from their own parents for economic or other reasons, and so on, tended to be more involved in the confederation. The detachment from relatives on the part of members of families with a higher social standing directed them to the world outside the family. Once so directed, the members increased their understanding and use of English, sought to attain a higher social position, and projected themselves into the confederation. The mastery of English probably also increased the members' social position in Maplewood. These interpretations are tentative, but they are consistent with the pattern of correlations.

The members who were more solidly entrenched in the city's stratification system and who were more culturally assimilated and integrated into the American world because of their understanding of English were more accepting of the value of trust. They could insulate themselves more effectively from the waves of suspicion sweeping the ethnic community. Others who were locked into the ethnic group, who were not carrying on meaningful interaction with Americans, who were doubtful of the unknown social rules they might be violating, and who were fearful that other persons might conspire to take advantage of them subscribed less to the value of trust. Their attitudes affected their participation in the confederation.

Although aware of the impediments to social mobility, those members who ranked high in activism believed that Maplewood offered them and their children opportunities for improvement and felt, individually, that the social system in the host society was basically fair. Instead of advocating revolutionary change, they found in their belief in activism a way of sanctifying social mobility. As the member experienced a release from the values integrating him with relatives and implanted himself more solidly in the stratification system, he came to view himself as master of his own future. With the acceptance of the value of trust, he was less fearful of other peoples' attempts to cheat him and was able to assimilate more easily into the dominant culture.

Table 14-1 summarizes the t_b correlations between the members' social position, their detachment from the value of integration with relatives, and their acceptance of the values of trust and activism with their reliability of attendance at confederation meetings. The correlations are presented first with no other variables controlled, then with the other variables controlled one at a time. The last column demonstrates that attendance is correlated with each variable when the remaining variables are controlled one at a time.

Of the variables discussed so far, not included in Table 14-1 are the social standings of the members' fathers and the ability to use and understand English. This is because the fathers' social position is the initial variable in the two-step historical sequence; since it necessarily comes before the other variables, it does not have a proximate relationship with the members' attendance. The understanding-and-use-of-English variable appears also to be somewhat more removed from the reliability of attendance. Both variables, however, have been discussed as if they had an effect upon some of the variables in the table impinging directly upon attendance.

Thus, the reliability of attendance is the critical variable linking the member to the group and has been treated as the terminal point in the two-step sequence. It is the main dependent variable. This was done because 12 of the 26 months of keeping attendance records came after the systematic interviews were conducted. With the exception of attendance, the variables were extracted from the data in the systematic interviews. Thus, if group participation affected the variables, the influence had to be registered prior to the systematic interviews. Chronologically, this appears to be a long period of time, but it is important to keep in mind that, even for the most reliable members, the meetings comprised a very small portion of their daily lives. As the narrative demonstrates, interaction at meetings was diffuse, conflict-ridden, and confused; moments of group unity were few and far between. Such experiences were not likely to have had a significant effect upon the members' basic values or upon their individual social positions in Maplewood.

Table 14-1

The tau b Rank Order Correlations between Reliability of Attendance at the Confederation's Meetings, the Members' Social Position, Their Detachment from the Value of Integration with Relatives, and Acceptance of the Values of Trust and Activism

Variables Correlated	Variables Controlled	Correlation without Control	Correlation with Control
Reliability of attendance &			
Members' social position	Value of trust	.3580	.2673
Members' social position	Value of activism	.3580	.2337
Members' social position	Detachment from value of integration with relatives	.3580	.2461
Detachment from value of integration with relatives	Members' social position	.3320	.2031
Detachment from value of integration with relatives	Value of trust	.3320	.2727
Detachment from value of integration with relatives	Value of activism	.3320	.2251
Value of trust	Members' social position	.3460	.2499
Value of trust	Value of activism	.3460	.2147
Value of trust	Detachment from value of integration with relatives	.3460	.2903
Value of activism	Members' social position	.4150	.3200
Value of activism	Value of trust	.4150	.3209
Value of activism	Detachment from value of integration with relatives	.4150	.3418

Before a person could attend a meeting, he had to know about the existence of the group. More than anyone else, Mrs. Estebán brought persons into the confederation: of the 42 members, 30 attended their first meeting at her invitation. But having once come to a meeting, the member's continuing participation depended, at least in part, upon his knowledge of when the meetings would be held and upon feeling welcome. Sometimes an announcement would be made at the end of a meeting about when the next meeting would be held. Usually the confederation mailed out invitations to those on a membership list, which supposedly was revised periodically according to the secretary's attendance records. Several times we checked on this point and discovered that among those who attended the meetings some were on the list and had received invitations, some were on the list and had not received invitations, and some were not on the list and had not received invitations but had heard about the meeting in some other way. It was not uncommon for the invitations to arrive after meetings had taken place.

No attempt was ever made to exclude any persons from meetings, even those meetings restricted to officers and advisors; it was understood that anyone who wanted to attend such a meeting would not be barred from participation. Several times Mrs. Estebán attempted to control attendance at meetings for various reasons by seeing to it that only certain persons were aware of the meetings, but these were few and marked exceptions to the usual pattern.

The open character of the group, its catch-as-catch-can procedure for announcing meetings, its disorganization, and its meeting place roughly equidistant from the city's main Puerto Rican neighborhoods tended, perhaps, to reduce differences among members in their opportunities for participation. Some persons chose to make use of these opportunities; others did not. The more deeply involved in the confederation, the more likely the member was to have also been a member of other organizations. The reliability of the members' participation in official activities of the confederation has a t_b correlation of .270 with membership in other organizations. Had there been more organizations available in the migrants' life space, the correlation would probably have been even greater. The correlation does suggest, however, a generalized tendency toward participation in formal groups among the more reliable members.

The inconsistency discussed in Chapter 13 — that persons, who were proud of their individual accomplishments, were optimistic, felt on a par with most persons in the city, and seemingly had little identification with the ethnic group, were indeed members of an action group that aimed to improve the welfare of this same ethnic group — becomes more sharply focused with the discovery that some of the basic elements in the inconsistency had little correlation with the rate of attendance: the t_b correlation between attendance and feelings of parity with most persons in the city was .004; with satisfaction with life in Maplewood,

.093; with feelings of accomplishment and optimism, .114.[7] The absence of high correlations indicates that this situation was shared by all persons regardless of how reliable they were as members of the confederation.

The variables correlated with attendance at meetings demonstrate, however, that the reliable members' participation was one way among many in which they were already extricating themselves from the inner core of the ethnic group while forging new links with the host society. Herein lies the solution to the inconsistency.

As compared to the casual members, the reliable members devalued customary binding obligations to their relatives. The prime example was Mrs. Estebán, the group's central leader and most reliable member; along with five others she had the top-rank position in the scale of detachment from the value of integration with relatives. So strong was her commitment to civic affairs that her life turned into a round of desperate efforts to respond to all that she felt was expected of her. Although she devalued obligations to relatives, she was the central person in her own extended family and was compelled to respond to her relatives' needs. Because of her attitude, however, she was able to disengage herself sufficiently from traditional kinship obligations to invest herself in the cause of the group.

The comparatively higher social position of the reliable members rooted them more securely into the new setting, at the same time enlarging their vision of Maplewood beyond that of the immediate ethnic group. Unfortunately, we were unable to ascertain how, if at all, their greater incorporation into the American world affected the idea of the stereotype, so often expressed, that Hispanos, virtuous and trustworthy in Puerto Rico, had developed many undesirable traits in Maplewood. The interview items dealing with the ethnic group were open-ended and, though revealing dimensions of the stereotype, did not allow the identification of differences between members in the strength of derogation of the ethnic group. Nevertheless, the stereotype was widely shared. Away from meetings it was expressed by even some of the reliable members, although they were not as likely as the unreliable members to use it to explain the confederation's problems. The reliable members thought the group's difficulties arose from the failure to define a purpose for meetings, to follow up organizational contacts, to set procedures for discussing topics, and to have continuity from one meeting to the next. Thus, they saw the group's problems as situational and not imbedded in the allegedly vulgar character of the ethnic group. Their stronger acceptance of the value of activism led them to capitalize more upon their opportunities to participate and upheld their problem-solving attitude towards the group.

On the other hand, the members who were lower in the scale of reliability connected the commotion and disorder of meetings to the common stereotype

of Puerto Ricans and, therefore, harbored fewer hopes of making the group better than it was. They thought the confederation's interpersonal difficulties
stemmed from the suspicious attitude they attributed to Puerto Ricans in general. They saw suspicion as a destructive factor in organizational efforts, but at
the same time they claimed that such suspicion arose from the calculated efforts
of some persons to take advantage of others. One person said, "The truth is that
some members have a personal interest. They want something for themselves.
That is why it is so difficult."

The members who were lower in the scale of reliability were less committed
to the value of activism, and they found it difficult to develop a pragmatic outlook towards the group's problems; less accepting of the value of trust, they felt
uncomfortable at meetings, and were suspicious that others were attempting to
take advantage of them in subtle and mysterious ways. Quickly, these members
withdrew from active participation in the confederation and reverted to their
former state of isolation.

The formulation stated above implies that reliable members were upwardly
mobile. To test this idea, the members were rank-ordered according to the disparity between their fathers' and their own scores on the *Index of Social Position*. The greater the disparity, the higher the member's rank position — a high
rank position meaning that the member had been upwardly mobile. We found
a direct correlation between social mobility and the rate of attendance at confederation meetings (t_b = .260). Those who were more upwardly mobile capi-
talized more upon their opportunities to participate in the confederation, as did
those who had greater mobility aspirations (t_b = .234). Participation, therefore,
had meaning in terms of attained and aspired upward mobility.

We found this puzzling at first because the confederation made determined
efforts to depersonalize goals and focus exclusively upon the collective welfare
of the city's Puerto Ricans. At meetings and in negotiations with city officials,
the confederation repeatedly dramatized the plight of the ethnic group by referring to the city's most disadvantaged Puerto Ricans — those the members felt
stood to gain the most from the group's objectives. Yet the members with a
comparatively lower social standing, who were at a disadvantage in the very
same way as the Puerto Ricans the group aimed to help, were the ones least
likely to support the group; those with a higher social standing became committed to the group. It would seem also that those persons, who more than others
had attained and aspired to upward social mobility and subscribed more to a
value system in support of upward mobility would avoid a group that attempted
officially to deny members individual or personal gains. Yet, just these persons
tended to be the group's supporters. It was possible that privately and in circum-
spect ways they sought to use the group as a means of enhancing their own
social standing. Shortly after the Hispanic Referral Office was established, waves

of gossip swept the membership about which member stood to gain the most by means of appointments to the office's jobs or by having the office open up valuable social contacts. But this situation was transitory and the group's control over the office was restricted sharply by the actions of the antipoverty agency. Neither before nor after the office was established did the confederation have the resources to improve materially the members' social standing. In addition, the group's links with the city's governing circles and controlling agencies were tenuous, and social contacts with them would have brought the members only minor gains at best. This fact was recognized by the group's secretary, Enrique Zamora, who said, "In the confederation there is nothing to gain, nothing that would be of personal benefit . . . so that it is not used. But had there been something to gain, it would have been used."

Though an explanation based upon tacit motives is always difficult to reject entirely, the confederation's public character itself provides a better explanation of the connection between social mobility and the reliability of membership. While attempting to depersonalize its goals and internal procedures, the confederation's thrust was toward the dominant American world, toward the city's organizations, agencies, and officers controlling resources of value to Puerto Ricans. The only meaning that social mobility can have — whether it be in terms of supporting values, actual mobility or aspired mobility — within the subordinate Puerto Rican minority, is a move toward and into the dominant American culture. Participation in the group took the members in the direction in which their social standing and social values were already leading them. What the group gained, the reliable members gained, immediately, in the context of participation. At this point, no distinction can be drawn between self-enhancement and the collective welfare of the city's migrant group, between selfishness and ethnic altruism. The basic congruence between the members' mobility orientation and the group's thrust towards external goals enabled them to develop a political stance and a political strategy, in the generic sense of the word — even though they lacked strongly favorable ethnic identification.

Had the confederation devoted itself to the celebration of Puerto Rican cultural traditions or to mutual help within the membership, very likely the characteristics of the reliable members would have been different. But there was a close convergence of interests between the reliable members and the group; they became intertwined and mutually supportive. In brief, the confederation stabilized the participation of members who already, in myriad ways, had embarked upon the course the group was to take, toward the American world.

Table 14-2 demonstrates, however, that the confederation succeeded in stabilizing the participation of only a small minority of its members. The table presents data on the reliability of membership according to the percentage of meetings each person attended out of those he could have attended, the rank order of membership reliability, and the cumulative percentage by rank order of the confederation's total attendance during the 26 months in which attendance records were kept.

Table 14-2

Membership Reliability of Confederation Members

Name	Rank	Reliability*	Cumulative Percentage of Total Attendance
		%	%
Cristina Estebán	1	90	13.0
Alfonso Vilá	2	76	24.1
Enrique Zamora	3	71	31.7
David Alemán	4	65	38.9
Justino Vilá	5	52	45.0
Irma Amador	6	49	50.9
Diego Zayas	7	45	57.4
Eduardo Estebán	8	42	60.4
Rafael Zayas	9	39	66.1
Laura Cantero	10	38	70.7
Alejandro Rico	11	27	74.0
Matilda Abelando	12	26	77.0
. . .			
†			
Conchita Caballero	42	1	100.0

*Percentage of meetings each person attended of all the meetings he could have attended.

†Information is omitted on the members whose rank order was between 12 and 42. The 30 persons with a rank order between Mrs. Abelando and Mrs. Caballero account for only 23 percent of the total attendance. With but few exceptions, their names would be unfamiliar to even the most studious reader of the confederation's history.

The arithmetic mean of membership reliability is 20 percent, and the median about 10 percent, which indicates that the very high percentage scores of the most reliable members increased the mean over the median. If the mean is taken as the summary measure, the "typical" member attended one out of five meetings he could have attended; if the median is taken, he attended one of ten. Table 14-2 shows that the 12 most reliable members exceeded both the mean and the median figures of membership reliability, almost all of them by a wide margin. The third column of Table 14-2 indicates that the 12 persons at the top of the rank order accounted for more than 75 percent of the group's total attendance.

The highly differentiated structure of participation therefore means that a small proportion of the membership dominated the group's total attendance and that the confederation's history is a history of the collective acts of a minority of reliable members. Most members were members in name only; they participated briefly in the confederation's activities; they did not have a value system conducive to sustained participation in the confederation; and their comparatively lower social position in Maplewood denied them a sense of commitment to the new social setting; at the same time, the constricted scope of their effective social world succeeded in keeping them turned inwards toward the ethnic group.

Mrs. Estebán who attended 90 percent of the meetings that she could have attended is at the top of the rank order; by herself she accounts for 13 percent of the group's total attendance. Her attendance, combined with that of her brother, Alfonso Vilá, comprises one-fourth of the total confederation attendance. The seven most reliable members account for over one-half of the total attendance even though they represent only one-sixth of the membership. With the exception of Justino Vilá (fifth in rank order of reliability),[8] the seven top-ranked members were also group officers representing the nucleus of leadership, for nothing occurred in the confederation that did not involve them individually or collectively.

Two persons who were not among the most reliable members were at one time or another confederation officers: Fidel Amador (22 in rank order) was the second vice-president; Fernando Vilá (16 in rank order) was the third and last president. Both joined the confederation early in its life but came to few meetings. Vilá became actively involved only after he was elected president as a result of his sister's success in starting a family dynasty in the confederation.

There were 28 men and 14 women in the group's membership. This overrepresentation of men reflects Puerto Rican cultural traditions, which grant men freedom to participate in activities away from home while tending to confine women to the family. Nonetheless, within the confederation the women were about as reliable as the men in their rate of attendance; the mean of membership reliability of the women is 19 percent, of the men 20 percent. There was no notable sex difference in any of the variables discussed in relation to group participation. The data also show that 36 percent of the female and 32 percent of the male members belonged to organizations other than the confederation, thus suggesting that the pattern of equal reliability of attendance between the sexes was not uniquely tied to this specific group. The blood and affinal ties present amont the members of the confederation probably tended to suppress differences between the sexes in the reliability of their participation.

The women, however, had a more difficult time in arranging for participation. Not only did housework and child-rearing keep them busy until the early hours of the evening when the group met, but some had to overcome their husbands' resistance in order to attend meetings. To be as reliable as the men, the women had to overcome impediments stemming from traditional sex-role differences.

In brief, a sequence of interconnected life events led persons into the group. Some chose to remain with it and to participate actively; others did not. The ones who participated reliably had a comparatively higher social position and an attachment to values supporting upward mobility into the American world. They were committed to forging the confederation into a successful action group by attempting to attain goals that had eluded other Puerto Rican groups.

NOTES

1. Kendall's tau b (t_b) was used as the measure of correlation between variables. Kendall's tau b measures the relationship between ordinal rankings, contains a correction for ties in the rankings, and yields numerical values which range from −1.0 to 1.0. Three statisticians familiar with this measure were consulted, and the problem of analyzing the statistical data explained to them. The statistician who first recommended the use of the measure felt that taus of .2 or above were "worthwhile" in the context of this study. Another said that by current standards taus of .2 "are respectable but not exciting." The third statistician evidenced more enthusiasm over a tau of .2 but advised that its statistical significance be compared to that of the Pearson product moment correlation coefficient. To be significant at the .05 level, one-tailed test, with an n of 42 (df = 40), the number of members in the group, a Pearsonian r must be about .257. On the other hand, all of the zero-order tau b correlations of .200 or above reported in this study are significant at the .05 level, one-tailed test. Tau b correlations of .200 or above, therefore, will be considered here as both "worthwhile" and "respectable." We shall be more restrictive, however, in discussing the correlation between two specific variables, in the set of variables composed of social position, social values, use and understanding of English, and involvement in the confederation, and deal in this instance only with zero-order correlations of .200 or above that are maintained at least at this level when the other variables are controlled serially, one by one, not simultaneously. This will provide some evidence, by no means complete, of the proximate connection between the specific variables being considered. For a discussion of Kendall's tau b, see Maurice G. Kendall, *Rank Correlation Methods*, 3rd ed. (New York: Hafner, 1962); Hubert M. Blalock, *Social Statistics* (New York: McGraw-Hill, 1960), pp. 319-325; William L. Hays, *Statistics for Psychologists* (New York: Holt, Rinehart, & Winston, 1963), pp. 647-655.

2. August B. Hollingshead, *Two Factor Index of Social Position*, (copyrighted 1957; Yale Station, New Haven, Conn.: privately printed, 1965). The *Index* uses as indicators of class position for members of a household the occupation and years of school completed by the head of the household. To calculate the position of the head of the household by this method, the scale value for occupation is multiplied by the factor weight for occupation (7), and the scale value for education is multiplied by the factor weight for education (4). The scores are then added and indicate, in a range from a low of 11 to a high of 77, the social position of the individual. In the ordering procedures that we used, the top rank represents the persons with the highest social position.

3. See Appendix.

4. The five statements and procedure for rank-ordering members are presented in the Appendix.

5. See Appendix.

6. See Appendix.

7. Following the same kinds of procedures described in the Appendix, the members were rank-ordered on their feelings of parity, social position, importance, and influence such as shown in Chapter 13, Tables 13-4 and 13-5; they also were ranked on satisfaction with life

in Maplewood and on feelings of accomplishment and optimism.

8. Justino Vilá is Mrs. Estebán's 69-year-old father. Although he was present very often, he was never considered in any way even an informal leader. He listened attentively at meetings but seldom spoke. Sometimes he appeared to be withdrawing into himself, muttering barely audible words, as if age had suddenly disconnected him from the give-and-take of the meetings. Some time later, I discovered by listening carefully to the tape recordings of the meetings that the elder Vilá was actually serving as an unobtrusive advisor to his daughter. Sitting close to her, he was giving her fatherly advice: "Cristina, you are repeating yourself," or "Cristina, you have spoken too much; let others speak." The words were meant to control her tendency towards excitability and to sound reassuring and supportive. Very likely, they helped her. Thus, as a reliable member, Justino Vilá's involvement in the group produced an effect that probably was much greater than what it appeared to be on the surface.

15

Social Change in the Confederation

•

The confederation was a small social system in which conduct was guided by old and new norms and by an unfolding common goal. It was a group in flux, caught in the process of reorganization in response to internal and external influences. No law of inexorable development guided its trajectory. Social change was uneven and fitful; its direction sometimes even regressive. At first the group was docile and uncertain in contacts with the city's governmental and service organizations. Then it grew more forceful until eventually it became militant in its negotiations. Consensus among the members was difficult to attain and group survival always remained a problem, but the group changed because of the conscious efforts of the reliable members and as a result of the unplanned, crescive processes that shaped its life. Norms emerged to regulate the conduct of the members and to change their traditional relationships. With the reorganization of roles came the attempt to develop an ideology supporting the direction of change and culminating in a precedent for the actions of a politically independent group in the migrant community.

Thus, if the confederation is compared to an ideal of how an action group should conduct its business, its shortcomings are clearly evident. But if it is considered in relation to the history of Puerto Rican organizational failures in Maplewood or to what it was when it started, its success demonstrates not only changes in the group but development as well.

The confederation's birth was the unexpected and unwanted result of an attempt by one community worker to bring Puerto Ricans into the established groups of the neighborhood to which he was assigned. The Puerto Ricans, however, formed an Hispano group with the goal of helping Puerto Ricans. Fearing the failures they remembered in other such groups, they were cautious to avoid divisive issues: they decided their group would not be political, would not be religious, and would not collect membership dues. After visiting the city's several Puerto Rican neighborhoods, they concluded that there was support for the group in the ethnic community, that it was in fact a legitimate organization. The choice of name, the Hispanic Confederation, expressed a lofty wish — but only a vague plan — for the group to be composed of the leaders of neighborhood subgroups. By virtue of its name, the confederation was to monopolize control of all Puerto Rican groups in Maplewood. These decisions, along with the election of officers, comprised the confederation's original legacy and starting point.

The early directing influence of American advisors led the members to treat the group's goal as if it involved only the helping of Puerto Rican nonmembers, so the possibility of mutual help among the members was not discussed. The subject matter of the meetings, however, was only loosely related to the group's official purpose. The informality and lack of structure at meetings immediately set the tone of a primary group: the meetings were always late in starting, and the detailed ritual introduction of members elicited personal questions or was taken as a point of departure for the recounting of personal experiences. This form of interaction was encouraged by the members' yearning to recreate in the new social setting a sense of the intimate community with those sharing their culture and language. At the same time, the group's goal of helping Puerto Ricans encouraged revelation of the members' personal problems concerning housing, employment, medical care, prejudice, and discrimination.

Stimulated by the group goal and the spirit of the primary group, the members gave free rein to the expression of their grievances. Each revelation, in turn, stimulated further and more extensive revelations. Even when the speaker at a meeting was an agency official who could have provided a target for sustained group pressure, the discussion and the angry outbursts inevitably came to rest on the discrete, individual problems of individual members. As one meeting followed another, the relief of unburdening themselves was seldom complete, for interruptions by one person followed by another would occur. The meeting would dissolve into confusion, and the members, cut off in the midst of their recitations, were frustrated and unhappy. The president and vice-president were locked in conflict, as were the other members, relatives, and friends, each blaming the other for the group's troubles. Some members quit because they felt that what they would not express in public — the vulgar stereotype of the Puerto Rican — was being publicly demonstrated. All the American advisors withdrew from the group, their humanitarian concern for helping Puerto Ricans having been sorely tested.

The members were unable to extract a common denominator from their personal complaints and act in a unified manner toward an external goal, and they were not involved in mutual help. Therefore, they were being denied not only the feeling of accomplishment of successful group action but also the rich primary relationships for which they longed. Power, control, and responsibility were diffused because membership roles were barely differentiated. At that point, the group was in an organizational limbo, unable to develop mechanisms for coping with the crisis. It was close to dissolution.

To understand what happened next it is necessary to turn to the city's partisan political system which is a source of external influence on migrant organizations. Although the migrant is culturally and linguistically marginal, he is deeply involved in the task of understanding the terms that the new environment is exacting from him and what, in turn, it can offer him. A welter of public agencies and departments — welfare, antipoverty, employment, education — surrounds him as a broad system with which he must contend. The gaps in the communicative and control structure of the agencies — differences in the orientation of their staffs, the social cleavages, and rivalries endemic to large-scale organizations — are at best only dimly perceived by the migrant who, nevertheless, must cope with them. He sees a bureaucratic design behind the most casual, even gratuitous comments of agency officials. He attributes to the system much greater unity and coherence than, in fact, exists.

At the same time, the influence of the migrant extends only into his own ethnic group at the lowest level of the city's power structure; it does not rise vertically. No informal web of stable interpersonal relations links him to the focal points of decision-making. Thus, to be a successful action group, the confederation had to get to such focal points. The political system was not just one way of getting there; it was the only way. No other established channel for upward influence was available to the members.

In a migrant organization this understanding leads to an advocacy of political activity. If memories of a homeland *patrón* who looked after his welfare still linger, the migrant decides it is now the politician who has parallel resources in the form of agencies affecting the grass-roots level of his life. The political system, however, poses a dilemma for migrant organizations: being apolitical means surrendering the possible benefits accruing from affiliation with the party in power, but being political means surrendering control to the political boss. Organizations and the political system surrounding the boss are locked into a system of tensions: what one gains, the other loses. Thus, the confederation was an immediate threat to the Puerto Rican political boss of Maplewood. Vicente de Serrano was known as a brilliant political tactician, skillful in subverting organizations to bring them under party control. His role as political boss mediated between the migrants' daily life and the power structure of the city, and it required that he control Puerto Rican organizational life, but, from the very start, the confederation policy to be apolitical was designed to protect the group from Serrano.

Diego Zayas, the first president of the confederation, thought the crisis in the group meant that there was a desperate need for progress toward the goal of helping Puerto Ricans. Although earlier in the confederation's life he had sworn he was against political involvement, his ideas inevitably began to gravitate toward the political party system. He thought there was a middle alternative between the horns of the dilemma, what he called "liberal politics" or the "politics of the empty stomach." This course would keep the confederation outside the party structure yet would allow for political action according to what would most benefit the group. This course, however, assumed that the members could agree upon the best individual candidates or political party, and then, disciplined and unified, vote according to group decision. By invoking the confederation to be *and* not to be political, Zayas was attempting to resolve a perennial problem of migrant organizations, but he neglected to consider the difficult organizational requirements "liberal politics" would impose upon the confederation precisely at a time when the group was in internal disarray.

A group such as the confederation is not disposed to experiment with a policy already established. Even in time of crisis when group survival itself was at stake, there was still resistance to sudden change involving internal revisions. Just by the passage of time the policy had become suffused with emotional feelings because it represented a point of consensus in a setting where disagreement was much more prevalent. In brief, the decision to remain apolitical had become almost sacred. Regardless of what advantages "liberal politics" might have brought to the group and regardless, too, of how poorly his political viewpoint was understood by the members, Zayas was seen as having betrayed the confederation. Later, even he felt guilt about this.

Although there were members of the group who shared Zayas's political beliefs, he never had the opportunity of explaining fully the value of his plan. In the confusion of the meeting, Serrano's political aides unexpectedly turned against Zayas on an issue which was incidental to the plan. Also, by then, Mrs. Estebán had crystallized her opposition to Zayas and, because she was a powerful, informal leader among the city's Puerto Ricans, she was able to attract to the meeting friends and relatives who would oppose him. Forcing Zayas out of office was, perhaps, as personal as it was political. At meetings he was volatile and explosive and repeatedly violated Puerto Rican cultural norms of cordiality and respect; his behavior contradicted the primary group solidarity that the members were seeking in the organization. In deposing Zayas the group rejected a political plan by the rejection of a deviant member. Twice, at later meetings, the members broke into a spontaneous round of condemnation of Zayas as if they were purging themselves of a moral affliction. This unsuccessful attempt to turn the group in the direction of "liberal politics" unwittingly served the cause of group unity.

The acceptance of "liberal politics" would have meant the acceptance of internal revolutionary change, although, externally, partisan politics was the institutional channel for attaining upward influence. By reaffirming its apolitical character, the confederation renounced with finality the only known access to the most evident instrumentality for upward influence. To succeed, it had to overcome its self-imposed isolation by forging new links with the city's governing circles — without any solid precedents in migrant experience.

Unlike Zayas, Mrs. Estebán was not concerned as much with the group's effectiveness as she was with the members' reactions to the meetings. She realized that the repeated recitation of personal experiences was time-consuming and confusing and that the members had grown tired of hearing each other's personal problems. She had no theory of group development, but she identified the problem accurately and set out to solve it by introducing a rule that nothing personal would be discussed at meetings. There was no discussion of the advantages or disadvantages of the rule; it was never voted on. As vice-president, Mrs. Estebán had no official authority to pass regulations or to control discussion, but when members failed to comply with the rule she declared them out of order, and the esteem in which she was held by the members was such that the rule was followed.

At first, a specific reaction to the crisis, the rule soon acquired broader meaning. When one of Serrano's aides argued that there should be mutual help among the membership, Mrs. Estebán silenced him with the admonition that "by law" the confederation did not permit discussion of the members' problems. The authoritative way in which she expressed the point, to repel another attack by the unwanted "outsiders," served to link the rule to the members' emerging feelings of solidarity and their consensus as a group. Although the rule had been suddenly improvised as a protective device, it was entirely consistent with the group's goals: if personal problems could not be discussed, then a member could not be given help. The old and the emerging policies were being brought together through repetition as if they were all equally legitimate.

On the surface, there appears to be little difference between the goals of improving the collective welfare of the migrant community and of mutual help among members, for both involve helping compatriots. Sociologically, however, they differ sharply. One set of principles directs the group toward traditional cultural norms; the other towards new requirements involving instrumental goals.

When a Puerto Rican group accepts mutual help among its members as a goal, it is reenacting patterns which are customary in the culture and, at the same time, stabilizing the primary group system and its associated values. When a group takes on the goal of improving the collective welfare of nonmembers, it must reach out far beyond the immediate situation of meetings to focus its attention upon organizations that command the resources useful to the total migrant community. The group must organize itself to sustain pressure upon such organizations and develop a political stance in negotiations. To do this the group must either depart from customary primary relations among members *or* develop procedures for bridging and reconciling different principles of organization. Mrs.

Estebán's insistence upon obedience to the rule represented the choice of the first alternative and it had an implicit but immediate effect upon the group: it outlined the group goal. Henceforth, the confederation would restrict itself to helping Puerto Ricans outside the group.

Obedience to the new rule meant that each member was expected to suppress his natural volubility, no matter how strongly he felt about a personal problem.

We have seen that in private situations the members stereotyped and derogated Puerto Ricans, felt that they were above their own ethnic group, and were satisfied with their material progress in Maplewood. In the group context, however, the member could no longer maintain the tendency to separate himself mentally from the Puerto Rican community, not if he wanted to participate in the give-and-take of meetings. To speak he had to submit to the intellectual and emotional discipline of translating his own personal problems into the collective problems of the ethnic community; otherwise, he would be criticized by the group's main norm enforcer, Mrs. Estebán. Thus, what appeared on the surface of meetings to have been a sudden shift toward an altruistic devotion to the ethnic group was in fact an intricate response to the terms of participation introduced by the new rule. Combined with the adoption of an external goal, this was a basic step the members took to become politicized, in the nonpartisan sense of the word.

The rule's enforcement sharpened the group boundary: interaction at meetings was no longer the same as it had been in the migrant community. Thus, in coping with the crisis, the group moved away from what it had been before and separated itself from the usual conversational patterns in the ethnic community, in an effort to serve the community itself.

As the new goal was being assimilated into the group's internal life, the expectation grew that progress would soon be made. The members' increasing identification with the goal gave rise to a new functional standard: the frequency of group meetings was to be weighed against group progress toward the goal. During Zayas's term of office, power, control, and responsibility had been diffused; then power quickly gravitated into the hands of Mrs. Estebán who not only kept the group alive but directed it toward an external goal as well. But to sustain action toward the exterior, a group must have an essential continuity in its life; it must store memories of its relevant past, conceptualize and put into use the information it acquires and the decisions it has made. It cannot start anew at every meeting. Before the rebirth of the confederation, the problem of discontinuity from one meeting to another had passed by unnoticed, because the members' attention was rooted on the immediate situation of each meeting. With the new orientation toward a distant goal, the members became aware that the meetings were disconnected.

The problem of discontinuity was too pervasive to be solved by anything less than concerted action among the members, particularly since the president herself was the main culprit. But the sharp organizational split between the formidably active leader and the passive faithful followers was an impediment to such action.

As an informal leader Mrs. Estebán had succeeded in bringing persons into the group who felt obligated to her for personal favors. This, by itself, tended to encourage passivity among the members. Had they reacted more forcefully, she might have realized that she was failing as president by leaving things undone. In addition, her personal problems had aggravated her tendency to launch into endless stories, and she brought into the meetings her confusion at the many contradictory items of information she had picked up in her contacts with other organizations. Her friends and relatives, not wanting to appear ungrateful, vacillated between hesitation and withdrawal. Nonetheless, as tensions mounted, the new members who did not feel indebted to her made her the target of unorganized sporadic attacks. Their restiveness was nurtured by feeling that the number of meetings convened was disproportionate to the group's progress.

Suddenly, unexpectedly, a procedure evolved — rehearsing the president in her role as spokesman for the confederation — which enabled the members to break out of their passivity by becoming involved in playing the role of city officials. By this means, they vented their criticisms of the president and sought to improve her performance without the appearance of ungratefulness. Soon, they no longer needed this form of pretense.

In their quest for action, the members found it necessary to turn to the mayor for assistance. As a result they ran into the same type of social-structural problem encountered with Serrano, the political boss. When persons or organizations play a mediating role between those in power and those not in power, any attempt to circumvent the hierarchy poses a threat. In the case of the political boss the threat was potential; in the case of the antipoverty agency, which they had overlooked in their attempts to deal with the mayor, the threat was actual for the group had requested in writing an appointment with the mayor. The result was unique in interactions in the city's political power structure, for an independent Puerto Rican civic group had bypassed political intermediaries and gone directly to what was thought to be the source of power.

Unaware of the precedent they had established, the members focused their attention upon the president and criticized her for violating at city hall the rule not to discuss personal problems. The rule had taken hold in the group's system of sanctions and even the president was not exempt from its conditions. The rule had become the group's property, and they could see its applicability to contacts with city officials: obedience to the rule would impress upon city officials the group's unselfish devotion to the welfare of Puerto Ricans. An ingroup virtue acquired outgroup merit as the confederation attempted to define a political stance in negotiations. The mayor's favorable reaction to the confederation's requests gave the members a sense of greater urgency to move ahead in order to capitalize on the opportunities being made available. When the president did not attend the next meeting, they appointed another spokesman to represent them at a meeting with the director of the antipoverty agency. At the following meeting of the confederation, Mrs. Estebán insisted that her plan be followed instead of the new one formulated in her absence, and a full-scale rebellion erupted.

Beneath the conflict, a new and different form of group organization was straining to emerge. The reliable members were demanding a stronger voice in the group's affairs and a dissolution of the pattern of powerful leader and passive followers. Although Mrs. Estebán, herself, had initiated the change during the group's rebirth, she fought to resist it. She had countered the political assault, implanted with almost sacred fervor into the group the goal of helping Puerto Ricans, and taken a step to depersonalize the interaction at meetings. Unwittingly, her own forceful actions created among the members a new vision of the group effort. Once the changes took root, the group's evolving character clashed with its authoritarian structure. Her opposition brought the struggle out into the open and solidified group feeling against her. The revolt came to an end when the members forced the unwilling president to take the action they wished. The victory was won. A more democratic structure was established.

The attack on Mrs. Estebán, however, did not signify personal rejection as in the case of Diego Zayas. It was a revolt against a style of leadership and against authoritarian group structure. It established the fact that the group interests were not always the same as those of the president.

Mrs. Estebán's leadership had introduced a wide range of changes involving norms, goals, and outlook, but it had also introduced changes in the reliability of the members. Of the 42 members interviewed, 23 had joined while Diego Zayas was president and 19 after Mrs. Estebán took charge. Thus, we can divide the membership into the newcomers and the veterans, the dividing line coinciding with the change of presidency. The recentness of joining the group is directly correlated with the reliability of the members in attending meetings (t_b = .394). The median membership reliability of the newcomers is .264 and of the veterans .029. The correlation and the difference in medians, in turn, are reduced by the fact that the two most reliable members, Mrs. Estebán and her brother Alfonso Vilá, were indeed veterans.

The newcomers were not only more reliable than the veterans, they tended also to have a higher social-class position (t_b = .270) and to have been more upward in social mobility (t_b = .302). The organizational changes were accompanied by the incoming flux of more reliable newcomers and their class-related socially mobile experiences. The evolving character of the group and the changing composition of the incoming members interacted to form a mutually supportive system of influences: group changes stabilized the attendance rate of the newcomers, and the newcomers, in turn, were contributing to the group's evolution toward activism. Their more reliable participation lessened the discontinuity between meetings.

Among the newcomers were David Alemán and Enrique Zamora, both recent migrants to Maplewood and, therefore, marginal to the network of social relations that Mrs. Estebán had incorporated into the confederation. These two newcomers began to provide, then, the main stimulus to social change because, without violating the obligations imbedded in the president's immediate circle, they could turn their attention to what they felt were the confederation's needs as an action group. Nonetheless, they could not have been effective as agents of social change if the group had not been intensely committed to external goals.

Usually, Alemán and Zamora made specific proposals, explained them, and gained support from the reliable members who were close to Mrs. Estebán. Gradually pressure was built up until, as the terminal point of the sequence, she was the last member to accept them. Thus, during the rebellious aftermath, suddenly she discovered that all the members had turned against her — "Even my brother," she complained. The repetition of this sequence over time altered the role Mrs. Estebán had assumed as well as the social organization of the group. Her immediate network of relations did stabilize the group but it also provided effective channels for the diffusion of social change in the confederation.

The presence of an organization such as the antipoverty agency is by itself a politicizing force among the disadvantaged minorities it attempts to serve. As it makes available new resources, it stimulates competition between minorities and an awareness of the need for concerted action. This was the case with the confederation. Yet the group's change toward an ever-increasing militancy against the agency must be understood in terms of the specific contacts with the agency: the ups and the downs, the resistance, the frustration, the promises made and not fulfilled.

In negotiating for the establishment of the Hispanic Referral Office, the group had to counter an array of arguments from agency officials: the office would open a Pandora's box of conflicting demands from other minority groups; it would violate an agency policy that the city's inner-city neighborhoods had to be treated — in the agency vernacular — as "integrated communities" without regard to the Puerto Ricans' linguistic and cultural isolation; the office would duplicate ongoing poverty programs; if such programs were not reaching Puerto Ricans, the solution was to scatter a few Spanish speakers throughout the programs. The arguments imposed upon the members the task of reviewing the broad spectrum of agency programs and of demonstrating their ineffectiveness in the Puerto Rican community. Heart-warming pleas in behalf of Puerto Ricans were not sufficient. While learning the politics of minority group representation, the more contacts with the agency, the more the members' hostility toward the agency grew (see Epilogue).

Even when impartially enforced and fully obeyed, the rule not to discuss personal problems distinctly favored the loquacious president. Because her involvement in civic affairs was far greater than that of anyone else, she could dominate talk at meetings with seemingly endless resumés of her outside activities. The information she brought the group was not personal, but it did confuse the members and frustrate their abiding wish to move ahead. The impact of Mrs. Amador's angry resignation led the members to instruct the president that henceforth each meeting had to have a purpose, and the purpose would determine the topics for discussion. In fact, this was a more refined version of the standard already accepted, that the more frequent the meetings, the more the group should progress. A more specific criterion of what was relevant talk, therefore, was derived from the group's evolving system of norms.

While social interaction in the confederation was being progressively shaped by norms and standards linked to the overall goals and by contacts with the outside world, the group was changing through gradual accretions to its fund of norms and total legacy. The meetings themselves did not contribute equally to social change: some meetings pushed the group ahead more than others. Quiet meetings usually meant that the conditions governing the past were being reenacted, obeyed, perhaps extended slightly, or that consensus on some issue was on its way to being established. Noisy meetings with heated arguments meant that basic issues were usually at stake: some event had precipitated awareness that an unresolved problem still lingered, that little or no consensus had developed on a fundamental point, that there was a sharp edge to the old and new principles of group organization, or that an important person was being evicted from the group's inner life or being pressured into acceptance of the emerging social mold. The pattern that developed was that the more unpleasant the member's subjective experience of a meeting, the more likely this was to signal a new sequence of social change. This pattern remained true as long as the group could preserve minimal conditions for its continuing existence.

Often the heated debate on a point turned the members' attention to the meaning and consequences of the group's social change. The confederation was putting its house in order after being swept forward by social change. It was attempting to construct an ideology. Painful as the decisions sometimes were, they did contain principles extending into the future. The future became linked to the present as the present was to the past. Meetings, therefore, became points in a continuum of the group's history, not discrete and isolated happenings. This was a major departure from the confederation's early life when the members' views of the group were bound and circumscribed by the immediate experience of each meeting.

The thrust toward ideology came late in the group's life after much had been accomplished. Surprisingly, with the exception of occasional, incidental comments, the members never had dealt with the inconsistency between the group's evolving normative system and Puerto Rican cultural traditions. As the emerging norms took hold in the system of group sanctions, however, pressure emanating from the group itself kept the system working: outside the group the members could participate in the traditional form of help-giving, but within the confederation help had to be given through the group's increasingly impersonal normative system. The role of a member had to be compartmentalized from the person's other roles. In brief, the spirit of help-giving imbedded in the tradition was to be kept intact, but its means of expression was to be changed. The new and the traditional, the sacred and the utilitarian, were being woven together into a coherent belief system whose essential purpose was to rationalize the confederation's change into an action group.

Unfortunately, circumstances did not provide a test of whether or not the ideology would have taken hold in the group's inner life or of its effect, if any, upon the group's ever-increasing activism. Despite the many changes in the confederation, there had been no preparation for the contingency that occurred. Although participation among reliable members had become much more egalitarian, group survival still depended upon the person of the president. When Mrs. Esteban was paralyzed into inactivity, the group collapsed and momentum was never fully restored.

Mrs. Esteban's failure to convene meetings for nine weeks stemmed directly from the threat of the group's social change to her leadership in the confederation and to her relationships in the community. She wanted to retain the affection and respect of her compatriots and at the same time not offend agency officials, but what the new leaders were advocating was taking hold. They wanted negotiations with the agency to be premised upon the assumption that the agency was obligated to help Puerto Ricans and Puerto Ricans, in turn, had the right to demand help. This view originated after the visit to city hall when it was decided that negotiations should be conducted according to the group's own internally derived system of impersonal norms; it was refined into the coupling together of the concepts of obligations and rights as a result of the unhappy entanglements with the agency. Thus, the group had become a vehicle which moved the president into an ever-deeper identification with the agency precisely at a time when the members' opposition towards the agency was hardening. This complication trapped her. The sequence of group change had begun again, but this time it posed a serious threat to the president's way of life and her relationship with others.

The nine-week lapse of activity wiped out the taste of triumph and opened the way for new conflict among the membership. Although social change favored the new leaders, if the disciplined enforcement of parliamentary procedures had been carried out, it would have probably culminated in the problem of sustaining motivation to participate even among the reliable members. The meeting chaired by Alemán as vice-president carried this ominous hint: too many procedural rules — involving quorums, motions presented, seconded, debated, voted upon, old business, new business, strict criteria of relevance — could have wiped out a lingering, but critically important, expressive component in the group's life. And neither of the two new leaders had Mrs. Estebán's breadth of influence among the city's Hispanos to be able to compensate for such a loss. Thus, there were even deeper organizational dilemmas in the confederation. Disillusionment gave birth to passivity, indifference, and withdrawal. The group was burned out!

An attempt to understand the downturn in the confederation's affairs unexpectedly led to the sudden acceptance of a plan to sponsor a social event. The official purpose was to recruit new members, but actually it was a legitimate way of suspending the wearisome grind toward the group goal and the austere norms of interaction at meetings. In the interlude of fun, the failure to bring in new members was hardly noticed, and, still relishing the memories of the party, the members found it difficult to resume the tiring business of an action group.

Five weeks later Mrs. Estebán imposed her family dynasty on the confederation. The control was kept where she wanted it — in her immediate network of relations. Continuity was preserved, along with the strong voice of the old leader. Nonetheless, when the group tried again to pressure the agency, old themes began to echo: the need for organized procedures at meetings and a stronger, impersonal stand against the agency.

The goal of elevating the Puerto Rican minority to a higher level of community involvement fit the traditions of a democratic society and it suffused the confederation with a democratic ethos. Yet the group was strikingly undemocratic in relation to the ethnic minority it sought to represent and, internally, in the preponderant influence of a handful of members. Although the members rejected policies of exclusion, only 46 Hispanos, out of an estimated population of about 4,500 Puerto Ricans in Maplewood, had been induced to come to at least one meeting during the first 19 months of the group's life. Less than 30 percent of those who came to at least one meeting accounted for more than 75 percent of the group's total attendance. The democratizing trend associated with the rebellious aftermath affected only the small handful of reliable members. In brief, a monopoly in attendance led to a monopoly of control over the group. Small in relation to the ethnic community, the group was small, too, in the size of its effective leadership. At no time ever in its formation or evolution did its strength derive from a broad base of participation, either within the total membership or outside in the migrant community. It derived from a small oligarchy of committed members, practically all of whom had been recruited from the president's circle of friends and relatives.

The history of the confederation substantiates Robert Michel's "iron law of oligarchy" and the observations of modern organizational theorists that membership in associations divides itself into an active, leading minority and a passive, uninvolved majority.[1] This division restricted the group's sphere of internal controls and denied it a numerical show of force in vying for community resources. On the balance, however, the processes which created and sustained the highly differentiated structure of reliability in membership — the oligarchical structure — introduced into the group a resilient stabilizing force and protected it from the full thrust of disruptions endemic to the Puerto Ricans' organizational efforts.

Thus, Mrs. Estebán's long tenure as group leader was protected by the unreliability of most members. A uniformly high invariant rate of attendance among members would have increased the opportunities for organizing and launching attacks against her leadership. To depose a leader, the person, clique, or subgroup must be sufficiently committed to the parent group to be present at meetings, and the confederation had very little of such commitment among members.

If all the persons who came to at least one meeting had become reliable members, the group would have extended itself far beyond the immediate network of social relations of the leader, but membership of many more persons outside the leader's social circle might well have destroyed the precarious balance between the forces of stability and change.

Although the size of the effective membership was small, the confederation's history attests to the tribulations of developing consensus in the group. Yet there were unusual advantages to the size: its small oligarchy shared a set of achievement values and class-related experiences which were functionally related to the group goal. More than the unreliable members, these persons believed in social values which: freed them from traditional obligations to relatives and conferred worth upon the stability of social contacts outside the family; entailed the belief that other persons ought to be trusted; and gave them a vision of the future as dependent upon man's present deeds. Along with a higher social-class position, they had experienced greater upward social mobility than the less reliable members. All of these oriented them toward incorporation into American life. Yet the congenial fit between the activistic character of the confederation and the character of the oligarchy, itself, by no means made it easy to attain consensus. To the very last, the members never fully agreed on the important issues of how to conduct meetings and what stance to take in negotiations with the antipoverty agency. Had the effective membership been larger, more diverse in values and life experiences, and outside the main leader's primary group associations, the confederation would likely have confronted an insurmountable task in the development of even an elementary consensus.

As first-generation migrants with limited formal education and a different culture and language, the Puerto Ricans of Maplewood had had few experiences from which they could draw in developing effective action groups. The array of voluntary associations that proliferates in middle-class American life does not have a counterpart in the migrants' experiences either on the island or on the mainland. But if, in the absence of such learning, the fund of skills and attitudes needed to maintain organizations remains undeveloped, the tasks of an action group seeking to represent an ethnic minority are difficult indeed. The stable operation of social forces impinging upon the Puerto Rican serves, in an ironic manner, to perpetuate his unorganized position and to deny him a voice he very much wants. This is the lot of the migrant in the city.

NOTES

1. See David L. Sills, "Voluntary Associations: Sociological Aspects," *International Encylopedia of the Social Sciences* vol. 16 (New York: The Macmillan Co. & The Free Press, 1968), pp. 362-379.

Epilogue

•

For everything we've done, there are five things we
haven't done, or five things we've failed at. If Maplewood is a model city, then God help urban America.
— Maplewood's Mayor,
commenting on the riot.

The end of August of the third summer of the confederation's life brought an
outbreak of rioting in Maplewood's racially mixed inner-city neighborhoods. The
glass-front windows of grocery stores, pawnshops, clothing stores, and liquor
shops were smashed, and the stores were looted. Fire bombs were thrown into
buildings, and when firemen attempted to extinguish the flames, they were
pelted with bottles and rocks, as were the policemen who tried to protect them.
Late in the afternoon of the second day, the mayor declared a state of emergency, and 200 state troopers were rushed into the stricken area to assist the
400-man city police force. To contain the disturbance, the neighborhoods were
cordoned off and a strict curfew was enforced. By the end of the second day,
more than 200 persons had been arrested for looting, disorderly conduct, violation of the curfew, and other similar offenses. The "show of force" was calculated to impress upon the residents of the neighborhoods the determination of
the city authorities to restore order.

The expectation had been that Maplewood would not succumb to the rash of
urban-centered, race-related riots that swept the country during that "long hot
summer," even though a year before a riot had almost erupted. No other city had
as successful an urban redevelopment program. In 13 years, slums had been torn
down and replaced with high-rise apartment buildings, elegant shops, and hotels.
New schools and public-housing developments were built. For the commuters,
there was easy access from the core of the city to the outlying turnpikes and
highways over a new connecting road. Nor had the needs of the poor been disregarded: The city authorities could and did point proudly to the many projects
sponsored by APA that had preceded by two years President Lyndon Johnson's
declaration of war against poverty. The projects completed and those being
planned formed a seemingly endless list. The mayor considered references to
Maplewood as a "model city" inaccurate, but this was actually the city's reputation among urban planners throughout the nation. Maplewood stood as an exam-

ple of the collaboration of imaginative and intelligent community and political leaders, with experts on urbanization and on the reconstruction of their city physically, socially, and economically, assisted by federal money grants. Many of the nation's urban programs were born in Maplewood. Thus, the riot came as a stunning surprise.

To María Porrata, a former member of the Pan-American Association, the riot came as more than a surprise but not because of Maplewood's vaunted reputation. Not knowing English, she had not read but had been told of the newspaper account which claimed that the riot began when a restaurant owner shot a Puerto Rican for throwing a rock through his front window. The Puerto Rican was her son Juan. Although she was deeply worried about Juan's chest wound, Mrs. Porrato was offended that her son was being blamed instead of the *Molletes* ("American blacks"). She explained to me what had actually happened.

> The *Molletes* are in revolt. They have been burning buildings and doing all kinds of dirty crazy things in the neighborhood. I don't know where all this will end. And now everyone is blaming my son Pablo for having started the riots. You see, Saturday night Pablo went to a snack bar in the neighborhood and asked the owner for a sandwich and the owner replied that he did not serve Puerto Ricans. Pablo told him he had a right to be served, but the owner, who is an Italian, refused, and they got into an argument. Then a *Mollete* standing near by punched Pablo in the face, knocked him down, and held him while the owner's son beat him up. Pablo finally got loose and came running home to get a knife, but at that moment my other son Juan walked into the snack bar. By this time the owner's son had a revolver and he shot Juan through the chest. And there I was at home when Pablo came running in to get his knife, and I chased after him in my bare feet. There on the sidewalk staggering home was my son Juan, blood dripping from a hole in his chest. He said, "Mother, they shot me." And he collapsed at my feet. The Italian shot him four times, but hit him only once. A police car rushed Juan to the hospital where they opened him up and took out a lead slug and then closed him up with 18 stitches. The doctors said he was lucky to be alive.
>
> Juan and the *Mollete* were arrested and had to post bond for $15,000, but the Italian who shot Juan — imagine this! — had to post only $5,000. When other *Molletes* heard that one of their own had to post more bond than the Italian who had actually done the shooting, they started to riot. Now they say my sons started the riot. We Puerto Ricans have to have faith in God. My son lives by a miracle.

Accompanied by two daughters and a grandson, Mrs. Porrata was among the approximately 300 residents evacuated from the inner-city neighborhoods by Maplewood's private organizations. They were taken to outlying suburban towns to stay in churches or in the homes of middle-class residents until the riot was over. Mrs. Porrata liked the family with whom she was staying, and she marvelled at the spacious green lawns, the neat flower beds, and the many trees in the neighborhoods, but no one in the host family knew Spanish and, in the hectic rush to be evacuated, she had forgotten to bring a change of clothing. She felt lonely, out of place, and disheveled. After one night in the suburbs, she returned to her own apartment in the inner city.

The police discovered caches of guns and molotov cocktails in the cordoned-off area. Because liquor stores had been looted, they expected drunken violence. Rumors flew on both sides. The residents heard that the Ku Klux Klan stood ready to storm the area with the full cooperation of the police. In the general confusion, the police began to arrest local black leaders who were walking the streets trying to quiet their neighbors.

After five days the riot ended, but even before the debris was cleared scores of explanations were advanced for its occurrence in a city with such exemplary urban programs. The causes or alleged causes centered upon the shooting of the Puerto Rican, police brutality, defiance of law and order, the "breakdown" of American society. Others blamed "people who thought they could get away with it [rioting]" and "bored individuals not in the forefront of correcting social ills." The system of social inequality and discrimination which victimized the black and the Puerto Rican and the failure of poverty programs to reach the poor were blamed too. One observer recommended that to prevent riots ". . . the city has got to got to start taking seriously the community leadership of the poor people." Another person said, "Once and for all, people must have the opportunity for full participation in bringing about the kind of social change which can break up the vicious cycle of the ghetto." Yet no one mentioned that for three years the Hispanic Confederation had been waging an uneven struggle to obtain full participation for Maplewood's Puerto Ricans.

During the aftermath of the riot the confederation's members were angry about a proclamation of alliance between blacks and Puerto Ricans issued by a black organization in the neighborhood of the Hispanic Referral Office. They felt that only an organization within the ethnic ingroup could speak rightfully on behalf of the Puerto Ricans, but serious internal problems kept the confederation from adding its voice to that of the other minorities who sought to impose demands upon the city authorities in the wake of the riot. Meetings of the confederation had been convened irregularly; invitations to meetings arrived late; few members attended them; and interest in the group waned. To broaden its appeal, the group was renamed the Hispanic-American Confederation, but with little success. Another attempt at drafting a constitution had ended in frustration. Some of the officers had resigned, and others were elected. So disorganized had the group become that Mrs. Estebán proposed the suspension of all activities for a year until stability could be restored.

Half a year later when the group had all but collapsed, word spread that the antipoverty agency had issued an order disbanding the Hispanic Referral Office.

242

That year the office's staff had been reduced from three to two persons — only Carlos Otero and his secretary remained. The confederation members believed the rumor and were aroused. Fernando Vilá, who was still president, organized a meeting of 40 persons, and invited the director of APA to explain his plans for the office. Although Bartola, the tape recorder, had not been used for almost a year, Vilá requested that she be brought back to record the important meeting.

The director denied the rumor, then promised to transfer into the office within a week two APA Puerto Rican fieldworkers. He promised also to recruit two Puerto Ricans from outside APA to work in the office. Thus, the staff would be increased from two to six. He went on to encourage the group to formulate plans for the development of a Spanish center for the migrant community. His promises were clear and firm; his attitude conciliatory, cooperative, and sympathetic. Never before had an APA official shown such concern for the Puerto Ricans. But suddenly, Carlos Otero launched an impassioned attack against APA and vowed to resign as coordinator of the office if the staff was not increased even more than what had been promised. The members, remembering APA's many duplicities, became aroused and one person after another rallied to his support. One said, "APA always relegated us to the garbage heap." Another proposed that Puerto Ricans picket the agency. There was a full and bitter release of the anger and frustration accumulated over the years of contact with APA. Toward the end the meeting became even more unruly, and Vilá finally accepted the APA's promise and explained that the group had not meant to offend the director.

The promise to transfer within a week two full-time employees to the office was not fulfilled, but the confederation had learned to use new sources of power as leverage against the agency. When doubts arose as to whether or not the promise had actually been made, the group contacted the Commission on Equal Opportunities to listen to Bartola's tape recording of the meeting and to examine the correspondence between APA and the confederation. A notarized statement of complaint was written and signed by Fernando Vilá as the president. As a result, one of Maplewood's newspapers carried the following front-page article:

CITY'S HISPANIC CONFEDERATION FLAYS APA PRACTICES

A Spanish-speaking group added its voice to local antipoverty discontent this week, as Maplewood's Hispanic Confederation demanded a "full investigation" of APA with respect to servicing and hiring of Spanish-speaking people.

In writing to the APA president, the confederation's president, Fernando Vilá, charged APA with giving the confederation the "run-around" and "discriminatory practices." . . . Citing promises "not kept," the letter specifically dealt with requests made at an April 1 meeting with APA, although it also stated APA had given it the "run-around" for the past four years. . . . Two additional workers to be assigned to the unit immediately was not done. The two workers are still part-time workers and nothing else. . . .

That summer the confederation finally began to publish its own newspaper, fully two years after it was first planned. One of the first issues of the "Latin Voice of Maplewood" contained the following article about the confederation:

This organization was founded by a group of persons who, observing the need for unity among the Hispanos and, even more, the need for adequate representation, decided to unite voluntarily but determined to improve the critical situation in which we found ourselves.

These persons sacrificed a great deal of their valuable time to develop the Hispanic Confederation. The group was made up of members of this community: workers, parents of families, housewives, in brief persons from all walks of life and social classes. These persons possessed integrity and did not need very much professional assistance in order to influence the chiefs of different agencies and the leaders of the community. . . .

The next edition will speak more of the organization, its members, and directors. . . .

Appendix

•

The subdimensions of achievement values — integration with relatives, activism, and trust — were taken from Joseph A. Kahl, "Some Measurements of Achievement Orientation," *The American Journal of Sociology*, 70, no. 6 (May 1965): 669-681. Many of the items pertaining to these subdimensions, which were included in the systematic interview schedule, also were taken from this source. Each of the items had four alternative choices: "Strongly Agree," "Agree a Little," "Disagree a Little," "Strongly Disagree." In turn, each alternative was assigned an arbitrary weight of 1, 2, 3, or 4, from "Strongly Agree" to "Strongly Disagree." After the weights for the items in each subdimension were added, the total score for each member was used to give him a rank order in relation to the scores of the other members. The following were the items used for each subdimension.

Integration with Relatives

1. If one has the opportunity of helping a person get a job, it is always better to choose a relative rather than a friend.
2. When one has true problems, only a relative helps one.
3. When a person is looking for a job, he should look for one near his parents' home, even though this would mean losing a better job opportunity elsewhere.
4. Nothing in the world is worth it if we have to separate from our parents.
5. Even though one is married, the first love is given to one's parents and not to one's spouse.

Activism

1. Children should be taught that when a person is born, his future or success is already written in his destiny; therefore, he should accept it and not try to fight it.
2. Children should be taught not to expect too much from life, so that they are not disillusioned.
3. Nowadays, parents should teach their children to live in the present, and not to worry about tomorrow.

4. Children should learn that to make plans by oneself makes one un-happy because these plans are almost never realized.
5. It is important that one always have clear plans about the future.
6. It is important to make plans for our lives and not only accept what is to come.
7. True happiness in life consists in accepting what one has and taking advantage of what comes along.
8. We, the Puerto Ricans, have great illusions, but in reality we don't know modern industry.
9. In political life, it doesn't matter very much which candidate is elected since nothing changes.

Trust

1. Children should learn that one cannot trust in most people.
2. Children should learn that if they do not take care of themselves people will take advantage of them.
3. Children should be taught that in this day and age one does not know whom he can count on.
4. One can only trust in the persons one knows well.
5. Many people whom one has helped help one, not for charity, but because it suits them to do so.
6. Some people are honest and don't try to take advantage of one.
7. Many people pay kindness with ingratitude.
8. It is not good for friends to know all about one's life because they would take advantage of one.
9. It is not good for relatives to know all about one's private life because they would take advantage of one.

The systematic interview schedules also included a series of items, each with fixed alternatives, to determine the extent to which the members understood and used English. For example, each member was asked how well he understood English — "Very Well," "Somewhat," "Very Little," and "Not at All." He was provided with the same alternatives when asked how well he read English, spoke it, and wrote it. After these four questions, he was asked four questions about which of the two languages — English or Spanish or both — he used in daily life, at work, and at home; which, also, he preferred to use. Finally, we asked him a series of seven additional questions as to his use of English — "Frequently," "Occasionally," or "Never" — in speaking to adults at home, to children, while shopping, with friends, while at work, at public places, and at meetings. The alternatives in each question were given equal weights. After the weights for all the items were added, the total score was used to give him a rank order in relation to the scores of the other members.

INDEX

Index